KARL WILLIAMS is a singer-songwriter, musician and model who performs under the name Ceaser London. He is a classically trained pianist and accomplished flute player and has recently been on tour with Maverick Sabre. He models for clothing brand Gabicci and his debut album, *Killing Time*, which is about his incarceration in Dubai, is being released later this year.

Instagram: iamceaserlondon
Twitter: @iamceaserlondon
Facebook: Ceaser London
iamceaserlondon.com

JUSTIN PENROSE was a reporter for seventeen years, working for a range of national media outlets including the Press Association and the *Sun*, before spending ten years at the *Sunday Mirror*. He was the paper's crime correspondent for nine years and has broken dozens of exclusives during his career. He now works in PR.

D1392554

KILLING TIME

SURVIVING DUBAI'S MOST NOTORIOUS PRISONS

KARL WILLIAMS
with JUSTIN PENROSE

SIDGWICK & JACKSON

First published 2016 by Sidgwick & Jackson
an imprint of Pan Macmillan
20 New Wharf Road, London N1 9RR
Associated companies throughout the world
www.panmacmillan.com

ISBN 978-0-283-07239-0

1 3 5 7 9 8 6 4 2

A CIP catalogue record for this book is available from the British Library.

Typeset by Ellipsis Digital Limited, Glasgow
Printed and bound by CPI Group (UK) Ltd, Croydon, CR0 4YY

Visit www.panmacmillan.com to read more about all our books
and to buy them. You will also find features, author interviews and
news of any author events, and you can sign up for e-newsletters
so that you're always first to hear about our new releases.

*To all the people who have fallen foul
of justice systems around the world.*

CONTENTS

1

PARADISE TO HELL

'*Yallah! Yallah! Yallah!* Go! Go! Go!' screamed the man in the Manchester United shirt as he dragged me out of the car and jammed a gun into my ribs. Pain seared through my chest as I fell to my knees. I looked up to see another gun pointed directly at my face. As I looked down the barrel, terror filled me to the core.

My friend Harry and I were being attacked in the desert paradise of Dubai, in the luxurious area of the city's yacht club and marina. Million-pound boats were moored in an inlet that led onto the green water of the Persian Gulf, less than 100 metres from where we feared for our lives. A group of six men brandishing pistols were stood around Harry and me, spouting words in Arabic that we didn't understand. I looked over and saw that our hire car, which was in a layby, had been penned in by two cars and a van. They were parked in the road, causing a traffic jam. Some of those stuck sounded their horns, but stopped when they saw the gang of men armed with guns. People across the street looked on, trying to see what was happening. They heard our cries but no one was willing to help us. I could hardly blame them.

As the intense desert sun was setting in the evening sky, I

honestly believed I was about to be killed. I am in no way a religious person, but at that moment I prayed to God, asking for him to save me.

I looked up to see one of the men, shabbily dressed in flip-flops, tracksuit bottoms and a yellow skin-tight cycling jersey, his distinguishing feature a quiff like the Fonz, leering down at me with a sadistic grin. Before I had a chance to ask why we were being attacked he administered a brutal slap to my face then pulled me up onto my feet and clasped handcuffs tightly around my wrists. The Sixties' throwback fastened them as hard as he could, pushing my hands up so they were at a 90-degree angle. The pain was excruciating, and a feeling of nausea swept over me. Next I heard Harry screaming in agony as the Fonz was now pulling his arm back as far as he could before administering a slap that made a horrific cracking sound which echoed in my ears. Everything seemed to slip into slow motion.

'Where is the stuff, you black shit?!' shouted the psychopathic-looking Arab in the football shirt. In a detached kind of way I noticed it had 'Rooney' written on the back. He stuck his face mere centimetres away from mine until I could almost taste the smell of tobacco on his breath. I was in a daze from the shock but I was quickly brought back to the horrific reality of the situation when the Fonz slammed his elbow into my ribs.

'Please, what do you want?' I begged.

I had instantly assumed we were being attacked by a gang intent on robbing and beating us. Nothing else made sense, as we had done nothing wrong and hadn't committed any crimes. Harry, who was on his knees beside me, said, 'What the fuck is going on?'

'Bruv, I don't have a clue,' I responded.

'Can we duck?' Harry asked, meaning could we make a run for it.

'Nah, man, this is one we can't duck from. We'd get lenged,' I said, using the street slang for shot. We both switched to East End London street talk, hoping our attackers wouldn't understand.

Our conversation was interrupted when the Man U thug shouted in my face, 'You black shit! Where are the drugs?'

I looked up at him, confusion spread across my face. I'm no angel and admit to having had the odd smoke when younger, at home in London, but I would never have been so stupid as to indulge in illegal substances in a country that has some of the strictest narcotics laws in the world.

'Drugs?' I said, starting to feel even more terrified now as it slowly dawned on me that the men currently attacking us had to be police officers. 'We don't have any drugs.'

Another cop came over to join his colleagues. He was dressed in a tracksuit, but what stood out the most was the Ferrari cap he was wearing on his head.

'You're going to tell us where the drugs are,' he said in a gruff voice.

'We're on holiday, mate,' I pleaded. 'I don't know anything about any drugs.'

Despite this being the truth, the last comment infuriated my attackers and they all started to kick and slap Harry and me as we tried to dodge the blows.

'You sure about that, you African piece of shit?' Rooney screamed as he kicked me, my body lurching to one side and forcing me to topple over with the pain. Another cop who had been watching on, laughing, came forward and pulled me back up onto my knees before delivering a hard slap to the face. The most alarming aspect of my new attacker was that he appeared to be about fifteen years old. I realized this slight boy was the sickest of them all, and seemed to delight in causing maximum pain. He seemed to gain confidence from each slap and the look in his eyes was one of sadistic enjoyment.

I was about to respond to his comments about my heritage, and tell him that I was a British citizen who happens to be black, but then I heard my friend Tariq being dragged around the corner by two more undercover cops.

'Get off me, you mugs!' he shouted, as the cops pulled him from his apartment entrance to the cars. Despite his aggressiveness towards his attackers, Tariq had a look of absolute terror on his face. He stared at me on my knees and his mouth dropped open.

'What the fuck is going on, man?!' he shouted before he was shoved into a black VW Passat.

I felt completely helpless. I was desperate to help my friend but could not even see how I was going to survive.

'It's time to talk, you Sudani piece of shit!' spat kid cop, as he came up close to my face.

'I'm a British citizen, I'm from England,' I said, but this seemed to enrage them even more. They could not believe that a black man in their country could be anything but an African. For them that was absolute justification for the beating they were dishing out.

'You Sudani! You Sudani! You black pig!' kid cop screamed, spitting the words at me. 'You African piece of shit! You not British, you black! Tell us where are the drugs? Tell us or we kill you and murder your friends. We are the police, we do what the fuck we like.'

As a fairly streetwise lad from east London I like to think I can judge when somebody is having you over or bluffing. The cold look of pure hatred in this teenage boy's eyes told me one thing: he meant every word he said and what happened over the next few minutes would determine whether we were to live or die.

This was the start of a year-long nightmare that would see us tortured and jailed with some of the world's most dangerous criminals. All for a crime we did not commit. We were to be victims of rogue elements within Dubai's police force, fitted up on spurious drugs charges and then punished further when we had the temerity to complain.

We were to discover that beneath the veneer of opulence and glittering lights, Dubai has a corrupt and festering underbelly. It is a nation that sells itself to westerners as a safe and tolerant dream holiday destination, with 15 million tourists having enjoyed its stunning beaches and party lifestyle last year. For many who do not know better it is a playground for adults in the desert. In reality people are jailed for owning a single codeine tablet, rape victims are arrested for having sex outside of marriage and the police 'create' their own cases. It has hypocrisy and corruption running through its veins. Sex outside of marriage is illegal, yet it has one of the biggest markets in prostitution in the world. It has a prison system that can be bypassed by paying corrupt prosecutors and those with *wasta*, or influence, can get out in days. Others on much lesser crimes are incarcerated with dangerous serial killers for the rest of their lives as they are unable to pay off the right people. Traces of certain drugs in the body is enough to see somebody jailed for years, yet the authorities use those exact same illegal pills to sedate inmates.

In Dubai's worst jail prisoners with HIV are used by gangsters to infect other prisoners as a form of sick retribution and punishment, murders happen on a weekly basis and rape is common. No police patrol Central 'Top Security' Jail, it is run by the Russian Mafia. It was only with their protection that we survived.

2

LIVING IN DUBAI

Harry and I have been best mates since we were eleven. We grew up two streets away from each other and first met on Wanstead Flats, a vast green area a few miles from the centre of London, but a stone's throw from both our parents' homes. I used to take the mick out of him and his younger brother's massive heads, which always appeared way too big for their bodies, and he mocked me for my massive clown feet and my 'bean head'. Harry and I lived the highs and lows of our teenage years together. He always called me Ceaze, which was short for my nickname of Ceaser. He was like a brother to me.

My dad, Roy Gumbs, was former British and Commonwealth middleweight boxing champion, but my mum was the rock in my life and brought me up well with my two older brothers Ross and Alex. I owe her everything. I've always been passionate about music and that is down to her, and my granddad, who paid for my music lessons. She made me sit at the piano and learn classical music until I was up to Grade 6. I also learnt how to play the flute and the saxophone. Alex played the clarinet so I dabbled in that as well.

I loved sitting around the piano with my family from the Caribbean, singing for hours. We used to go to Pontins as a family and take part in talent shows, where we would sing and where the artist Ceaser was born. I'd always win in my age category and my brothers also won theirs. The prize for each of us was next year's holiday. So it seemed obvious to me that music would be my career.

When I was eleven I did my first gig as an MC at a house party. I remember practising my lyrics all week and when the party came I ripped it up. I started spending a lot of time with my friend Alan Hodder and his brother Lewi who had a music studio in their loft where we'd hone our lyrics and practise our routine. When I started the group Deadly Soldiers with them and my friend Sammy Porter it felt like my life was beginning. I was in my element and knew this was what I wanted to do. Over my teenage years most of my mates lost interest, but Sammy and I kept going strong. We started hosting club nights at the Legends Nightclub in Barking.

It was only when I met a producer called Steel Banglez that I realized I had a genuine talent as a singer as well as a musician and a rapper. He was the first person in the music industry who made me believe I had a voice that people wanted to hear. He would say: 'Your voice is so different. It's deep, man.'

While music was my dream I knew, at the age of twenty-two, I had to earn some cash and I moved to Colchester with Sammy. He was at university at the time and we started a booze delivery business called Dial A Pint where students would put in orders and we would drop off cut-price alcohol. It was an instant hit, but we didn't have the necessary licences and got shut down after four months. The success whetted my appetite for making cash out of the entertainment side of things, so when my brother

Ross told me there were opportunities in Dubai I jumped at the chance.

He had moved out there three years before to work in publishing and told me he could get me a job. He set me up with a position at a company called Naseba, where I would be events manager for the Saudi Arabian government, which would include booking clients and sponsorship. I was due to start in June 2011, and I decided to go out a month early and have some fun.

As I got off the plane the heat hit me in the face, sapping all of the energy from my body. I had never experienced anything like it. I had been to my family's home island of Anguilla several times in my childhood but the heat there was never this intense. My brother picked me up and took me to his apartment where I was to stay for the next six weeks. Ross lived with his wife, Diana, and their three-year-old son. His spacious three-bedroom apartment was on the third floor of an eight-storey block. It was luxuriously fitted out and bigger than any flat I'd seen in London. The apartment was situated two minutes away from the Mall of the Emirates, one of the biggest in Dubai, so I said I would walk over there to take a look.

'Yeah, all right, mate,' Ross laughed. 'Good luck with that. It's almost 40 degrees out there.'

I didn't understand why he was being so funny about it until I started walking. By the time I arrived in the air-conditioned oasis I was almost passing out from the heat. Dubai was going to take some acclimatizing to. I took a cab back to his apartment. Ross laughed as I staggered in the door and said, 'I told you bruv, but you wouldn't listen!'

Later that night we went out to a local bar called Trader Vic's in Madinat Jumeirah on the waterfront. This stunning part of the city blew my mind. The old-style sandstone buildings looked like an Arabian Palace reflecting in the crystal clear water, and it became one of my favourite places in the city to go out. In the distance I could see the Burj Al Arab, a skyscraper shaped like a huge letter D, set on its own artificial island. Ancient met modern to create one of the most beautiful places I have ever seen. I was immediately hooked and vowed to make the most of my time there.

That night we bumped into one of my brother's friends, Zain. The last time I'd seen him was when I was fifteen and he'd rescued me and my pals when the car we were in broke down. We were to become close over the following months.

'What you doing here, boy?' Zain said, delighted to see me.

'Yeah, mate, I'm out here for a bit and Ross's trying to set me up with a job.'

'Mate, we're gonna have it up. Boy, I'm gonna take you brassing,' he joked, pretending he was going to introduce me to hookers and the seedier side of the city. Zain is about five foot six and a little overweight. With his squeaky cockney accent he is hilarious.

'Nah, man,' I said. 'My brassing days are behind me.'

Zain laughed, 'Yeah, whatever mate.'

As part of my initiation into Dubai we ordered a round of zombies, a heady mix of various spirits so strong that the bar owners would only serve two to each person. My brother thought it would be a good idea to add extra vodka from a bottle he was holding in his bag. Each drink was passed around the group and whoever pulled out of drinking first had to buy the round. My brother and I stumbled home and were both sick. Only then did it strike me that I was in an Islamic country, where it was illegal for anyone to drink without their own alcohol licence, yet nobody had batted an eyelid. This was the permissive side of Dubai and one which I was to enjoy as much as I could. If you are young, working and earning cash, Dubai is a wonderful place to live where you can suspend reality and have a great time. It was only later that I was to learn that it has a twisted core.

Zain had promised to show me around so I went to see him at his apartment. It was a huge split-level flat on the ground floor of one of several tall yellow towers overlooking the ocean. The tiles were pure marble but the floors were all heated so the stone never felt cold to the touch. The bathroom and kitchen wouldn't have been out of place in a mansion in the UK and this was costing him just 3,500D a month (£700). Over the next few weeks we spent a lot of our time playing *Street Fighter* on the PS3. The loser would have to down a shot of vodka. He also took me to the Crystal nightclub and I was in awe. I'd been to many clubs but this place was like nothing I had ever seen. Ferraris, Bugattis and Lamborghinis were parked outside – the only vehicles deemed worthy of gracing the front of the building. The club is at the top of a pyramid-shaped building, with floor-to-ceiling windows giving you a complete 360-degree view. As I stared out I marvelled at the sight of Dubai's vista shimmering in the evening sky.

'This is the life, Jimmy,' Zain said. He never explained to me why he called me Jimmy. Zain could be a bit of a nutter sometimes but he was a fun guy to be around.

This was indeed the life. There were so many beautiful women in the club I thought I was in heaven. I didn't realize that many were hookers until one offered to spend the night with me for 3,000D. I politely refused.

I ended up spending so much time with Zain in that first week that he suggested I move in with him. As part payment I said I'd teach him to swim and help him lose weight. I became an amateur personal trainer and made him run up and down flights of stairs in the blistering heat. My life became like the nineties' sitcom *Men Behaving Badly* but based in Dubai. Instead of a local dingy pub we had the Armani nightclub or stunning bars on the water.

After about a month of partying I had to get back to reality and start my job. It felt like joining the army. Even though my brother had lined the position up for me I had to go through a gruelling interview process. Then when I started they told me I had be clean-shaven and if I wasn't they would send me to the shop to get a razor. The idea was that everybody had to look like the boss, James. After three weeks of working there booking sponsors for events, I secured sales that got me £20,000 in commission in a single day and I started slacking off. I didn't hide the fact that I hated being there. When the boss pulled me up on my recent performance in front of the staff I told him where he could stick his job. I hated working in such a restrictive, controlled environment and had earned enough to fund my life in Dubai for the next year.

During my time in that amazing city I spent a lot of time in clubs. Many of the events were organized by a promoter called Bill who would always sort me out at his nights and introduce me to the acts performing. With my musical background, I was in my element.

Bill was constantly splashing the cash and ordering champagne for everyone. He was a funny guy. We'd go back to his apartment, order food and play pool. As I looked at him I could see he was living the Dubai life, making good money and spending time with beautiful women.

Life became one long party and Zain was my right-hand man always ready to go messing about when he finished work for the day. One night we were out at Chi, a huge outdoor club with a massive dance floor. After hours of boozing I went out the front of the club and found a drunken Zain arguing with a cocky English bloke I'd never seen before. In his early twenties, he was a tall guy with hair that was short down the sides but floppy on top, and wore a grey Gucci tracksuit. I was later to learn he was called Matt.

'Come on Zain, man, I don't want to get barred from this place,' I said, trying to break them up. 'You, fuck off,' I said pointing at Matt.

'Who you pointing at you prick?' he shouted at me in a north London accent.

'Sorry, mate, I didn't mean to point but there's no need to fight over nothing.'

'Who the fuck do you think you are?' he said, getting more irate.

Not only was my attempt to diffuse the situation not working but I was getting pissed off myself. This guy clearly wanted a fight. It was only when two of my other mates – Brooksie, a bald south London guy, and Junior – came out and pulled me away that we dispersed.

In my first couple of weeks in Dubai, I met a British girl called Amy. We met outside a nightclub and started chatting after I heard her accent. She was a stewardess with the airline Emirates and we immediately hit it off. It turned out we had several mutual friends. Amy had an Emirates card which gave her a huge discount on anything she bought, including drinks.

'That's crazy,' I said when she explained the benefits of working for the airline. 'If you flash your card in the club then I'll pay for the drinks.'

We ended up having one of those drunken nights where you just click with a person. I immediately liked the girl but we were just really good friends at first, even though I fancied her. Normally when I meet a pretty girl I try to make a move on the sexual side of things straight away, but when I met Amy it was different. We connected as friends. After a couple of weeks I was honest and told her that I had grown to like her more than that.

'No, this will ruin our friendship,' she said. I tried to persuade her otherwise but she wasn't having any of it. I was crestfallen, but vowed not to let it ruin the bond we had. I also promised myself to keep on trying.

Two weeks later, around a month into my time in Dubai, we went out with Zain and his girlfriend to a club called 400, a small nightspot by Dubai standards. Zain was in a foul mood and ridiculously thought I was trying it on with his girlfriend. He could be a bit insecure sometimes and would take it out on others.

'Zain, mate, come on, you know I wouldn't do that,' I said.

'I know you, you're trying to fuck my girl,' he shouted.

This was stupid and there was no reasoning with him. I grabbed Amy and jumped in a taxi, allowing him to cool down for a bit.

Back at the apartment Amy and I sat on the sofa. 'Why is he acting like that?' she said.

'I have no idea but the geezer can act a bit crazy sometimes.'

She let the subject go and we relaxed, listening to some music. The next minute Zain burst through the door and we ducked down in front of the sofa so he couldn't see us. He was so irate he stormed past oblivious to our presence. Amy and I were trying to suppress our laughter as an angry Zain slammed the door to his room. At that moment I looked into Amy's eyes and kissed her for the first time. We started seeing each other, staying at her plush Emirates apartment and exploring Dubai together. I'm not one for getting tied down, but because we'd been such close friends she was special.

After Zain's recent outbursts I decided to move out of his place and in with a friend called Junior, in Jumeirah Lake Towers. We had a two-bedroom, open-plan flat on the twenty-sixth floor, in a beautiful modern forty-storey tower block. Junior was a big, butch black professional footballer who played for one of Dubai's top teams. Football wasn't going too well for him so he had started to do personal fitness training. I was still lounging around doing nothing. Junior moaned at the state of the place and suggested I needed to pull my weight and tidy up, but I wasn't going to clean the apartment for anyone. We needed a maid.

I was out shopping with Amy one day telling her about it when I suddenly heard a quiet voice behind me.

'I'll clean your place for you,' said a curvy black woman in her early thirties. She was well dressed and looked respectable.

'Sorry, who are you?' I said.

'I'm Alem and I'd like to be your cleaner.

'OK, have you got a passport and papers?'

She admitted that she was from Ethiopia and was staying in the country illegally so now she was struggling to survive. She had overstayed her visa and had no way of working and no money. Amy persuaded me to give her a chance and she came to work for Junior and me. I'm glad as she was a wonderful lady.

She was the first person to open my eyes to the brutal side of Dubai. She told us how her past employers used to rape her, beat her, and one even kept her in a small dog cage. She was so desperate she ran away. I was stunned as it was the last thing I would ever have expected. Everything here was so organized, beautiful and civilized. Crime was almost unheard of, or at least that's what I believed, and I hardly saw a police officer during my time there. When I saw other maids walking around with their employers it all appeared to be happy families, with them all eating together. It seemed in some cases that veneer shattered at home.

There are moments in your life that change everything, so that every time you look back you wish you could do things differently. I had no idea that one fairly innocuous incident would, much later, destroy my world.

I was in a club one night when some girls caught my eye and I walked over to talk to them. I was just going to have a bit of a flirt. I didn't realize they were in a private section and the next thing I knew I was dodging punches. I was pulling my best boxer moves as several Arab guys dressed in shirts and jeans tried to lay into me when two guys who I assumed were club security came to my rescue, dragging me away and into an office.

'What you doing going through this section? This is a private party, man,' a big black African guy dressed in a black shirt and trousers said in an American accent.

'Sorry, man, I didn't realize.'

'You need to leave. There are lots of people who want to get you now. These guys are with lots of police officers and you mustn't go near them. They have a lot of *wasta*. They're important people.'

A short chubby Arabic man with zigzag sideburns came into the office and introduced himself as Hamza. He revealed he was an undercover police officer.

'Why did you go into that area?' he asked. 'Are you crazy?'

'I didn't know it was a private party. I was just walking about.'

'Yeah, man, that's why they tried to fight you as they thought you were trying to steal their women. I like the way you dodged those punches, you move like Neo out of the *Matrix*. Just leave. If these guys see you again they will get you.'

'I'll just party at the other side of the club. I don't want any trouble.'

'No, we know they'll start. Finish your drink and go.'

I had no idea then that meeting those two men in that club was both one of the worst and the best things to have happened to me. At that moment I was just annoyed that the idiots who attacked me had ruined my night.

I noticed I had a little bit of blood on my cheek so thought I could have been caught by a swipe. Enraged, I put two bottles in my back pockets as potential weapons and walked out of the club. I had every intention of attacking them when they came out of the club. Being an east London lad, I had been in a fair few fights in my time and I refuse to take shit from anyone. I know how to look after myself and, although I don't go looking for fights, I won't tolerate being pushed around. In that moment I wanted revenge. I hid behind what looked like a Roman column a short distance from the entrance.

It was only after fifteen minutes of standing there that I realized I didn't know what my attackers looked like. Two friendly Arabic guys came up and said, 'Man, we saw that fight in the club. Are you okay? We'll back you up if they come out again.'

Before I had a chance to thank them a large group of men came charging out, shouted something in Arabic and ran at my two new friends. I watched on, shocked, as the group of thirty seriously beat them. Although the two guys had offered me kindness, I didn't know who they were and why this group was attacking them so viciously. I quickly walked off and made my way home after what had been a particularly bizarre night.

*

In July I was becoming concerned for Amy as she kept complaining of stomach pains and I persuaded her to go to the doctor. She insisted on going by herself and called me on her way home in tears.

'I'm pregnant,' she said as I picked up the phone. 'I'm scared and I don't know what do.'

I froze and immediately felt nauseous. I'd never even thought about having children. I was too busy having the time of my life and the last thing I needed was somebody depending on me when I could barely look after myself.

'It's okay, calm down,' I said. 'Come round and we'll talk about it.'

I gave her a big hug as she walked through the door. 'What do you want to do?' I said. 'I will support you no matter what you decide.'

'I don't know,' she said, looking panicky. None of this was planned and we didn't have the answers. Tonight wasn't the time for making decisions so I told her to go home and to think about what she wanted. We needed to make a decision quickly as this was incontrovertible proof that we had had sex out of wedlock, a serious criminal offence in Dubai.

It was a couple of days before she called me again.

'I want to go home to the UK and have an abortion,' she said.

My heart sank, yet I have to admit a little part of me was relieved at the same time. I didn't want my baby to be destroyed but the selfish part of me realized I could carry on enjoying everything Dubai had to offer.

But after a few days at home in England Amy returned with another bombshell. She got a cab straight to my apartment and I could immediately see she seemed a bit uneasy.

'I've decided to keep the baby,' she announced.

My emotions flipped once again. I wasn't ready to have a

child but I was a little bit excited. I was also in a little bit of shock.

'How are we going to do this?' I said, trying to remain calm.

'I want to go back to the UK.'

'Okay, when are you leaving?'

'In the next few days,' she said. 'I want our baby, but there's no way I can stay in Dubai with it.'

'Okay, well, I'll sort a few things out and then I will come back with you.'

I helped pack up Amy's stuff and put her on a flight a few days later. The thought of returning to grey and dingy England for a screaming child and dirty nappies did not fill me with joy. But I had grown up without a dad and I didn't want my child to not have me around when they were small. Although I was supposed to be going home after a month, it ended up being four. I managed to string it out as I simply did not want to leave. It was my last chance to enjoy everything Dubai had to offer before I had to start acting responsibly.

It was a sad day when I got on my Emirates flight home. I was starting a new life but I knew I would come back to the place I had come to love, eventually. Little did I know that when I did return, it wouldn't be like the dream I had been living for the past year, but would turn into a nightmare.

3

LADS' TRIP

My beautiful daughter Faith was born on 18 April 2012. It was one of the happiest moments of my life.

Amy had wanted to find out the sex of our child beforehand so I knew we were expecting a girl. I was excited to meet her but that feeling was mixed with sadness because my granddad James was seriously ill. In the weeks before my little girl was brought into the world I'd been to visit him on Anguilla, with the rest of the family, to say goodbye. Whenever I'm going through difficult times I've always turned to music, and that's exactly what I did on that trip. During one particularly contemplative moment I wrote a song entitled 'Blue Lights' about avoiding the CID. On my return I went to the studio to record it, but when I was in the middle of the session I got a message saying Amy had gone into labour.

I was terrified and froze. In my state of shock I carried on recording the song for half an hour before announcing to my producer pal Will that Amy had gone into labour.

'Woah!' he said. 'You gotta go!'

He was right but I wasn't thinking straight. Sammy came to pick me up and we headed to Bedford Hospital, close to where

Amy lives. After a few hours of labour Amy was rushed in for an emergency caesarean section as Faith's heart rate had dropped. I was terrified as I didn't know what was going to happen to Amy and my little girl. I put on a hospital gown and sat in theatre by her bedside holding her hand. The whole operation seemed to be over in a couple of minutes, and Faith was brought into the world. The doctors handed her to me. I looked down on this tiny beautiful bundle and was the happiest man alive.

The previous five months had been pretty intense with recording music and a bit of modelling work. I'd first started modelling when my friend Ben Drew, who is better known as rapper and musician Plan B, wanted me involved in promotion photos for the bestselling LP *The Defamation of Strickland Banks*. Some were used on the inside sleeve of the record in 2010. Then when I returned from Dubai my stylist and fashion PR friend Rich London asked if I wanted to do some modelling for cloth-ing brand Gabicci. I was particularly fond of one of the outfits – this included a black trilby, grey trousers and a brownish coloured shirt with sunglasses. This old-school suited look was to inspire my image as the artist Ceaser London.

In 2011 I had recorded a song with rapper Dream McLean who was signed to Chase & Status's record label MTA records. The song, which was called 'Golden', was released when I was living the high life in the UAE and got a massive response on BBC Radio 1 Extra and in the music scene generally. It had been my first step into the industry. It was a good start but I knew that if I wanted to support Amy and Faith properly I would have to work hard and try to fulfil my dream. She was living in Bedford while I was at my mum's in London trying to make it work in the music industry, and going to see them whenever I could.

'Get a real job Karl,' my mum would moan, but I refused. I was confident in my own talents.

'Blue Lights' was my first solo single and was well received by the critics. Publicity was beginning to build around me and I was starting to do a lot of modelling for Gabicci. I planned to release more singles throughout the year to help build my profile.

The foundations for my life-changing second trip to Dubai were formed when I met Tariq through a mutual friend. Tariq approached me about getting a job in the Emirates as he knew my brother had a business out there. He was an electrician by trade but was looking to do something different in Dubai. I met him for some food in north London and I immediately liked this short Indian cockney with a massive monobrow. We had an instant connection and had loads of friends in common.

'So what's Dubai like, mate?' he asked.

'It's one of the sickest places you will ever go,' I said.

'What are the birds saying out there?'

'All the girls are brasses and you'll eat some of the best food you ever had,' I enthused. 'Make sure you take loads of money as you'll spend it in a week. But there's no weed out there, mate, and whatever you do don't even think about doing any drugs.'

'What the fuck?'

'Yeah, mate, you'll get beheaded or something.'

Ross had a vacancy, and after a chat with me Tariq was off to Dubai. I knew I had to be in the UK for my daughter, but I dreamt of returning and was a little jealous of my new friend.

During a night out with Harry a few weeks later I told him how I'd met a guy called Tariq and helped him out.

'Tariq from Ilford?' he said, a huge smile spreading across his face.

Bizarrely it turned out that they were already friends. We

started hatching a plan to visit him and I put aside some money from MCing to pay for the trip. Tariq had been out there for two months by the time we had booked our flights to Dubai. He was enjoying the high life, partying most nights and working for my brother in advertising. He was loving it. He was living with four girls and had fallen head over heels in love with a woman he said he was going to marry. We weren't so sure, but he seemed to be happy.

The plan was for Harry and me to travel to Dubai, have a drunken holiday and return refreshed.

We decided not to let on to Tariq that Harry was coming along for the trip, to surprise him. He had no idea Harry and I even knew each other.

We were like children the night before Christmas as we boarded our Emirates flight to Dubai. I knew the delights this amazing city had to offer and I was excited that I'd be showing them off to my best mate. We started as we meant to go on, ordering endless bottles of red wine and Jack Daniel's. The only bad thing about the timing of our trip was that my brother Ross was flying the other way for a holiday in Europe and North America. It meant I would miss him but I was sure we'd catch up soon enough.

By the time we arrived in Dubai we were steaming drunk. The first thing I did was try and call Zain. He'd been my right-hand man when I had lived in the city and, despite his annoying tendencies, I missed him. His number went straight to voicemail. This was strange. Zain always had his phone on him and never turned it off. I resolved to try him again in a few hours.

We jumped in a cab at the airport and went to the Jumeirah Beach Hotel for a buffet breakfast. We ate everything on the menu. There was English, continental, pancakes, waffles and pastries and we worked our way through the lot. I was over the moon to be back in Dubai. I loved this place and leaving before had been a real wrench. Now I was here with my best friend and we were ready to party. Harry was stunned by how beautiful it was and couldn't believe it was real. He immediately loved this man-made paradise as much as I did.

After stuffing our faces, we made our way to our hotel, the Five Star Media Rotana. Like many hotels in the city, everything was included in our stay . . . Well, almost everything. As we walked in the entrance we were immediately approached by a group of pretty Chinese girls. There seemed to be several of them hanging around in the lobby.

'You want special massage, sirs, or special entertainment?' one said as she handed us a business card.

It was clear to us what kind of party they were suggesting so we made our excuses and left.

I called Tariq and told him to come to my hotel room. When he arrived, Harry answered the door and Tariq couldn't believe his eyes.

'What the fuck are you doing here?' Tariq screamed as he embraced Harry. 'I can't believe he's here! How do you two know each other?'

We got on it straight away by heading down to the pool. Dozens of stunning women were lounging around in bikinis while others were at the bar.

'How the fuck is this shit allowed in a Muslim country?' Harry said. 'I never thought there would be anything like this here.'

'This place is sick,' Tariq said. 'I've been having it, getting drunk and banging lots of birds. You should both move here.'

'Yeah, Dubai is wonderful, mate, but I don't think my missus would be too pleased,' I said.

We had started as we meant to go on, drinking in the sun and having a good time. But the party had only just begun. Despite being up for the mother of all sessions we knew from the start that we would not be touching any drugs. When I lived in the city I had been told that if you are ever offered any narcotics it will probably be from an undercover police officer. It was a risk I never took in the country and a message I hammered home to Harry and Tariq.

That night Harry and I headed to the Armani nightclub as Tariq was with his fiancée. I wanted to show Harry what Dubai was all about. Situated in the basement of the Burj Khalifa, the tallest building in the world, the club oozed extravagance, luxury and wealth.

I had hung around with a big shot called Brian when I lived in Dubai. I'd met him through Zain and had partied at his apartment with some of the most powerful men and the most beautiful women in Dubai. I remembered that he always had a table at the Armani club – whether he was going that night or not.

'I'm on Brian's table,' I said to the beautiful hostess on reception.

She looked at me quizzically and said, 'Brian's not in tonight.'

'I know,' I said, trying to act cool. Brian had said to me previously that I was always welcome to use his table, anytime.

We were led to one of the best tables in the club. A hostess immediately brought us a magnum of Grey Goose vodka in an ice bucket with sparklers attached. If it hadn't been for my connection to Brian the table and bottle would have cost us a cool £500.

Harry could not believe his eyes. 'Who the fuck's Brian, bruv?' he asked.

'Just somebody I know,' I said coolly.

Groups of beautiful women kept trying to get onto our table, believing we were big players. One stunning blonde Russian woman took a particular liking to me and kept trying to kiss and fondle me.

'Why do brasses keep kissing you?' Harry said.

It was time to leave. Things were all getting a bit much. I decided to show him the seedier and more sinister side of Dubai so we jumped into a taxi and headed towards the Rattlesnake Club, a rundown 1980s building that used to be a hotel, with big, gold Arabic writing on the outside.

By the time we arrived the club was shutting and there was chaos on the streets outside, which resembled a cattle market, but women were the livestock. There were hundreds of hookers, all done up to the nines in skimpy outfits, trying to sell themselves. Women of all shapes, sizes and colours were bartering with prospective punters, who all appeared to be Arabs, shouting and screaming. It was unbelievable. *'Yallah! Yallah! Yallah!'* men shouted, shoving girls into cars and into boots or wherever they could stash them.

'This is unreal,' Harry said as he turned to me, a shocked look on his face. 'How can this be happening in a Muslim country?'

'Welcome to Dubai, my friend,' I said.

The following days passed by in a drunken haze. The next night Harry, Tariq and I went to the Crystal nightclub. It attracts some of the wealthiest people in Dubai so it shouldn't have been a surprise when we saw then Manchester United and England striker Danny Welbeck on the table next to ours, surrounded by women. I had managed to blag a table through another friend of mine who was filming footage for the club for a promotional video. I didn't even know who Danny Welbeck was as I'm not into football, but Harry and Tariq were excited.

He was in Dubai with his brother two days after scoring a belting goal for his club. Tariq and Harry were chatting to him about football and downing drinks. I was spending more time talking to his brother who was his agent. He mentioned that Danny was interested in getting into the music business so we swapped details and promised to get in touch when we were both in the UK.

All the time the star was hanging out with us our table was surrounded by security guards, making sure that only the prettiest girls got anywhere near him.

At one point I overheard Tariq chatting to one of the girls and bragging that he was a footballer. Nothing was further from the truth, but it was hilarious to hear his tragic attempt at claiming he was a Premier League star.

As the night came to a close we were shown into a private lift that opened up into a lobby that was inaccessible by the general public. Danny was sitting there surrounded by more beautiful women. He was talking about going on to another party and we were trying to blag an invite. Unfortunately our plan was scuppered by Tariq who was very drunk and staggering all over the place.

'There's no way your friend is coming along,' one of Danny's huge security guards said.

We tried to persuade him but he was having none of it. Instead we stumbled into a taxi and headed back to the apartment where we spent the night finishing off a bottle of vodka and ordering things from room service including miniature steaks, cupcakes and breakfast at 4 a.m. By this time Tariq had passed out and when Harry shook him to make sure he was okay he completely freaked out.

'Where the fuck am I?!' he screamed. Harry and I wet ourselves. We were to find Tariq had a fairly nervous disposition. He went home shortly afterwards.

We woke up the following day with a raging hangover. What

better way to cure it than with more booze? We started drinking in the bar downstairs and were quickly catapulted back into drunkenness. When I went to the toilet I decided to check out the club opposite called Rock Bottom. It was a cool retro bar decorated like an American diner and was a nice change from the trendy top-end clubs we had been to on the rest of the trip.

As I looked across the bar I saw an old friend of mine from my time in Dubai. Vladimir was a six-foot-four wall of muscle who I used to train with at a local boxing club. With his short brown hair and dark glasses, this Russian man mountain, who was in his late thirties, reminded me of Arnold Schwarzenegger in *Terminator*. I never got into the ring with him, but we took various classes together and always got on well.

'Hey, Karl, how are you doing, man?' he said with a Russian accent. 'Are you still fighting and being a nutter?'

'I'm good, mate, how are you? How's the fighting going?'

He proudly got out his phone and showed me a video of him sparring with Royce Gracie, a member of the Ultimate Fighting Championship hall of fame.

'So, bruv, what are you up to these days?' I asked.

'I'm bodyguard.' It turned out he worked for a top Dubai official, looking after his son.

He introduced me to a small, dark skinned Arab with short hair who was skinny and quite effeminate. He didn't speak a lot because his English wasn't good.

After a while of catching up with Vlad I realized I had forgotten all about Harry and messaged him to come across the road to the bar.

'You prick, you left me with the bill,' Harry said with a big smile on his face as he walked in. He was soon placated when he saw the video of Vlad and Gracie.

'That's fucking amazing,' Harry said.

He's a big UFC fan so seeing one of his heroes fight the man in front of him on video was quite a big deal for him.

We proceeded to have a few more drinks before we invited them and a prostitute Vlad had taken a shine to, along with a few girls who had attached themselves to our group, back to our suite for a mini party.

'Hey, Karl, how's your fighting these days?' Vlad said as he grabbed me around the neck and put me in a full nelson head-lock. He was clearly drunk and wanted to show Harry and the girls he hadn't lost any of his UFC fighting skills.

'Fuck off, man! What are you doing?' I said, unhappy at the messy turn of events. We were all steaming drunk but I didn't enjoy being manhandled by a Russian monster of a man. If it had been anybody else I may have reacted with more venom but Vlad was, firstly, a beast who could batter me and, secondly, an old mate. We wrestled on the ground for a minute.

'Come on, mate, it's only a bit of fun,' he said. I laughed and said nothing, as I started walking to our hotel. The official's son, who I just realized had never even told us his name, seemed unperturbed by his bodyguard's strange behaviour.

'Karl, can I fuck in your bedroom?' Vlad asked as we walked through the door.

This was a bit weird, but Vlad isn't the kind of person you say no to, especially after he'd just got you in a headlock. Anyway, it wasn't that big a deal so Harry and I agreed. We continued chatting to the girls while the official's son sat in the corner. He seemed to be eyeing Harry up.

'I think you've pulled, mate,' I said to Harry.

'Shut up, man, no I haven't.'

'He keeps eyeing you up. It must be your lovely hairy chest.'

'Fuck off, mate,' he said angrily. I always took the piss out of Harry for his pretty-boy looks and soft mannerisms.

A very dishevelled-looking hooker and a very happy Vlad came out of the room and the whole group swiftly left. There was blood on the bed and the bed covers were all over the floor. Neither Harry nor I thought it would be a good idea to ask what had been going on. It had been a weird night.

The following day we met up with Tariq again and told him about the night's events.

'That's fucking ridiculous, mate,' he said, laughing at our crazy evening with an official's son, a UFC fighter and a hooker. 'It sounds like the title of a fucked-up book.'

That night my old mate Bill was holding a club night at one of the big hotels. I recognized the girl on the door and she got Bill for me.

'Oh, man! It's been such a long time. I hope everything's okay? I thought you'd left for good,' he said.

'Yeah, man, I'm back for a little bit.' I introduced Harry and Tariq.

'Oh yeah, I've seen you around at a few events,' he said to Tariq. 'Good to meet you, bruv.'

Bill took us through to the club and got us a table in a prime location. I saw my old pals Junior and Brooksie across the club so they joined the table with a load of girls they knew, including a good friend of mine called Laura. Bill kept plying the table with shots and gave us a massive discount on bottles of vodka. It was turning into quite a party.

As I looked across to the other table I saw a group of Emirati men and recognized one of them immediately by his strange sideburns. It was the undercover cop Hamza who had spoken to me after that bunch of men had attacked me in a club several months before.

'Hey, man, how you doing?' I said drunkenly.

'Hey, you recognize me?' he replied.

'Of course, man, do you want a drink?'

Hamza said he wasn't drinking and started talking about how he could get me involved in buying properties in Dubai. I was out getting drunk with my friends so I wasn't interested.

'I do music, mate, I don't buy property,' I said. 'It's not what I do.'

'No problem. Well, one of my friends could be a good hook-up for you for cheap club entry and hire cars if you want?'

He introduced me to a muscle-bound Arab with jet-black hair called Maz.

'If you're friends with Hamza I can sort anything you want at a super-cheap price,' Maz said, slipping me his card. 'Just give me a shout.'

'Sweet, thanks mate.'

Trusting Maz was one of the worst mistakes I have ever made.

Later in the evening we headed back to the hotel room for another party. I called a bunch of dodgy characters who dealt in unlicensed alcohol. You buy booze in Dubai in the same way you might buy drugs in the UK as there are no off-licences. I met one guy in a car park and he handed me a couple of bottles of vodka and some sambuca.

We eventually passed out as the sun was coming up, unaware that this was to be our last night of freedom for a year.

4

ARREST AND TORTURE

After four days of ridiculous partying we decided to slow down, see some sights and get some gifts for our loved ones. Although Dubai has a Metro it is not as extensive as the London Underground. In any case, we were on holiday and were not planning on slumming it with the masses. We had taken taxis around the city so far but what we really needed was a hire car. I immediately thought of Maz and his offer to sort us out with a motor at a knocked-down price.

'Hey, man, how's it going?' I said as the huge Arab answered the phone. 'We met you the other night, you remember us?'

'Yeah, of course I remember you!' he laughed. 'You boys are crazy!'

As much as I would normally have reminisced about the previous night's antics my head was hurting so I cut to the chase.

'Can you still get us a car?'

'Yeah, what do you want?'

Tariq was the only one of us with a licence and was talking in my ear, saying that he wanted a Porsche Cayenne. We had been living the life of hotshots for the past four days so he figured we needed a car to match.

Maz told us he had just the car but we would have to go to a garage in the Al Barsha district of the city to sign some paperwork and pick it up. We were dropped by cab at a small warehouse and walked through a sliding garage door to see a small fleet of flash cars. A Porsche Cayenne sat alongside a Maybach, a huge Mercedes and a Bentley. The lads from the hire car company were expecting us, as Maz had told them we were coming, and they greeted us warmly before telling us the bad news that the Porsche's battery was flat.

It didn't make any sense to me, as this was a brand-new car. As far as I was aware batteries don't tend to go flat on cars like that, especially in the desert. But when they said they would have a BMW 6 series convertible available in a couple of hours we were happy. In addition, they said that Maz would deliver the car personally to us at the Mall of the Emirates.

We caught a taxi to the mall and spent a bit of time shopping and messing about on some rides before I called Maz who said he was on his way. We waited outside to be greeted by the sight of a beautiful white BMW convertible with a red roof.

'Hey, boys, here's your car. We need it back by tomorrow,' Maz said as he handed us the keys.

We were suitably impressed and thanked him for his kindness and generosity as it was a great car at an exceptionally low price. After all, he was just somebody we had met the night before through an acquaintance I had made when I had been living in Dubai; he didn't need to help us. Tariq jumped in the driver's seat and put the roof down before carrying out a few wheelspins around the car park. When we had finished messing about we put our shopping behind the front passenger seat of the car – where we found a white plastic bag that was not ours.

I immediately feared the worst, as I had heard of people being fitted up for things in Dubai – my imagination running wild, I expected to find a gun or something in the bag. I peered cautiously inside, and instead there was a package the size of a shoebox covered in an unopened thick cellophane wrapper. Inside were dozens of small silver foil bags bundled together with an elastic band. It looked like they had been packaged ready for market. A label on the cover stated that the substance was 'legal in the UK' and 'not for human consumption'. I relaxed a little but was still suspicious and, since Maz had already left, I called him to ask what to do with the strange-looking parcel.

'What's up, bruv?' I said as he answered the phone. 'We've found a package underneath the passenger seat and it's full of little bags.'

'I don't know what that is. Take a picture and send it to me.'

I took a quick shot on my phone, sent it to Maz and called him back.

'That's the local tobacco called *dokha*,' Maz said.

'What's that?'

'It's legal tobacco that gets you high for a couple of seconds. Don't worry about it and just drop it back when you bring the car to me.'

'Okay, bruv, no problem.'

Maz's reassurance and the fact it said it was legal in the UK on the front put my mind at rest. It is a mistake I will regret for the rest of my life.

After buying a few items for our family, cash was getting short. 'Tariq, any chance you could spot us a few quid until we get back to our hotel?' I asked. His apartment was closer so it made sense to swing by there instead of traipsing back to the hotel.

'Sure, man, no problem, let's go and pick some up.'

As we waited in the car for Tariq outside his apartment, the cops swooped. It was like a SWAT team descending on us, except these guys were dressed like they were going down the gym. We were completely stunned; there was no chance to react. We were dragged out of our car at gunpoint and put on our knees. A terrified Tariq was ambushed as he walked out of his apartment and dragged screaming into a VW.

'Tell us where are the drugs? Tell us or we kill you and murder your friends. We are the police, we do what the fuck we like,' kid cop yelled at me.

'Search the car, you can come to our hotel, we have nothing. We are here on holiday,' I said.

'Keep your mouth shut, you black shit,' the Fonz screamed before kicking me in the ribs. I buckled over, wheezing, desperately trying to get my breath back.

After what seemed like an eternity, but was probably just a few minutes, the officers started to search our car. Kid cop stood over us, continuing to administer blows.

'Where are the drugs? We know you have them. You think you can bring drugs into our country and get away with it? We kill you,' he said again.

Considering the fact the officers had enough information to target us, it seemed strange that they were not aware of exactly what they were looking for. Believing the left package was tobacco, we had put it openly on the back seat of the car. As far as we were concerned we had nothing to hide. The officers went over the car at least twice before one of them looked in the bag and triumphantly held it aloft as though he had just won the World Cup.

The cops started to whoop and high five each other.

'*Haram!*' shouted the cop in the Ferrari cap, which means sinful in Arabic. 'You pieces of shit. You should never have lied to us about the drugs. You are all liars. For this you will pay.'

'What are you talking about? Drugs?' I said. 'I never lied to you about anything, there are no drugs.'

Rooney held up the bag which had been left in the car. 'What is this then?' he said.

'I don't have a clue. I thought it was some form of tobacco.'

Although that was the truth, I realized as soon as I said it that it just sounded like a hollow excuse. If what he had in his hands was drugs, we were in serious trouble. I felt a wave of nausea flood over me. You hear of people being fitted up for crimes they never committed in foreign lands and you can't help feel they were at least partly culpable. How could anyone be stupid enough to let something be planted in their car? But here we were. On our knees, staring down the barrel of a gun and fearing for our very existence.

'Where did you get this from?' shouted Man U cop.

'It was in the car when we hired it.

'You lie again!' the Fonz screamed. 'Why you lie?' He slapped me again.

Harry looked at me, a wide-eyed look of shock on his face, and said, 'Ceaze, what the fuck, man?!'

'Mate, I don't have a clue what's going on.'

I was in shock at what was happening to us. We had been fitted up.

'We have the spice, now tell us who supplied!' shouted Man U cop, who seemed to gain a whole new lease of life after finding the contraband. I tried again to explain that the bag did not belong to us and that we had only hired the car for the day. The response was a kick to the ribs.

'Who your supplier?' bellowed kid cop.

At that point they seemed to realize there was a small crowd of people on the opposite side of the road watching us get beaten. After a short conversation in Arabic, Ferrari cop and another officer picked Harry up under his arms and dragged him to the white jeep.

'Where am I going? Where am I going?' Harry cried in panic, before being silenced by another slap to the face.

'Where are you taking him?' I said, terrified for my friend.

Rooney stared down at me and screamed, 'Shut up! You are all going to the same place and you will tell us the truth. You will die unless you talk.'

'We've told you the truth. I'm not lying to you. I don't know what you're talking about. It's not ours.'

'You lie.'

Rooney and kid cop hoisted me up to my feet and pushed towards our BMW. *'Yallah! Yallah!* Go! Get in the car!' they shouted at me.

I was shaking in terror. I was in a foreign land with cops saying they had found drugs in my car. I felt like I was in a nightmare that I couldn't wake up from. I had no idea where they were taking us and I was scared for my life. I sat in the back of the car stunned at how a debauched holiday with my friends had turned into something out of *Midnight Express*.

'Please, where are we going?' I begged.

'Shut up. You will see,' kid cop said with a smile on his face.

The unmarked cop cars and our BMW sped through Dubai, onto the motorway and out of the city. As we entered the desert, fear and adrenaline rose up through me as I realized things could be about to get a whole lot worse. All I could see out of my window was sand dunes and desolation. The sun was setting over Dubai and I desperately hoped it wasn't representative of what was about to happen to our lives. We were being taken to a place away from prying eyes. Nobody was going to rescue us.

I was in our BMW hire car with Man U thug and kid cop. The

child was smoking, taking long drags on his cigarette as if it was almost post-coital. He looked very happy with himself. I've always thought it best to try and get on with everyone you ever meet, in whatever circumstances. Rightly or wrongly, and it was quite clearly the latter, these people were doing their job. Being pleasant to them could actually save our lives.

'So what's going on, man? Where are we going?' I said to the cops. I was met with a torrent of Arabic that I didn't understand, screamed in my face by the kid.

Man U cop, the leader of the group, looked in his rear-view mirror and smiled at me. 'You will see when we get there.'

'Seriously, what's going on here? Where are we going?'

He responded, with a sinister smile on his face, 'We're going to find out the truth.'

'I've already told you the truth,' I whimpered.

He emitted a snide laugh. It was clear that whatever we said they were not going to believe us. We were being fucked.

My whole body ached with the need for a cigarette after the trauma I had just been through so I thought I would try a different tack. 'Please, can I have a cigarette? I'd really appreciate it, I'm gasping.'

The kid looked at me as though I had just insulted his mother, absolute hatred in his eyes as he leant back, blew smoke in my face and tried to slap me. I ducked his blow and shut up.

We drove for what seemed like forever, deep into the desert past never-ending sand dunes. By the time we reached our destination the sun had gone down and a large full moon was in the sky. Man U cop got out of the car and dragged me out of the back door into the darkness. On my knees, I lifted my head up and I was met by a brutal slap to the face. I fell to the floor and knew things were about to get serious.

The bright moonlight gave everything an ethereal-looking quality. Hundreds of stars twinkled in the desert sky, free from the city's bright lights. Normally I would have appreciated the beauty of the stars, but at that moment the scene terrified me to the bone. We were beside a large two-storey building that resembled a car park that had been under construction before being abandoned. The metal girders were still visible, while bits of tarpaulin attached to the structure flapped around in the desert breeze. I froze. I truly believed we had been brought miles away from the nearest human being to die. We all experience moments of fear in our lives but until you actually feel extreme terror, it is not something that you can possibly imagine. I am told it affects people in different ways but for me I felt sick to my stomach and my whole body went numb.

'Your name is Maz,' Rooney cop said.

'No, it's not, it's Karl.'

'You lie!' He slapped me a few more times. I was confused. Why did they think I was Maz when I didn't look anything like him?

Just then the cops' jeep and VW Passat pulled up and formed a loose triangle with our BMW. I couldn't see what was happening to my friends through the tinted glass. Then the window of the black Passat was wound down and I could see Tariq's tear-covered face. The Fonz got out of their car and shouted, 'What's his name?'

'Tariq, his name's Tariq,' I said. We had nothing to hide and lying didn't seem to be the best policy under the circumstances.

'You lie!' the cop screamed. It was only later that I realized the confusion over Tariq's name would have come from the fact that his real name was Jamal Tariq, but his middle name was not on the paperwork for the hire car. Now I watched in horror as Ferrari cop got out a cattle prod and electrocuted my friend. Tariq screamed out in agony. That was the first time I had seen a mini taser. My mouth fell open and I felt nausea rise up into my throat. The shot of electricity given to Tariq was followed by a series of slaps to the face. He was shaking.

'What are you doing? Why are you doing this to us? We are British citizens.'

Rooney slapped me and shouted, 'No you're not, you're Sudani!'

I could still see Tariq crying in the back of the Passat, tears flowing down his face.

'What's his name?!' the Fonz said to Tariq, pointing at me.

My friend could hardly speak. He was stuttering over his words but this infuriated the cops even more. Struggling through the tears Tariq said: 'R-R-Robert, his name is Robert . . .'

If the situation had not been so serious it would have been funny. 'Tariq you prick, what are you doing?' I shouted as more slaps and kicks struck me, punishing me for Tariq's ridiculous lie.

They asked him again and Tariq said 'Ceaze' in reference to my stage name. I was kicked in the ribs and Tariq was given another electric shock. This was getting beyond a joke. As more blows rained down on me I said, 'Tell them my real name, for fuck's sake!'

'Ceaser,' Tariq said and I realized that he didn't actually know my real name as I had only met him a few months before and he had always known me as Ceaser.

'Tariq you prick, tell them my name's Karl.'

The cops at last seemed to believe I wasn't Maz. They told me to call him to arrange a drug deal but I refused.

'Mate, I've never sold anything to him or bought anything from him so why would that make sense?' I said. I was also aware that if I did that to save my own skin I would be committing a crime in front of the officers who had arrested me.

I realized I hadn't seen Harry since we had stopped in the desert and that he had been left in the jeep. Had they injured him so badly that they were hiding it from us or was he dead? Now I was panicking for Harry as well as myself. Every part of me wanted to make sure he was okay and to protect him. But I was helpless.

'Who is Al Shebab?' the Fonz said as he stood over me. I hadn't noticed him walk over from Tariq's car. 'Call your supplier and we will make it easier for you,' he added as another slap struck my face.

'If I knew what you were talking about, man, I would say, but this shit isn't ours,' I said. 'We're just tourists—' That's all I managed to utter before the wind was kicked out of me.

The Fonz came up to within a couple of inches of my face. With a twisted smile he whispered to me, 'You're nothing. You will never see your family again. You will do twenty-five years before you finish and that's if you ever leave this desert alive. People will never know where you are, we have a big desert for you to disappear in.'

The implication was clear: that they had done this before and they had got away with it. From the evil look in his eyes I believed him.

We were in a vast area of desert and I had never felt so small and insignificant. I had been in a few sticky situations in my time but nothing could ever have prepared me for this. As the desert wind blew sand in my eyes I thought of my little girl. A tear fell at the thought I was never going to see her again.

At that moment the jeep Harry was in started to rock. The police had wound down one of the windows, so I could hear his cries of pain and the cracking sound of electricity touching skin. The car was moving in such a way that I was terrified my friend was being raped. Despite the constant blows to my body, I found that the worst feeling of all in that desperate situation was not fear for myself. It was hearing my friends screaming in agony and being unable to help. I wanted to save them, and I knew they wanted to save me, but we were all helpless. Every cry of pain hurt me as much as the blows that continued to rain down upon me.

'You call your supplier,' Man U cop demanded, giving me another slap for good measure. For a lot of this interrogation the cops would all be shouting at the same time, making it difficult to understand what was going on and disorientating me even more. I received a few more slaps to the face before they dragged me back into the rental car.

Man U cop got into the BMW holding a large battery with wires sticking out of the top. 'You want to have children in the future?' he said.

'Yeah.'

'Do what we say or you will never have kids.'

I didn't have time to think about the implications before Tariq was dragged into the back with me. He was working himself up into a state, shaking and struggling to breathe.

'What do I do? What do I do? My handcuffs hurt so fucking bad,' he said. I told him to move his body round to face me so his hands weren't being pushed into the seat.

We set off back towards the city, giving us hope that we were not going to die today. Not in the desert at least. Eventually we pulled up to the side of our hotel and sat for what seemed like an eternity. Man U cop was on his phone shouting at some unfortunate person at the other end.

We sat in silence for a while before there was a sudden burst of activity. The hotel manager had come outside and we were dragged out of the car. The cops pushed us down a slope into the underground car park where we were walked into a service lift. The hotel owners and the police did not want to draw attention to what was happening to us.

Then the jeep pulled up alongside the lift and, to my relief, Harry was pushed out. It was the first time I had seen him in over an hour. Despite his slightly swollen face he was alive.

'Are you okay, mate?' I said.

'Yeah, mate, I just held a few licks,' he said, referring to the blows that had hit him.

I turned to Tariq and said, 'Bruv, I took licks because of you. You couldn't even get my name right.' I was annoyed that I had received even more of a beating because of my friend, even though I knew he hadn't done it on purpose.

'Shut up!' kid cop said. 'Don't speak.'

We went up to our floor in silence and were led to our hotel room. The hotel manager opened the door and we were shoved inside. As we were ushered in he caught sight of a cattle prod sticking out of the Fonz's belt and his mouth fell open. I gave him my most pleading look, desperate for somebody to help us and stop the torment we were going through. But he was obviously terrified and there was no chance he was going to put his own safety on the line for us. He turned and ran down the corridor before disappearing into the lift, away from the torture that we were about to be subjected to in his own hotel.

If we thought we were over the worst of our 'interrogation', we had seen nothing yet. I don't know whether it was because of the colour of my skin or whether they just took a particular dislike to me, but the police reserved an especially hard beating for me.

To start with we were pushed onto the sofa. All of them started shouting at once.

'Where's the drugs then?'

'Tell us where they are and everything will be okay.'

It was chaos and difficult to hear what was being said.

'Mate, we have no drugs in here, we don't know what you're talking about,' I said through the melee.

The Fonz lost patience and went to slap Harry but stopped when my friend shouted, 'No, no! I'm sick. I'm diabetic. I need sugar. I need chocolate,' before doing a passing out motion.

It was a complete lie, but was a little act of genius as it stopped the cops from attacking him. Despite their threats and the force with which they were attacking us they clearly didn't want the death of a tourist on their hands. Tariq was having a panic attack and was breathing heavily.

'What is wrong with your friend?' Man U cop asked me.

'He has panic attacks. He is asthmatic,' I said.

The cops must have thought I was the captive least likely to die on them, as they dragged me into the bedroom of our suite where the torture really began. I stood with my hands still cuffed behind my back while the cops started pulling the room apart, emptying the drawers and pulling off the bedclothes. They went through our shopping bags and put some fake watches we had bought in their pockets.

'Who is Al Shebab? Where are the drugs? Where is the money?' they kept asking. I tried to tell them that they wouldn't find anything as we had done nothing wrong. A cry of anger and disgust from the Fonz suggested otherwise.

'What is this?!' he screamed, holding up a condom. 'You fuck?! In my country?!'

Raging, he punched me in the side of the ribs. I have been involved in fights in the past, but I can honestly say that this was the hardest punch I have ever felt. It came out of pure anger and hatred. The wind was knocked out of me and I started wheezing. Struggling to regain my composure, I said, 'It's not mine,' but they didn't believe me. It probably belonged to the bodyguard Vlad.

Reinvigorated, perhaps by their pure anger at what they had found, I was shoved onto the bed and the officers started to attack me like I was a piece of meat. There were eight officers in the room and it was like they were trying to fight each other to get to me and slap me.

I was asked question after question about supposed drug dealers I had never heard of. I didn't know who to look at as I was dodging slaps. I said, 'You have to stop otherwise I can't talk.' This infuriated them further.

The Fonz screamed, 'Stop?! No! We do what we want, this is our country.'

In a moment of respite I overheard the officers in the other room telling Tariq and Harry, 'We kill your friend. Tell us who is your supplier or we kill him.' My friends were begging for my life but it was clear I was being used to try and get them to talk.

A cop came out of the bathroom and pulled a towel over my face. I was struggling to breathe as I tried to dodge blows and kicks I could not see coming. I felt two of the officers grab hold of my legs and pull them apart. I braced myself as I expected them to start kicking me in the balls.

'What are you doing? What are you going to do to me?' I screamed.

'Have you ever been fucked like a whore?' Man U cop said. I thought they were going to take it in turns to rape me and I was petrified.

I struggled to break free, shouting, 'Get off me, you cunts!' But my resistance was met by more blows to my legs.

'Call your supplier!' one repeated. I shouted that I didn't have one.

I suddenly felt a sharp pain running up my arms. An electric cattle prod was being used to torture me, sending waves of electricity into my body. It was like thousands of needles being stabbed into me. I screamed out in pain as the prod was run up the inside of my legs and onto my testicles. The pain was intense and I shouted for them to stop. I also thought that if I screamed louder somebody in the hotel would hear my cries.

It was only then that I remembered that when we checked in we had asked for a room away from others as we were likely to be making noise. Our room was next to the janitor's room and the stairs. Nobody was going to hear my screams.

Suddenly I could breathe again as the towel was whipped away from me. As I regained my vision I found myself staring down the barrel of a gun and all the fight fell away from me. In that split second I thought I was dead. I thought of my daughter, my family, my friends and the life I would not see again. Then I noticed that there was no clip. The realization that the weapon being used to threaten me had no bullets in it gave me new vigour. I felt like I had caught life as it was tumbling out of my grasp.

The cop hit me twice on my leg with the gun and then tried to carry out an elbow drop on me. But when I saw him launch himself up I took the opportunity to roll off the bed. What ensued was like something out of *Keystone Cops*. The officers were slapping each other to get to me as I rolled around on the floor trying to dodge the blows.

I was dragged up onto a chair but a sharp blow across my face knocked me onto my knees. The Fonz had had enough. He kicked me time and time again. Each blow forced me to twist my body to avoid it, but my wrists were clasped so tightly by the handcuffs it was putting severe pressure on them. I lost count of how many times he kicked me, but eventually I felt and heard my hand crack. I screamed like I had never screamed before. The pain was nothing like I had ever experienced, worse even that the cattle prod.

When they eventually stopped slapping me, telling me to shut up, I slumped onto the floor. The pain from all the torture was intense and I was beaten. Tears were flowing down my face but as the door opened I could just see Tariq in the bathroom. He asked, 'Man, are you all right?'

'I'm fucked, mate,' I replied. 'They fucked me up.'

It was Tariq's turn for a beating and I could hear his cries coming from the other room. Man U thug could see torture was not garnering any results from me and tried a change of tack, putting on his best good cop impression.

'You give me one or two names and you go home,' he said. 'Was it your friends? Just tell me it's theirs and no problem, you go home. They tell us the drugs belong to you, but if you say it was theirs, you are free.'

I knew instantly that this was a complete lie. No matter what torture we had been subjected to none of us would drop our friends in trouble just to escape ourselves. I had absolute faith that they would all be telling the truth like me. We simply didn't know about the 'drugs'.

I tried reiterating that we found the package in the rental car but as soon as the subject came up they didn't want to hear anything. It seemed to me that they knew exactly how the drugs had got into the car, they just wanted me to blame somebody so they would have a case.

'Where are your passports?' Man U cop said.

I told him they were in the safe in the wardrobe, which they had somehow missed when they turned over our room. I didn't know the combination so Harry was dragged in to open it. He was trying to input the numbers but kept getting slapped. The officers looked excited, believing they were about to find bundles of cash and more 'drugs'. Their bubble was soon to burst when all they found was a few thousand dirhams and our British passports.

'I told you I was British,' I said to the cops.

The tone of the interrogation changed immediately. The racist officers had assumed throughout that because of the colour of our skin we had been lying about our nationality. When they saw we were British they started to treat us more like human beings.

'I am sorry, sir, I know you are ill but drugs in our country are a big problem,' Man U cop said to Harry. 'Please understand why we had to do this. Tell us who supplied you and you go home.'

When you are being framed for a crime you are in an impossible situation and the cops knew that. If we said the package in our car was somebody else's then they would be the ones facing the rest of their lives in jail. Tell the truth and we would be the ones carrying the can as the 'drugs' had been found in our car. As we were led away from the hotel and put back in the cars I was thankful I was alive, but conscious that my future was on the edge of a precipice.

5

FALSE CONFESSIONS

Bloodied, bruised and beaten, we were taken to CID headquarters for interrogation. The two-storey white building was illuminated by street lights and had a huge compound the size of several football fields. Despite its vast expanse the station was eerily quiet. All I could hear was Tariq's panicky breathing. We were led into a freezing cold reception area where our phones and cigarettes were taken away from us before we were asked to pee in a pot for a urine sample.

'You smoke any drugs?' Man U cop asked, handing us a pot each.

Harry admitted that he'd smoked cannabis a few days before, but I denied taking anything. We had got stoned together the evening before we left for Dubai, but I didn't want to give the cops any more ammunition than they already had.

As we walked into the cell block the unbearable stench of unwashed, blood-caked bodies hit me around the face like a sledgehammer, making me heave. Yet more pervasive than any other smell was the desperation all around us. It lingered in the air and seeped out of every poor soul incarcerated in that modern-day dungeon.

'Bruv, I think this is the place that that English guy got beaten and died,' Harry said.

'Shit, man,' I said. I had read the newspaper article on British tourist Lee Bradley Brown, who had been carried out of a police station in Dubai in a body bag. There were disputed reports he'd been beaten by police officers.

Tariq looked terrified and I could understand why. We thought getting out of the desert was a good sign, but we could be in just as much danger in the police station.

The door of our cell creaked open and we could see ten men staring back at us, hollow-eyed, like they'd lost a piece of their souls. The cell was twelve by six feet with concrete walls and floors. There was no bed, no toilet, and there was barely enough room to move let alone lie down. All surfaces were white and reflected the bright strip light that was constantly on. White bars went along the top of the wall where the door was situated but were too high for us to see out of.

'Enjoy your stay,' the Fonz laughed as he shoved us into the cell before slamming the door shut.

We were terrified. Harry and I were just about holding it together, realizing we had to look tough to prevent any of the current inmates taking a fancy to us. Tariq, however, was not faring so well. It was hardly surprising as we were being detained in a horrific cell after being arrested for a crime we hadn't committed. He started to hyperventilate again.

'It's all going to be okay, bruv, but you have to hold it together,' Harry said.

'Yeah, mate, come on, we're going to get through this,' I said. 'Everything is gonna be all right.'

Tariq's rapid heart rate and out-of-control breathing weren't helped when we heard a woman's ear-piercing scream from down the cell block.

We slowly managed to calm Tariq down while watching our backs at the same time. There were Arabic and Indian men on the floor, some lying in their own faeces and smeared with blood. One had a bone protruding through the skin on his arm. The guards didn't seem to care that this man was in absolute agony.

'There is no fucking way I'm going to get bum raped,' Harry said in a hushed voice as we sat in the corner of the cell. It was like he had read my mind. I would rather die than have that happen to me. 'We have to watch each other's backs in here. There are ten of these fuckers and if they wanted to overpower us they could.'

I agreed. Torture and death were bad enough but rape was out of the question. The thought of being sexually abused by several men was my greatest fear. We had all heard about inhumane foreign prisons. None of us had any intention of letting anyone near our arses.

Tariq started to look panicked again. 'There's no fucking way some dirty prisoner or cop is coming anywhere near me,' he said.

'We have to think about this tactically,' I said. 'We have to try to stay together at all times but we also need to be aware that we could be forced to split up. If that happens we need a plan.'

We agreed that the only way of avoiding rape when up against a group was to offer to give the attackers a blow job first and then bite the rapist. You know you are in serious trouble when, as a totally heterosexual guy, you are discussing putting another man's penis in your mouth.

'But then what?' Harry said. 'You're going to get the shit kicked out of you.'

'That I can handle,' I replied. 'Rape, I can't.'

We all agreed that was the best course of action and made sure one of us would always be awake.

Throughout this time there had been little movement in the cell. Those inside seemed barely alive, almost waiting to die. The one exception to this was an Iranian guy in his mid-twenties who was sitting silently in the corner with a massive smile on his face. His eyes were so bloodshot that they were like red beacons.

'Hey, man, what's going on?' he suddenly said, before bursting into a fit of giggles. 'You in for drugs too?'

'We are but we have no idea what the drugs were,' I said.

'You took drugs without knowing what they were? Drugs roulette, man, I like your style.'

'No, no, the drugs were planted in our car,' I said. 'It was spice or something but we've never heard of it.'

'Oh, spice,' our high cellmate said. 'That's good shit. You should've tried some.'

He introduced himself as Sofian and explained that he had been caught smoking spice which was a synthetic form of cannabis. I had never heard of it before, let alone smoked it. It appeared that the police had launched a crackdown on the substance with several others arrested around the same time as us.

During the round-up we had obviously come onto their radars when they met us in the club. We looked like we had money as we were on a big boys' table. We were prime targets to fit up. The cops' mistaken perception of us as big players had ended up with us being in this concrete hellhole terrified we were going to be raped and unsure if we would ever get out.

I looked around and realized there was no food or water anywhere to be seen. We had not had a drink since we had been arrested near Tariq's flat several hours ago and we were all gasping. When the guards walked past, dragging another poor man, blood spread around his face, I shouted, 'Excuse me, mate, any chance of a drink?'

A small guard with a moustache came up to the door and shouted, 'You drink when we say you drink! Ask again and see what happens to you!'

Despite my desperation for some water asking again was out of the question. As well as being sadists the police officers were lazy. There was no toilet in our cell which meant that they had to come and let us out if we needed to go.

Minutes seemed like hours. I sat in the corner and exhaustion flooded over me. I had never felt so tired. The adrenaline of the torture and arrest had started to fade. The pain in my hand was excruciating and, along with the stench of putrid, dirty bodies, made it difficult to settle on the concrete floor. Every part of my body ached and as I closed my eyes I dreamt of home, and of this nightmare being over.

I must have been asleep for a matter of minutes when there was a disturbance outside the door – a demonic scream that made everyone in the cell sit up. The sound of the key in the lock warned us that whatever had just made that noise was coming into our concrete box.

'Raaaaaaaaaar!' shouted a huge Arabic man, thrashing around as four guards struggled to contain him. They managed to throw him into the cell. Now he was our problem. The man mountain before us was about six foot four and built like an ox. His arms were covered in cuts and blood where he had been slicing himself open. He was wide-eyed, like he was crazed on drugs, his fists were clenched and he was breathing heavily, as if he was primed to attack. His face contorted in rage, he shouted, 'Fuck you, cunts!'

He punched the door and walls, splattering them with blood as the skin on his knuckles merged with the filth that adorned the concrete. We looked at him and thought he was going to kill us. Most of the men on the floor, who hadn't moved since we had entered the cell, sprang to their feet and tried to keep their distance from the psychotic madman in front of them. Two were so unwell that they stayed where they were, still lying in their own bodily fluids.

Harry, Tariq and I backed away as far as we could to bunch together in the corner.

'What the fuck?' Harry whispered to me.

'Just stay calm, we can take him if we have to,' I said.

'I'll hold him and you punch him, Ceaze, as you've got the fastest hands.'

I agreed while Tariq stayed silent. After a few minutes two of the Arabs in the cell started talking to him and managed to calm him down. An hour later the guards returned. They bundled the madman to the floor, handcuffed him and walked him, kicking and screaming, out of the cell. One of the officers looked straight at us and said, 'You like it here?' with a big grin on his face. We realized the mentally unhinged ogre had been put in our cell for our benefit.

After that I tried to sleep. I needed something, anything, to help me escape from my present reality. Within minutes Harry was being called to the door. Having been tortured just hours before, my friend was understandably terrified of what he was being called for. But in a rare show of humanity the cops had called for a couple of paramedics to check him over because of his 'diabetes'.

'It's fine, mate, I'm not diabetic,' Harry admitted to the ambulance men. 'They were hitting me and I said it to make them stop.'

Man U cop, who was standing alongside the paramedics as he said this, started abusing him in Arabic before saying with genuine hurt in his voice, 'You lied to us?' It was a touch ironic considering what they had put us through.

I came up to the bars to see what Harry was doing and shouted to the paramedics that my wrist was hurting. The cops let me out of the cell to be examined and one of the paramedics told me that I had to go to the hospital for an X-ray.

'No, no, no, he must stay here,' Man U cop said.

A furious exchange in Arabic between the officer and the medic started but there was only going to be one winner. The cops didn't want their brutality exposed by having me go to hospital. The fact I was in pain was just another tool to get me to admit to my 'crimes'. The paramedic was allowed to bandage my hand and put it in a sling, but it still ached intensely. I suppose I should have been grateful. There were people lying on the floor who were in a worse condition than I was and nobody cared. It wasn't long after that that the cops came and took Sofian away. He didn't return.

We had been in the holding cell for a couple of hours and I realized I was starving. 'Please can we have something to eat?' I begged a guard. He sneered at me without saying a word. About an hour later he came back with the most revolting substance I had ever seen or smelt. It was a brown goo and stank like dhal left for two months in the desert sun. Its rancid aroma made me heave. One of the Pakistani prisoners was so desperate for sustenance that he tried to eat the disgusting slop. As soon as it entered his mouth he retched and vomited on the floor. The hours passed before the door opened again and we were offered water by a guard I hadn't seen before. We hadn't had anything to drink for hours and my throat was dry. The cool, wet liquid felt like heaven as it went down my throat.

*

Our time came the next day, and we were taken out one by one for interrogation. I was led into a small office where the Fonz and Ferrari cop sat behind a desk. A small urn of hot water was in the corner while a window gave my first glimpse of the outside world since we'd arrived.

'Please can I have a lawyer?' I asked. 'Or at least can I speak to somebody at the British embassy?'

The men laughed. 'You don't need a lawyer,' Ferrari hat said. 'Say these drugs belong to your friends and you go home tomorrow.'

'Please can I have a lawyer?' I persisted.

I was met with a barrage of questions, 'Who is your supplier? What is this spice? What does it do?'

I told them I had never had spice, the drugs weren't ours and that I wanted legal representation.

Ferrari cop was getting frustrated. He stood up, went over to the urn and filled his cup with scalding hot water. I was mentally and physically scarred by the previous day's torture and was terrified that I was going to be subjected to another bout. But I knew that no matter what they did to me I wasn't going to say that the spice was my friends'. I was not going to trade my own freedom for that of my mates.

Ferrari cop started to flick water around me, so it just missed my skin.

'Come now,' he sneered. 'This can be so much easier for you. Just say it belongs to your friends and this all goes away. Tomorrow you go home and this whole nightmare is over.'

'No,' I said. 'We found it in the car and it is not ours. Please call my embassy.'

The Fonz spent the whole time writing in Arabic. I assumed he was taking down what I was saying to make a statement. I told them once again that we had found the package in the hire car. As I was saying it I realized again how it must have sounded. If I had been a cop I'm not sure I would have believed me either.

'Drugs were found in your car but they weren't yours?' Ferrari hat said. 'You seriously expect us to believe that? We don't care. Tell us it was your friends' and you go home. Who was the car registered to?'

'It was hired in Tariq's name.'

'So the drugs must be Tariq's then?'

'The car's in Tariq's name but the drugs aren't his. The package was in it when we got the car,' I said again. I kept repeating myself but it was exhausting. I was frustrated that, no matter what I said, they wouldn't believe me. 'We noticed the bag in the car when we came back from shopping,' I added.

'I don't care. Tell us it was your friends' and you go free.'

It was obvious to me that all they wanted was one of us implicating the other. Then they would have a cast-iron case.

After an hour of interrogation the Fonz read out the statement he had garnered from my interrogation. It was fabricated to the point of being laughable. It said that I was 'in the country to sell spice' and that we were 'regular spice takers'. It even said Harry was driving the rental car, yet he can barely drive a pushbike let alone a BMW.

'No, this is all wrong!' I said. 'Have you not been listening to anything I have said?'

Ferrari cop sauntered over to the urn and filled up his cup again. I could already feel the boiling water scalding my skin. I felt sick to the stomach. To my relief he sat down. 'Ok we change your statement to you deny,' he said.

As he scribbled alterations to my statement in Arabic, I was relieved that they were seemed to finally be starting to take notice of what I'd been saying.

'Sign this and you go home tomorrow,' he said.

I couldn't read the text and I told them I couldn't understand what they had written. I feared it was wrong, but I so desperately wanted to believe that if I simply signed the 'confession' my nightmare would end. I was sweating with fear as I thought that if I did not do what they wanted the torture would begin again.

I grabbed the pen and signed my name. As I scribbled my signature I felt nauseous. I was taking a gamble that they would let me go when they had a 'confession', but the main reason I signed on that fateful day was because I could not endure any more pain and I honestly believed they would not think twice about torturing me to death.

I was taken back to the cell to find we all had different experiences during our questioning. Harry had been told that Tariq and I had already grassed on him and said that the drugs were his.

'I didn't believe them of course,' he said. 'I just kept saying, "Can I have a lawyer, please? Please call the embassy." They didn't like that much. They were trying to play good cop with me, saying, "We aren't going to torture you like these crazy police officers. We are your brothers. Say it was your friends and you go home." When they read out my statement it was psychotic. According to that I admitted being a big spice trafficker. When they read it out I laughed and said there's no way I'm signing that.'

Harry was the only one of us to hold out and refuse to sign. I admired him for it but he wasn't so keen on our stance.

'Why the fuck did you sign that bullshit?' he said. 'You've admitted something when it wasn't true. You can't possibly believe them that they're going to let you go?'

'Fuck off, man,' I said. 'They were going to torture me again, flicking boiling hot water around me. I couldn't go through that again.'

Tariq was also so scared that he had agreed to sign. The thought of going home was just too enticing, making it impossible to hold out.

Harry told us that while he was being interrogated there was a small Filipino woman in the same office as him. She had been arrested for spice as well but was tucking into some Kentucky Fried Chicken.

'It was sick, man,' Harry said. 'I overheard the cops saying that she was doing the right thing by saying the drugs were her boyfriend's. She had shopped her own boyfriend for a Zinger burger and the promise of freedom. When they read the statement out it said her boyfriend had supplied her with the drugs and they had taken it together. They said he would get ten years for supplying. She didn't even bat an eyelid as she ate another handful of chips. It made me feel sick for that poor guy. How could anyone do that to anyone, let alone their own boyfriend?'

We expected some kind of resolution after our questioning but nothing happened. Haunting screams echoed around the cell block. The lack of sustenance made me feel weak. I could barely swallow from the lack of water. I closed my eyes and tried to sleep.

'When are they going to let us out of here?' Tariq said. 'Do you think they are ever going to?'

It was a good question but none of us knew the answer. We were trapped without representation and nobody knew we were here. Worse was the fact that nobody would even miss us for a few days. We were on holiday and our friends and family knew us better than to expect regular updates when we were having fun.

I was woken by the sound of sobbing from the next cell. A

young lad had been thrown in while I had been passed out. He hadn't stopped crying since.

'I didn't know it was illegal,' he whimpered. 'Please let me out. I want to go home. Please.' His begs for clemency were incessant.

Within minutes we heard several guards enter the young lad's cell. 'Shut the fuck up!' one screamed before a loud slap and a cry of pain could be heard. For five long minutes those guards laid into his body. I could not understand most of what the guards were saying or see what was going on, but the cries of agony that came from the lad, and the cruel laughs from the cops, made it obvious what they were doing. Irritated by his crying, they had decided to use him as a punchbag.

For a few moments after the guards left the lad was silent. We thought he might be dead.

'Are you okay, man?' Harry called to the boy.

His question was met by more sobs. Minutes later the officers barged back into the cell and took it in turns to beat him again. His screams rang around the cell block. He was just six inches away through the concrete wall but there was nothing we could do to help him. When the cops left again, laughing and joking about the torture they had meted out, Harry tried to calm the boy down.

'Bruv, what's your name?' he said, in his most soothing voice.

'Qumas,' he sobbed. He was twenty-one, from Iran, and had been caught with spice.

'Look, bruv, you have to stop crying,' Harry said. 'I know it's hard but the more you cry, the more they beat you.' He put his hand through the bars at the top of the wall and stretched it to the cell next door. 'Mate, hold my hand,' he said. 'It's going to be okay.' Harry is one of the nicest people you will ever meet.

Qumas calmed down but it didn't stop the beatings. He was

the guards' new plaything. Somebody to beat up when they got bored. Needless to say he wasn't the only victim. In the three days we spent in that cell I lost count of the number of desperate individuals that crossed our paths. Some looked like they had been in a car crash, with exposed, open wounds and broken bones. Those from countries that did not have an embassy in Dubai were treated the worst. The police knew they had no chance of complaining so were treated like dogs. Some were pulled out for interrogation and returned while others left for good. It wasn't clear whether they had been released or had been moved to jail. We feared some may have just disappeared. They were always replaced by more beaten and tortured souls.

When the moment came to leave I was barely able to move through fatigue. We were shown into the reception area of the police station, not knowing what to expect. 'What do you think they're going to do with us?' Tariq said.

We were led into the back of the van where the heat sapped all our energy. There were ten young lads sat in handcuffs, most looking like they had been crying for days.

'You all go home now,' Man U cop said. The feeling of excitement in the group was tangible. The kids, who looked about eighteen or nineteen, were all going hyper, saying, 'We're going home!' excitedly.

I was excited too and wanted to believe what the police were saying but after the past three days a part of me was sceptical that they were telling the truth.

After a few minutes we were told to get back out of the police vehicle and pick up our remaining belongings from the hire car. The police had forgotten that we needed to get our stuff before being released. We were then were led back into the reception area.

'Sign here for your belongings,' the desk sergeant said. He handed us a clear plastic bag with our mobile phones, money and watches inside. My heart rose with excitement. Could it be we were actually going home? For the first time in what felt like ages we had real hope.

6

DREAMS OF HOME

It is only when you truly reach your lowest ebb that you realize the power of hope. I had been electrocuted, beaten, starved, sleep deprived and locked up in a tiny cell with psychotic madmen, yet at that moment I had never felt so alive. Adrenaline raced through my exhausted body. We were going home.

Harry was talking to some of the kids, asking their names and what they had been arrested for. All ten, a mix of westerners and wealthy Arabs, had been arrested for possession of spice. Danny, a Welsh guy, was living in Dubai with his girlfriend when the police caught them smoking in a car.

'They arrested me and my girl in my car,' he said. 'Then they raided my apartment and found more. My girl then went and snitched on me and said it was all mine even though we were smoking it together and it was both of ours.'

Harry looked shocked. 'Shit, man, I think I saw her eating a KFC as she signed your life away, bruv.'

'Yeah, all for a chicken burger. That's fucked up,' he said. 'But she didn't mean to fuck me up. She was just naive. The police officers tricked her.'

'She ain't meant to stick you in it,' I said.

'Well, what was she supposed to do? She's just a girl.'

'She's supposed to look after you, bruv, and you're supposed to stick together.'

'She was tricked,' he claimed again.

'She didn't look that tricked when she was stuffing down a Zinger burger, did she?' Tariq joked.

'Come on, guys, lay off him,' Harry said. 'He's just a kid, leave him alone.'

I was bored of the conversation with Danny and turned to a young kid sitting nearby who looked like Uncle Fester from *The Addams Family* but chubbier. He introduced himself as Maroon.

'So you were caught with spice as well, were you?' I said.

'Yeah, man, I went to get some spice from my mate Bobby,' he said in an American drawl as he pointed to a guy at the front of the van. Bobby, a small, slight and hairy black guy from Sudan, had already been arrested when Maroon turned up, but the police had put a couple of officers in his flat to detain anyone who knocked on the door. Maroon was one of the unlucky ones.

'We've been smoking this shit for ages,' he said. 'It's become a big thing in Dubai. It's like weed but legal. Except now they're saying it isn't.'

Looking at the rest of the guys in the van, I thought they were potential rape candidates if they ever found themselves in jail. They were little more than children and looked petrified and vulnerable. I was scared but, being just a few years older at twenty-five, I knew I couldn't show it. If we were going to end up in jail – and there was a fairly high chance the cops were lying to us and we would – we needed to keep it together and look tough. If we were to walk into a jail crying, we would be first on the inmates' target list.

We were making our way through Dubai and I was desperate for us to get to our destination as the heat was intense. The metal seat was difficult to sit on, so hot it was burning my arse through my shorts. The heat was all-consuming and made it difficult to breathe. I'd had hardly anything to drink for three days and I was struggling not to pass out as sweat trickled down my back and drenched my vest.

Within minutes of leaving the police station we stopped and the doors were opened by Ferrari cop. The cooler air from outside revived me and I saw we had pulled up behind a large white building. A sudden panic seemed to strike the spice kids and they were all asking what was going on and where they had taken us.

'Shut up!' said Ferrari cop. 'This is the Dubai public prosecutor's building. All of you be quiet when you are inside here. No noise.'

I turned to Harry and Tariq and said, 'Shit, we ain't going home, boys.'

'What the fuck are we going to do now?' Harry asked.

I didn't know the answer but if we were being taken to see the prosecutor it did not bode well. We hadn't even spoken to the British embassy let alone a lawyer, yet it appeared likely that they were going to try to make a case against us.

'Just tell them that you smoked and you go home,' Man U cop said. I wasn't so sure, as I didn't trust these torturing cops. The police were talking to each other in Arabic, which we didn't understand. Fortunately for us Bobby did.

'He's saying we'll all be let off if we just admit smoking some spice,' Bobby said in an American accent, backing up what the police had said.

'Fuck that,' I said. 'I ain't gonna say I smoked anything when I didn't.'

'Look at these mugs,' Tariq said. 'They're gonna go into the prosecutor and say they smoked this shit. They're fucked.'

Still in handcuffs, we were led down a slope into the basement of the prosecutor's building. Suddenly we came into a brightly lit corridor, past what looked like a prisoners' exercise area. All of the walls and floors were bright white and made me squint in the sunlight.

We turned a corner and came face to face with the prisoners' holding area. Bars went from the floor to the ceiling at the cell front. We could see several Arabs in white jail outfits inside. We were shoved into a huge empty cell that could have held at least 200 people.

We hadn't eaten for three days and we were starving, so when a glorious smell of fried meat wafted into our cell it was like a mirage in the desert.

'Burgers, anyone want burgers?' shouted a little Indian guy at the door to our cell.

I couldn't believe my eyes. The whole group of us swarmed towards the door. Most of the spice kids didn't have any cash on them but we did. We handed the vendor 200D and told him to give us all of his burgers, chocolate and water. A couple of the kids also had money and put their notes in to buy as much as we could. That Indian guy's trolley was like a vision from heaven. We handed out the haul to all of the kids and feasted on the food. A burger and Kit Kat have never tasted so sweet.

As I finished my burger Harry was called out of the cell by the guards. He looked scared as he was led away. I was worried for my friend and tried to distract myself by listening in to others' conversations. I could overhear the spice kids talking.

'Hey, man, you better not snitch on me,' Bobby was saying to the other kids.

'I'm not saying anything until I get a lawyer,' Maroon said. The others agreed. If there was one thing I knew, it was that snitches don't last long inside. It appeared that the kids knew that too.

I tried to lighten the mood. 'Hey, you lot. Does anyone know how to play penny up the wall?' I said.

Bobby, Maroon, Danny, a fat kid called Sharia and an American kid called David crowded round. 'No, man, what's that?' Maroon said.

I explained it was a simple game where you all threw a coin and whoever got it closest to the wall kept all of the coins. I used to play it all the time at school. There was a sudden burst of enthusiasm as we started playing the game.

After a while Harry returned, looking concerned, and I immediately stopped messing about to ask him what had happened.

'I was shown into a room with the prosecutor and an interpreter,' he said. 'He told me to sign the statement but I told him I wanted to see a lawyer and my embassy. He just said, "You don't sign? No problem. I make life very difficult for you. Your file, it will go to the bottom of the pile and will take a long time. We are the prosecution, we do what we like." It was fucked up.'

Of course, I had already signed my statement through sheer terror. I hoped it meant I would be going home.

Next they called out my name, or something like it at least. 'Kerrol Errol Williams,' a guard said. Throughout my time in jail they never used my proper name of Karl Irving Williams. I was handcuffed to a guard and led out of the cell, into a lift and up to the prosecutor's office. The inside of the building was beautiful, with marble floors and walls lined with mahogany. I was told to sit down in a plastic chair before being led into an office. The room had the same decor as the rest of the building but with portraits on the wall and luxurious soft chairs. The man before me was wearing the best quality clothes and oozed wealth and power. A small man sat to the side of the desk while another sat behind a computer screen in the corner. The prosecutor started talking in Arabic and the man to the side of the desk translated.

'You are here because you have been trafficking drugs,' he said.

'Mate, what are you talking about?' I said, suddenly very awake to the seriousness of what we were facing. We had been in a hire car with a suspect package but that had suddenly become the much more serious offence of trafficking.

'Yes, you are charged with trafficking, possession and use. How do you plead?'

'Not guilty,' I said. My throat was dry and I was in a state of shock. I was sat in front of a prosecutor who was telling me I was a drugs smuggler. It doesn't get much scarier than that.

'Don't lie. Tell me you smoke and you go home.'

'Mate, I haven't smoked. I smoked back in my country but I haven't smoked anything here. I would never be that silly as to disrespect your country. I've just had a baby and want to go back to my daughter. I am a good family man and behave myself in the UK. I haven't done anything here at all. I was just on holiday with my friends and we found some stuff in the car but it wasn't ours.'

The translator said a couple of words to the prosecutor before moving on. I realized at this point that he wasn't directly translating everything that I said. I was filled with more fear. This was the next stage of the stitch-up.

'Please can I have a phone call? Please can I have a lawyer and see my embassy?' I asked pleadingly.

'You don't need this,' he said.

This was not good. I was being fobbed off just as Harry had been. They didn't want us getting any legal representation or letting our embassy know what had happened to us. They just wanted us to admit the charges against us so they could get more convictions.

'What happened to your hand?' the prosecutor asked through the translator.

'Apparently it's broken. It was done by your police officers in my hotel.'

The translator looked at me and said, 'I won't say this. You are lying.'

I repeated, 'The police officers beat me up and broke my hand.' I made a cracking noise to emphasize the point. 'Don't worry, I'm gonna tell the British embassy about this,' I added.

The translator said something in Arabic and the prosecutor nonchalantly shrugged his shoulders.

'So, your drug test has come back positive. Why have you lied?'

'My drug test will come back positive for cannabis in England.'

'No, for spice.'

I immediately knew that the whole drug test had been a farce and was fabricated. I knew I would test positive for cannabis but I had never touched spice.

I told them we had got the car from a rental firm but it had been delivered to us by Maz.

'Whose was the car?

'It was all of ours as we all put money in.'

'How can it be all of yours?'

'We all put in money but the car was in Tariq's name.'

'So the car was Tariq's? That means the drugs were Tariq's.'

'No, the drugs weren't his, they were in the car when we got it.'

'So they must be Maz's then?'

'I don't know whose they are. All I know is that they're not mine, Harry's or Tariq's.'

I wasn't defending Maz, I just didn't want to accuse anybody of the crime. I didn't know for sure that he had put the drugs there.

'The only thing he said to us was to leave the Arabic tobacco in the car as somebody had left it in the car before us,' I said. 'He told me to keep it in the car and give it back when we returned the BMW.'

'So who had the car before?'

'I don't know. If I knew that I would have called them, so I wasn't carrying somebody else's shit around. Then I could have avoided being beaten up by your police officers.'

I was presented with the statement I had signed at police headquarters. It was all in Arabic and I didn't understand a word.

'What does it say?' I said.

'It says you came here to sell spice, that the parcel was yours.'

'I only signed it as I thought they were going to torture me again and I didn't know what I was signing.'

They showed me a picture of the spice that had been in our car. The bags were open and the drugs were poured out. There was a lot of synthetic cannabis.

'Why are you showing me this?' I said. 'This isn't ours.'

'You smoke this in my country,' the prosecutor said in perfect Queen's English. I was taken aback. He had understood everything I had been saying and the whole process had been a charade.

I tried to tell him again that I had done nothing.

'Okay, you sign this paper and you go.'

'What does it say?'

'It just says your name and that you didn't smoke anything.'

'If I sign it, do I go home?'

'Yes, you go home.'

That was all I needed to hear. Looking back, I realize it was extremely naive but I badly wanted to believe it was true. I signed the paper and I was shown back to the cell. Tariq went through a similar experience and signed his name as he had done at the police office.

'You're mugs, mate,' Harry said. 'You think they're just going to let you go when you've signed this bullshit statement? That's bollocks, mate.'

'Come on, mate, think positive, we're going to be home soon.'

'Don't be a prick. They're not going to just let us go.'

Throughout the whole arrest and aftermath Tariq had been remarkably quiet for the chippy East End boy that he is. He seemed to be withdrawing into himself. He clearly needed some space so we let him be.

We were desperate for a smoke and started hounding the guards. One middle-aged cop with a moustache showed us some mercy and got out a box of cigarettes. We were led to an inner courtyard area where beautiful smoke filled our lungs. After three days of not smoking that small stick of heaven tasted like nectar. The kind guard asked us about our cases.

'What did you say?' he said to me.

'I said I didn't smoke.'

'Why you say that?' He looked surprised. 'You should have said you smoked and then you go home.'

'I'm not saying that when I didn't. It was nothing to do with me.'

'Don't worry, it doesn't matter. This stuff not even illegal. You will be going home.'

Although we had suffered horrifically at the hands of a few

cops, not all of them were bad. The man standing before me was testament to that. He didn't need to give us a cigarette or show us any kindness but here he was, handing out smokes to us and all of the spice kids.

When we had all been questioned we were taken to the reception area.

A balding guard led the way before announcing, 'Get your stuff. You are all going home.' The excitement in the air was tangible. The spice kids were all whooping with delight while nothing would have suppressed the smile on mine and my friends' faces. Could it really be that having been arrested and questioned by the prosecutor they were going to let us go? The guard was telling us we would be going home and we wanted nothing more than to believe every word he said.

'Mate, we're going to get some of those Chinese girls in and have a massage after all this shit,' I said to Tariq.

'Yeah, mate, I'm going to get a manicure, a pedicure and a massage.'

'And get your eyebrows plucked?' I joked.

'Fuck off, you prick,' he said with a smile on his face.

I picked up my phone and cash before we were led into the sweatbox van.

We were in better spirits than we had been for days as we were put in the back. All of the spice kids were chatting frantically and had been told the same thing: we were all going to be released. As we set off I called my brother Ross, even though I knew he was in Amsterdam.

'Mate, I've been arrested for some bollocks I didn't do.'

'You dickhead, what have you done?'

'We had some spice shit in our rental car but it wasn't ours.

It's fine, mate, I think we're going to be going home. That's what the guards have been saying, so don't tell Mum.'

I love my mum to bits but she is not a woman you would want to mess with.

'Okay, mate. Listen, you're gonna be all right,' Ross said. 'Hey, did you hear? Zain has been arrested as well.'

This was a complete bombshell, but now everything made sense. That's why I couldn't get hold of him.

'Fuck, that's mental. Do you know why he was lifted?'

'No, man, I'll try and find out. He's being held in Port Rashid. Look after yourself, bruv.'

I hung up, concerned for my friend. I hoped he wasn't in serious trouble and that he hadn't been through an ordeal like Harry, Tariq and I had.

We were driven out of the city and eventually stopped at a small, single-storey building that looked like three Portakabins pushed together. Maroon piped up that this was the Jebel Ali processing centre. My feeling of excitement grew as we made our way out of the van. Even the guards seemed more relaxed here.

'Come in, boys, you're going home,' the guard who opened the van door said.

As we walked into the reception area some of the spice kids' parents were inside waiting. Maroon burst into tears and screamed, 'Mum, Dad, please help me.' Pandemonium set in. His parents were crying, desperately trying to touch his hands while the guards pulled him away. Despite the general feeling that we were all going home, seeing their parents in the reception was too much for some of the kids' emotions after two days at CID Headquarters.

'*Yallah, yallah*, go.'

A handful of the other kids' parents were swarming around us.

'Mummy! Help me!' Sharia screamed, before he was dragged away.

This was the first time we had seen a westerner who had not been arrested for days. I was not going to pass up on this opportunity to try and let people know where we were.

'Please help us!' I shouted. 'They've beaten us really badly. They've broken my hand, please tell the British embassy.'

Tariq and Harry were shouting too. Maroon's parents promised to let our embassy know.

Around twenty of us were shown into a small room that had four chairs up against the wall. A small Arabic man was sitting handcuffed to one of the seats. He was slouched as we came through the door but his head shot up at the noise as we entered the room.

'Escape, escape, I need to go,' he shouted. 'I have been on this chair for two days. Please help me.'

We were to discover that the chair was a thing of legend. I was to meet dozens of people who had spent days sitting in it, simply being ignored. It was a symbol of the police's torturous power over those worthless enough to get arrested.

Maroon's parents came into the reception area and handed us bottles of water. We thanked them profusely. I guzzled it down, relishing the cold liquid. Everyone seemed to have calmed down after the initial emotion of seeing their parents. We were all feeling better than we had since our nightmare began. We were seeing movement. We were going home. As there was a large group of us they wanted to get us processed and out the door as soon as possible. They called us forward and took our mugshots. They read out our charges but we didn't understand what they were saying. We believed we were going home so we weren't even listening properly.

The guards kept saying, 'You going home, you going home.' We were elated, laughing and joking with each other.

Tariq looked at me and said, 'Ah, man, you can go back and see your daughter now.'

'Yeah, man, I miss her so much.' I was so full of emotion at the thought of holding my little girl again.

It's twisted how hopes and dreams can be shattered in a split second. My head swung round when someone let out an anguished scream. It was Maroon's mum, who had burst into tears. I figured she had just overheard something, and it wasn't good.

'What the fuck?' I said to my friends.

Maroon's dad was trying to console her but his own face was contorted in pain as he sobbed. His mum continued to wail, 'No, no, not my boy.'

All hell broke loose. Most of the spice kids burst into tears and started shouting towards their parents, 'Mummy, Daddy, help me, please!' At the same time the guards started to shove us out the door. The wind whipped up the sand in small tornadoes as the guards shouted, *'Yallah! Yallah! Yallah!'*

The acrid desert heat got to the back of my throat as sand blew around us and mingled with a feeling of terror in the pit of my stomach. We weren't going to the airport, we were going to jail.

7

ENTERING PORT RASHID

The human mind has an innate survival instinct. Harry had gone into Terminator mode, looking numb and emotionless. Tariq looked panicked and was hyperventilating. My mind started planning. I instantly knew we had to distance ourselves from the spice kids, who had gone from being slightly annoying, pretty, spoilt, rich teenagers to potential rape victims. If we were associated with them then we too could suffer their fate. Having been through torture, I had no intention of letting myself or my friends be raped too. We couldn't be caring for a bunch of kids. We had to look after ourselves.

I knew we needed to act tough but be respectful in prison. If you give people respect and act in the right way you have a much greater chance of getting through the ordeal alive. Most of these kids had been given everything by their parents and hadn't got the slightest clue of how to be streetwise. They didn't even know how to carry themselves properly. They would get eaten alive.

'Listen, don't panic, we've got a bloke inside,' I said to Tariq and Harry. I knew that, because of the area we were arrested in, we would probably be going to Port Rashid prison. 'Zain is there,' I added.

'That fucking muppet?' It turned out that Tariq and Zain had been out together in the past but Zain had a habit of getting into trouble. I could understand why Zain sometimes did Tariq's head in.

We were driven into a garage behind the prison and led like a chain gang, handcuffed to each other, into the jail. The long room we were in appeared to be some kind of visiting area. There were phone booths on both sides with a sheet of glass in between. Some of the kids were begging the guards to let them go.

'Please, we don't belong here. Let me go home,' Danny snivelled.

They lined us up so we were all facing the glass. The officers were laughing at the terrified group in front of them. A bunch of spoilt, rich teenagers were about to be thrown in with hardened criminals. They thought it was hilarious and decided to have some fun with us. A door on the other side of the glass was opened and the inmates started to come in. Crazed-looking madmen scoped us out through the glass, whooping at the sight of the younger, prettier looking boys. I thought we were fucked and would have to fight for our lives. They all looked unhinged. Huge shaven-headed blokes, who I was later to learn were Russian Mafia gangsters, were alongside menacing-looking Arabs. One psychotic-looking, bald, short stocky guy with a black eye and a bust lip came up close to the window and stared intensely at us. He looked insane and I was later to learn he was also from Russia.

Then I saw another taller shaven-headed Russian guy and my heart dropped. I can look after myself but this guy was massive. We could be in serious trouble here. The Arabs were all dressed in head scarves and looked intimidating.

The inmates walked up and down staring at us. It was as if they were selecting their victims, like we were in a brothel and they were punters choosing who to fuck. The guards were wetting themselves with laughter. They knew what was happening and it was all designed to freak us out. We all felt like targets, but I knew we had to hold it together and look tough. It is difficult to play it cool when all you feel is fear.

'Welcome to Port Rashid,' said a skinny police officer, with skin that was so bronzed he appeared to glow. He was clearly relishing the sight of the new inmates coming into the jail. He was dressed in a green uniform and had a name badge saying Mo.

We had been taken to Port Rashid Prison, effectively a holding jail that was attached to a police station. Despite being a jail all of the guards were police officers. It was a strange set-up but it was the same in all jails in Dubai. Prisoners here were either on minor charges or their cases were waiting to be progressed to trial. This overcrowded fleapit was to be our home for the next nine months. At that moment I never thought we would survive a day.

As we were being led through the main visitor's area, to my immense relief I soon saw Zain on the prisoners' side of the glass. He was sporting a serious black eye, which didn't bode well.

He picked up one of the phones on his side and gestured for me to do the same on my side of the glass.

'What the fuck are you doing here?' he said. He looked devastated that we had been arrested as well.

'Look, mate, I'll talk to you when we come through. What happened to your eye?

'We need to talk. I've got some serious beef in here. Look, you have to balls lots of money as you're going to need it in here.'

He meant we had to hide our cash wherever possible before it was taken off us. The guards were starting to check in the spice kids and take their possessions away so we had to act fast. We quickly scrunched up most of our money and hid the notes underneath our balls while the guards weren't looking.

'Any of you boys English?' The sound of another British voice was beautiful to my ears. I immediately recognized Matt, with brown curly hair, as the bloke who had been fighting Zain outside a club when I lived in Dubai. I couldn't believe that he was here too, on the other side of the glass. He told us to come and find him when we got in.

The time had come to enter and I felt sick to my stomach. Tariq was shaking. 'Just hold it together, bruv,' I said. 'It's going to be all right.'

Harry was attempting to hide at the back of the queue, but he was so much taller than the others the guards saw him trying to duck down and picked him out to go in first. He went up to a desk where he handed over his phone and some cash. We decided to give some to the guards so it wasn't obvious that we had hid most of our cash in our pants. Harry stood tall and tried to look as tough as possible as he went through the door and into the prison.

I was next and walked up to the desk where I handed over my British and Dubai phones and a few notes.

'You are only allowed 500D a week. That's it,' said the cop in a high-pitched squeaky voice. He was an overweight guy dressed in a sandy-coloured uniform, with the name badge saying he was called Captain Aziz. He patted me down, but didn't find my hidden stash of money.

'No smoking, otherwise you catch another case. *Yallah!* Go!'

I walked across the visitation area and through the door. I needed to look menacing to compensate for the fact my hand and wrist were in bandages, making me vulnerable. I couldn't defend myself.

I found myself in a thirty-foot room with three phones on the wall. There were three Indians on the phones with a queue eight-deep behind them. On another wall was a hatch through which a guard was talking to an inmate. I was later to learn that this was where we would go if we needed to speak to officers. The area was rammed with people and stank of sweating, unwashed bodies. I tried to stare ahead, walking as fast as I could to the other side. I entered another small room where I saw six people asleep on the floor, wrapped in blankets. I looked to my right to see a wall of white bars and through that I could see the main jail. The first thing that struck me was the sheer mass of humanity. Men were lying all the way down the long corridor. Bars went from floor to ceiling along the whole walkway.

I picked my way through the crowds, trying to look hard and putting on my best gangster swagger. To my surprise nobody was paying any attention to me. I'd thought dozens of muscle-bound men would be eyeing me up as I walked through, but it couldn't have been further from the truth. I also thought the jail would be hot, with large communal areas outside, surrounded by sand, but instead it was almost all inside, dingy with no natural light but air-conditioned. There were no windows in the jail and I was to discover that the lights were hardly ever turned off.

The corridor stretched about 300 feet and was roughly 10 feet wide. Small groups of men of all different faiths and nationalities were lying around on each side. The stench of unwashed bodies attacked my nostrils. A putrid smell of rotting faeces gradually got worse as I headed down the corridor. Eight cell doors lined each wall and a toilet and shower area could be seen at the end. I saw Matt standing about three quarters of the way down and walked as quickly as I could towards him.

I was so grateful to see a friendly face in Matt that I could have kissed him. Matt, who lived in Dubai and worked in recruitment, was with his friend Gary, a south London guy who was originally from Yemen. The pair were arrested together for possession of spice. They asked what had happened to me and I told them. Then they answered my prayers.

'Do you smoke?' Matt asked.

'Yeah, mate.'

'Come on, Harry's down here.'

Smoking had been outlawed in all detention centres after some bright spark had burned one down and six people had been killed. It made sense not to give inmates fire to play with, but I needed a cigarette so badly that my lungs ached. It was fortunate that there was a ready market in contraband in Port Rashid.

They took me to the end cell closest to the toilets, where the ubiquitous aroma of shit was at its strongest. Harry was in the cell smoking what looked like a home-made pipe constructed out of a biro and some foil. At first appearance it looked like a makeshift crack pipe, but it was being used to smoke a strange mint-like tobacco.

'Bruv, smoke some of this.'

'What is it?'

'It's *dokha*.'

I took a lung full and almost fell over. There was an intense head rush and I thought I was going to pass out.

'Woah, what the fuck, man?' I said as I came to. 'Is this legal?'

'Yeah, mate, it's only tobacco,' Matt said.

Harry and I both laughed. We had been arrested for having fake cannabis that wasn't ours, yet we were in jail smoking perfectly legal tobacco that got you high, albeit for about twenty seconds. The irony wasn't lost on us.

'Are you boys hungry?' Matt said. We were starving as we

hadn't eaten for hours. We went back to his cell where he undid a bundle of newspapers. Inside was half a chicken with rice. We demolished it with our hands and it tasted amazing. Tariq walked in as we were finishing.

'Fuck me, man, this place is insane,' he said.

'Yeah, it's rammed. Tariq, I've just seen your old man,' I joked.

'Where? Where?'

'Over there,' I said as I pointed towards one of the immigrant workers on the floor as Harry and I wet ourselves with laughter.

He pointed to a black guy and said, 'There's your twin brother.'

'Shut up, you little prick,' I said, laughing. Taking the piss out of each other helped us survive jail.

We went to a room known as 'the smoking room' near the toilets where people bought their cigarettes from an inmate. We spent 50D – £10 – on a single cigarette each. Demand for cigarettes was high, meaning the cost was even higher. With the spice kids boasting about the cash they had the cost was only going to increase.

Matt asked us what had happened to us and we explained how we were stopped by police when they found the package that wasn't ours. He then dropped a bombshell that shocked me to the core. He told me how he had gone to Zain's with Gary to get a small amount of spice. They had become friends after the incident outside the Chi nightclub. 'Seconds later we were jumped on by cops. Zain snitched on me, man. He got me arrested.'

'No, mate,' I said, stunned at what I was hearing. 'Zain is an honourable guy who would see himself arrested rather than rat on somebody.'

'No, man, he snitched on me. Bruv, when he walked into the jail I had to punch him in the face.'

Matt and Gary had told all of the inmates the story and as a result Zain had been exiled to the Pakistanis' room next to the toilet. If there is one thing I hate more than anything it's a snitch, but Zain was a good friend of mine and I knew he would never do this to anyone, let alone a mate. I had to see him. I walked into his cell and he was lying on his bed, looking forlorn.

'Jimmy, what's going on?' he said. 'What you doing talking to that snake? He punched me in the face as soon as I walked in.'

'Matt said you're a snake.'

'I'm no snitch. I've known you since you were a kid. How could you think I would do that?'

'Look, mate, I don't even really care. I just want to keep my head down.'

I felt for Zain but right then I was more concerned with surviving. My head was in a spin after everything that had happened.

'Fair enough, but you have to believe me,' Zain said. 'What happened to you?'

I told him about our arrest and torture.

'Shit, that's fucked up, mate,' he said. 'What now?'

I had had enough talking. I was shattered and I asked him if I could sleep in his room. He explained that I needed to get permission from the foreman of the jail, a prisoner who was in control of what we did, rather than the guards outside. This sounded bizarre.

'Yeah, mate, he's called Mohammed. I'll introduce you.'

We went and found Harry and Tariq so we could all meet Mohammed, who was a big fat, larger than life Emirati Arab in his late thirties. I immediately liked him.

'Yo! English boys, what's happening, my man?' he said in a

mock American accent that many Arabs seemed to adopt. He wore a white cloth wrapped around his bottom half and a Ralph Lauren T-shirt with 'Great Britain' plastered across it on top. His fat, hairy belly was sticking out in between. The little finger on his right hand was missing. He was like a funny caricature, but we weren't sure if laughing would be a good idea. I immediately knew he was not to be messed with. Two small Indian guys flanked him and looked like his pint-sized minion bodyguards.

'You boys have any problems in here then come to me,' Mohammed went on. 'If you want to see the doctor I will tell the guards and if you want to fight you come to me first.' Straight away he had stamped his authority and from that point it was never in doubt.

'British boys, you want a bed? Maybe you sleep on the floor with the immigrants,' he said with a smile on his face. 'No, seriously, it may take a couple of days as there are 350 people in a jail that holds 112. Just sleep where you can. What are you in for?'

'I dunno, we got caught with some shit in our car and got arrested.'

He asked what we did in the UK and when I said I was a musician Mohammed started dancing from foot to foot.

'You a rapper?' he said excitedly, a huge smile spreading across his face.

'Yeah, sort of, but I sing more really.'

'That's cool, man. Okay, boys, as long as Zain is okay with you sleeping on his floor that's cool.'

We were to find out that Mohammed, who was in for smuggling 350 kilograms of hashish into the Arab state, was in charge of everything at Port Rashid and was the person the jail captains approached to instil order. Officers generally only came into the detention centre for a few minutes every day for roll

call, but when they did come in they would speak to Mohammed. Even the police officers would kiss his head as he was a
member of a highly respected family.

I turned to Zain and said, 'What's the run-ins in here?', meaning what's going on and how do things work?

'You need to get a phonecard from the Bengalis in the front
cell nearest the entrance. They buy them all from the canteen
and resell them for profit. The whole jail is like one big hustle
club. For cigarettes and *dokha* you go to the cell near the toilets.
You see the Russian with the black eyes?' he said, pointing
towards the big guy I had seen earlier. 'Stay away from him, he's
a nutter. He will try and iron you out.' That meant he would try
to knock us out.

I thanked him for his help and we all went to get phonecards
to call home.

'Tariq, did you see Mohammed's finger was missing?' I said.
'Has he hidden it in your arse crack?'

'Fuck off, Ceaze. If anyone's gonna get fingered, it's you.'

I was just trying to distract us all from the calls home we were
all dreading. It had been four days since our arrest and we hadn't
had a chance to speak to anybody back in England. I bought one
for 40D and called my mum.

'Mum, I'm in jail,' I said when she picked up the phone.

'I've heard, Ross told me. Are you okay?' she said, trying to
stay calm. I know my mum would have been in bits inside but
she was holding it together for me. Knowing that I was putting
my mum through this made me feel guilty, even though I ultimately knew being inside wasn't my fault.

'Yeah, I'm fine,' I lied. I didn't want to worry or upset her
either. I didn't mention the torture we had been subjected to as
I didn't want to distress her further.

'Look after yourself. You know I love you and will be praying for you.'

'Have you spoken to Amy?'

'Yeah, you need to call her and let her know you're okay as she's really panicking.'

I thanked her and hung up. I called Amy and she answered the phone instantaneously. As soon as she heard my voice she burst into tears.

'Hey, it's all right,' I said, trying to soothe her. I was met by sobs down the phone. 'Don't worry, everything's gonna be all right.'

I had a feeling that it wasn't but I wanted to make her feel better. She had recently given birth to my child and now I had left her alone. Then I heard Faith crying in the background. I felt like the heart was being ripped out of my chest.

'Why did you go? Why did you leave me?' she sobbed.

'I'm sorry, Amy, but we've been arrested for something that wasn't anything to do with us.'

We talked for a bit and I explained what had happened.

'Look, Faith's crying,' she said. 'Can you call me soon?'

'Of course. Every day.'

I hung up and put my head in my hands, tears running down my face. The call brought it home to me what I had lost. I had to face up to the very real possibility that I would never see my little girl growing up. It broke my heart in two.

I walked down the main corridor to find my friends and hear how they had got on with their calls. Tariq had told his fiancée he was going to Qatar with his friends.

'You muppet,' I said. 'Why didn't you tell her the truth?'

'I don't know, man, we might be getting out soon anyway.'

'Bruv, you should have just told her. She deserves to know the truth.'

'Fuck off, mate. I was supposed to meet her family soon. What was I supposed to say? How about you?'

'Real bad, mate. Amy was in tears and Faith was crying. It was terrible.'

'Sorry to hear that, bruv. We are innocent of all this shit and we will be getting out, you know.'

I loved Tariq for his optimism at that moment and knew I had to hold onto that hope or I would go mad. Harry had also tried to lie to his girlfriend, Sarah, but had failed abysmally.

'I tried to tell her we were going to stay a couple of days more,' he said. 'But she said, "You little wanker, your friends have been coming round with money for me as you're in jail." I had to tell her the truth and she wasn't happy.

'Sarah was crying and then I called my mum and she was crying too. Everyone keeps on crying down the phone at me and it's doing me head in.'

Harry is the big softy out of all of us, but he was the most resilient at that moment. He didn't shed a tear while Tariq and I were in bits.

I went and bought another phonecard to call some of my friends. I needed to make sure there were people looking out for Faith and Amy while I was inside. I didn't even need to ask my pals Sam and Mytus before they offered.

'Look, bruv, keep your head down and don't worry about a thing,' Sam said. 'No matter how long it takes we'll look after them.'

It was exactly what I wanted to hear and I couldn't thank them enough. I felt impotent; unable to help the ones I loved the most. But having close friends to help would make it slightly less unbearable.

I also called the British embassy and told them what had happened. An official took down our names and said someone would come out to see us.

That night I slept on a two-foot-wide bug-infested piece of sponge on the floor of Zain's room. I could feel the bugs moving as I laid my head on it. The disgusting section of a chopped-up mattress had been thrown out in the rubbish for that reason, but I had nothing else and I was exhausted. The room was the closest to the rancid toilet. The stench of rotting faeces was like sweaty balls and arse mixed with sewage. You could almost taste it.

Tariq and Harry were on the floor in the hall next to the cell, covered in a blanket so riddled with bugs that it looked like the whole cloth was alive. Despite his size Harry had an insect phobia. Needless to say this wasn't his dream scenario. Cockroaches scuttled across the floor by his head, causing him to cry out and move rapidly away.

Zain laughed and said, 'Mate, you're going to have to get used to them. This place is a health hazard infested by bugs.'

He was right. Port Rashid was a dirty, sweaty, overcrowded jail and a few creepy crawlies were the least of our worries. I closed my eyes and passed out, falling into a restless sleep. I dreamt of my former life and being away from this hell. I woke up with a bug the size of my fingernail crawling across my face. I leapt up, sending it flying. The disgusting creature had been feeding on my body and I was covered in bites. I felt sick to the core. But this was my new reality and the most terrifying thing of all was that I had no idea how I was ever going to get out of it.

8

LIVING ON A KNIFE-EDGE

'*Allahu Akbar!*' bellowed a man at the top of his voice down the hall, rousing me out of sleep and galvanizing the quiet jail into a hive of activity. Dozens of Indians and Pakistanis who had been sleeping in the corridor quickly stirred as the booming voice continued to reverberate around the jail. Tariq and Harry were forced to stand up and the small square of floor they had been sleeping on moments before was hastily covered in prayer mats. Muslims bowing down and chanting to Allah took up every square centimetre of space.

Mohammed was stood at the end of the corridor furthest away from the toilet and was leading the prayers. Not only was he the prison foreman but he was also the imam. It was 5 a.m. We sat on the floor in Zain's room in a daze.

'What the fuck's going on, man?' I said.

Zain explained that this was just the first of five calls to prayer every day.

I realized that I hadn't been to the toilet since we had entered the jail twelve hours before. I was scared that if I went off by myself I would be set upon by other inmates.

'Let's all go to the toilet together to avoid getting jumped on,' I said. 'Tariq, you go first.'

'Ah, fuck off, mate,' he said as we pushed him to the loo. We agreed we would wait outside to make sure nothing happened.

There were four toilet cubicles and four showers with doors that could, thankfully, be locked. We had all seen enough movies to know that if you were going to get raped anywhere it was in the shower. The room itself was covered in grimy white tiles and the door was 'decorated' with Arabic graffiti and crudely drawn pictures of naked women.

'Fucking hell, you have to shit in a hole in the floor,' Tariq said when he came out.

The festering toilet was one of the worst things I had ever smelt. The stench never went away during my whole time in Port Rashid, but when you were squatting above the toilet itself it was on a whole new level. The toilet consisted of a metal slab on the floor with a hole in the middle. The smell of hundreds of men's rotting shit seeped up and made me wretch. I had feared wiping my arse may be a bit of an issue and my worries were confirmed when I saw there was no toilet paper and just a jug of water. I swiftly poured it down my back and washed myself with my hand.

As we walked out of the toilet block there was a sudden rush of activity. Everyone was heading towards the canteen and we eagerly fell in with the crowd. I was starving and, by the excitement the food was generating, I was expecting a good breakfast.

The canteen was an eighty-foot-long room with marble tables and benches. A hatch was in the side of the room where Indian staff served the food and there was a forty-two-inch flat-screen TV on the far wall. There was a cacophony of noise as inmates jostled for position in the queue. Some of the men were so filthy you could see the dirt ground into their skin. Many had yellow mould growing on their feet and their pungent aroma could be smelt from metres away. I resolved to find something to put on my feet before I took a shower.

Of the 350 people in the jail around half were visa over-stayers. They had been migrant labourers who were treated worse than animals and paid a pittance for working twelve-hour days in extreme conditions. In truth, many were arrested even if they had valid visas. Abu Dhabi paid Dubai 350D – £70 – each week for every prisoner they held. Justice was superfluous when there was a profit to be made.

Mohammed's minion bodyguards, who we learned were called Qasim and Babar, were in charge of the canteen queues – a powerful position in jail as it meant they could get as much food as they wanted.

When I got to the front of the queue I discovered the food was a far cry from the fry-up I was expecting. Instead I was handed a boiled egg, a small circular piece of bread and some *semiya*, a brown but transparent type of noodle that was covered in sugar. I was not impressed.

'Mate, what the fuck is this?' I said. 'Tariq, ask your old man to get me something decent,' I joked.

'Shut up, you Somalian pirate. Go and rob someone of their flip-flops.'

I swapped my *semiya* for a boiled egg with a small Indian guy. Little did I know it was a bad move as you could save the noodles and eat them throughout the week. It would have been even more useful for us as we had been arrested during Ramadan. Although we weren't Muslims we were not given any food while the other inmates fasted. It meant an early breakfast before the sun rose at 6 a.m. Zain explained that items such as slippers, toiletries and tea could be bought from the canteen every Monday and Friday.

After breakfast we went back to Zain's cell and changed. We were allowed our own clothes, but we only had the items we had bought the day we had been arrested. We seemed to be some kind of novelty, with inmates standing in the doorway to stare at us. Zain explained to the gawpers that we were his good friends and told them to leave.

Mohammed walked into our cell. 'Ah, British boys, how do you like my jail?'

'It's all right, man,' I said.

'You managed to call home yet?'

'Yes, thanks, but it was expensive, A phonecard cost me 40D.'

'What?' he shouted, a look of anger spreading across his face. 'I will not have extortion in my jail! Come!'

We went to find the little Bengali guy who had sold me the card. Mohammed immediately started berating him in Urdu, pointing in his face. It was clear to me now he had ripped me off but I felt sorry for the guy as he stared at his feet in shame. It was like he was being told off by the headmaster. Finally Mohammed ordered him to give me two phonecards by way of compensation.

'There you go, my man,' Mohammed said as he swaggered off.

The little Bengali turned to me. 'Please, sir, please continue to buy phonecards from me. I am sorry.'

I said I would. He was only trying to make some money to survive. In the end I spread my purchases around three Indians. These people are so poor and they have to rely on their wits to stay alive. There is no benefits system to catch them in Dubai. The workers from India and Pakistan have only got what they can make for themselves. Despite being banged up in a Dubai prison, I realized how blessed my life was in comparison to theirs.

After sorting out the phonecards, I decided to go for a wander to explore the jail. I walked into the canteen and saw one of my favourite films, *Dodgeball*, was on telly. The room was teeming with Indians and there were only two benches free, so I went and sat next to a stocky black guy with his hood up. He was built like a wrestler and resembled rapper 50 Cent. I immediately regretted sitting next to him. He turned and glanced at me before looking away.

'You've been here before, haven't you?' he said in a soft American accent. I was taken aback and alarmed. He looked terrifying and I was now engaged in conversation with this potentially dangerous criminal.

'Nah, mate, I've never been to jail,' I said.

'I know you, right?'

'No, mate, I don't think so. It's my first time in Dubai.'

'What's your case?'

'I don't know yet. Some spice was found in my car.'

'You got a brother in Dubai, don't you?'

My blood ran cold. Did this muscle-bound inmate know me or was he just trying to get into my head?

'No, mate, you must be mistaken.'

He looked at me, smiled and nodded his head, before turning back to the film. We sat in an awkward silence for a few minutes before I summoned up the courage to get up and walk away. I ran back to Zain's cell to find Harry and Tariq.

'Some big black geezer has been asking me loads of questions,' I said.

'Do you recognize him?' Tariq asked.

'No.'

'Is he your boyfriend or your long lost dad?'

'Shut up, you prick.'

We were laughing but I was concerned about who this mysterious black man was. How did he know I had been to Dubai before and that I had a brother here?

One thing you learn quickly in jail is to work out what's happening purely by sounds such as people's footfall. The first thing I discovered was that if there is mad shouting and the sound of flip-flops moving fast, it's a fight. Tariq and my conversation was halted by screaming and shouting from outside the cell.

'Raaaaaaaaaaaar!' screamed the psychotic-looking Russian who had been scoping us out as we entered the jail.

I looked out of the cell to see him piling into a six-foot-tall Arab with dark skin and short curly hair. Zain skirted the flying fists and came back into his cell. 'Shit, man, that crazy, unhinged Russian has just attacked Ayoop. He's the leader of the local gangsters. You wouldn't want to fuck with him, bruv.'

He explained the local gangsters were in for having fights with massive swords. They were mainly drug dealers, but in jail they kept themselves to themselves. We knew we had to respect them.

Within seconds the unhinged Russian was on the floor being pummelled by Ayoop. He was only saved from a much worse fate when Mohammed came rushing out of his cell and ordered the fight be stopped.

Port Rashid was like a tinderbox where violence could break out at any moment, and it often did. It was like living on a knife-edge.

I needed some fresh air so headed to the only place where you could find it in the entire jail, the hoosh. This thirty-foot-square area was surrounded by a twenty-five-foot wall. A wire mesh went across the top while the floor was made up of grey and white tiles. Inmates were asleep all over the floor despite the midday sun shining high in the sky. I was shocked at the sight before me and could see no way through, so went back inside.

The daylight hours in Port Rashid were for catching up on

your sleep. Prisoners would stir for a visit or to pray but generally it was a fairly quiet place. The night-time hours of 10 p.m. to 2 a.m. were when the jail came to life, when fewer guards were on duty and nefarious activity could take place.

As soon as the clock struck ten it was like a school bell had gone off, bringing everyone out of their slumber. The main corridor, where many of the Indians and Pakistanis slept, was affectionately dubbed 'the strip', but Las Vegas this was not. That evening I wandered down the corridor, taking in the remarkable sights and sounds. We were in jail but the strip resembled an Arabian street market or a souk. It was organized chaos, with cigarettes and *dokha* the main items on sale. I had no idea how they managed to get contraband into the jail, but clearly there was a way.

I passed Ayoop and the local gangsters playing cards on a blanket outside their cell. As I walked past the next cell I saw Mohammed engaged in serious conversation with the big black guy who had asked me about my brother earlier that day. It made me even more wary that the man who seemed to know things about me appeared to be close to Mohammed and was potentially a serious player in the jail.

Little Bengalis were rushing around doing everybody's washing while others were getting their hustle on trying to sell tea. It seemed everybody had something going on.

A group of Pakistanis were playing Ludo while others were putting some chicken and rice together. The Russians were in their cell and stared at me as I walked past. They were the individuals I was most scared of in the jail. They all looked like they could kill you with their little fingers.

As I headed back to Zain's cell, it was apparent that the closer you got to the toilet, the lower down the pecking order you were. We were on the floor in the end cell where Zain had been banished to for being a snitch. Things had to improve and I was determined to do something about it.

Mohammed breezed in. 'What's going on, British? Make sure you have your stuff ready to go tomorrow as I have a bed for you,' he said, pointing at me. I think he took mercy on me because of my hand which still constantly ached.

'Thank you so much, man.'

'All right, but don't say anything as others should have a bed before you. Don't worry, I will make a westerners' cell for you all. We have an Arab cell, now you get a westerners' cell.'

We were lucky. Mohammed had our back and was looking out for us – maybe because we were British or just because we got along. Whatever his reasons, I could have kissed him.

Dinner was some putrid, stringy chicken and rice. I was starving and tucked in, but within a couple of minutes I felt nauseous. I ran to the toilet and threw up while breathing in the disgusting smell of other men's rotting shit. I wandered back to the cell in a daze.

'You all right, bruv?' Harry said. 'I think there might be nuts in the rice, mate, so you'd better avoid it from now on.'

'Fuck, man, that's why I was sick.'

I'm seriously allergic to nuts and had been close to going into anaphylactic shock in the past. That was the last thing I wanted in a Dubai jail.

The next day I was shown my new bed in the Syrians' cell. It was three cells from the entrance end of the corridor. Three sets of bunk beds were up against the walls but, considering we were in a fleapit of a jail, it didn't feel too claustrophobic. Curtains, which appeared to be made out of bed sheets, hung down, concealing the bottom bunk and giving the owners of those beds some privacy. Samir, a fat Syrian, was the leader of the group and introduced himself and the other three men from his homeland. Mohammed had previously told me they were all in for fraud.

'There's a nice clean bed for you there,' he said to me. 'You can leave your stuff in this room, no problem. It will be safe.'

Mohammed swaggered in. 'Hey, man, you met everyone? You'll be safe here, British, the Syrians are good people.'

I expressed my gratitude to them all. I had been in the jail for two days and had been given a bed. Things were looking up.

Tariq, Harry and I were all starting to smell so made a pact to finally have a shower. We bought slippers and shower gel from the canteen and took it in turns to brave the fungus-ridden cubicles. The two of them stood guard while I cleaned myself for the first time in days. Little flies flew round my head as I put shampoo on the floor and in the shower head to cover up the rank smell. I let the boiling hot water wash over me, closing my eyes and pretending that I was home. But as soon as I opened my eyes there was the stinking hell that was Port Rashid.

Although things were grim, in those first few days we slowly began to assimilate ourselves into prison life. You have to adapt to survive. After a couple more days Harry was offered a bed in the room run by Mohammed's sidekicks Qasim and Babar. This odd pair, in their early twenties, were both manual labourers in for murder after Babar, a short but stocky Pakistani man, was raped and turned on his attacker. Mohammed told us that Babar stabbed the man to death. He then took the corpse around to his friend Qasim's flat where they stashed it. But this is where the story got really psychotic.

'So, man, they called this guy's brother,' Mohammed said, 'and they said, "We've killed your brother, we bummed him and killed him." So his brother called the police and they tracked them down and found the body still warm at Qasim's house.'

Master criminals these guys were not. Despite having to share a room with them Harry fell out with Qasim straight away. The Pakistani murderer had pictures of little girls aged three or four on his wall. This wasn't because they were his family, but because he found them sexually attractive.

'Take them down, man,' Harry said. 'In my country this is wrong. You are the lowest of the low if you hurt children.' Qasim and Babar didn't care. They had no sense of morality.

It may sound warped but part of adapting to prison life was accepting people for what they were. Even though one was a psychotic murderer and both displayed clear paedophilic tendencies, we had to learn to live with them. Harry, Tariq and I were quick to learn that we were powerless to change things. We could hate a guy all we liked for having pictures of kids on his walls but it was wasted energy. Sometimes it seemed my friends and I were the only ones in that jail with a set of morals. But we had to stay with these people for the foreseeable future and fighting the world would not make any difference, it would only make our time that much harder.

We learned that the Arab attitude to sexuality is totally different from our way of thinking. Most men we met would happily have sex with a man, but only if they were the one penetrating the other. They didn't consider that made them gay. I was walking down the strip when I heard one inmate talking to the mysterious black guy who seemed to know who I was.

'So, man, I had this male maid who had a cute arse so I bent him over and fucked him,' the inmate said. 'My wife found out and said I was gay! But how can I be gay if *I* fucked *him*?'

After a few days in Port Rashid I realized things could be a lot worse and the main reason they weren't was down to Mohammed. He was a crazy drug dealer on the one hand, but he would teach the Qur'an to inmates on the other. He was a very spiritual guy. He didn't drink tea or smoke, saying, 'This is not the way of Allah.' Our fears of being raped also turned out to be redundant, largely because of our friendly foreman. 'No fucking in my jail,' he said.

9

TWENTY-FIVE TO DEATH

When we heard the officials from the British embassy were coming to see us a week into our incarceration it was like the sun was finally breaking through the clouds. Surely after they heard our story they would be able to do something about our wrongful arrest and get us out of this hellhole?

Captain Aziz called us to the door where we had entered the jail to tell us we had a visit from the embassy officials.

'*Inshallah*, you boys will be going home,' he said. 'This spice isn't even illegal.'

This was music to our ears. I was with Harry, Tariq, Zain, Matt, his friend Gary and the spice kid Danny as we walked across the other side of the visitors' area and into the office of the main jail boss, Captain Abbas. Zain and Matt were keeping their distance from each other and I could feel the tension between them. I still didn't believe Zain could be a snitch, but Matt had been good to us since we had entered the jail so I wasn't sure of the truth. We had been playing a lot of blackjack to pass the time. The fact I had been winning made it better.

Harry and Danny were talking. They had started to get close which worried me. The spice kids were ruffling feathers, throwing their cash around and making themselves bigger targets than they already were. More than ever, I didn't want me and my friends lumped in with them.

'What do you think this is all about?' Danny said.

'I ain't got a clue, bruv, but it's got to be a good thing, right?' Harry said.

I didn't know what to expect as we entered the office. Aziz led us into the room where two smartly dressed women were sat behind a desk. The older and better-dressed of the two introduced herself as Mandy Smith, the vice consul. She was in her early fifties but was well groomed and, in my sex-starved state, my first impression was she was extremely hot. Sat beside her was a young Arab woman who introduced herself as Hibba. Without any pleasantries Mandy looked down at a sheet of paper in front of her and delivered the most shocking statement I have ever heard.

'So, we are here today so you can sign your paperwork. Karl Williams, you have been charged with drug trafficking and the maximum sentence is twenty-five years or the death penalty.'

It felt like all of the blood drained from my body and I was immediately sick on the ground. She went on to read the same charges to Tariq and Harry. They looked stunned and the colour drained from their cheeks. As a result of having some drugs planted in our car we were looking down the barrels of a firing squad. Twenty-five years or death. That moment everything changed. I was numb. All of the dreams I had for my life fell away. My throat was dry and I was in a daze. This couldn't be happening to us.

Mandy went on to read the charges to the others. Danny was charged with dealing after his girlfriend snitched on him.

'You are facing twenty-five years or the death penalty,' Mandy said to him too.

Danny started crying quietly to himself. There was no time to console him as Mandy went on to tell Zain and Matt their potential fate.

'You are charged with possession and use and you are facing up to four years' imprisonment,' she said.

'This is your fault, you prick!' Matt said to Zain.

'Shut up, I ain't a snitch.'

I wasn't interested in their petty squabbles. I was still reeling from the bombshell that had just been delivered.

'How have we been charged with trafficking when we weren't even at an airport?' I asked, struggling to get my words out.

'I don't know, that's what the police said,' Hibba replied.

'Tell them what happened to you,' Zain piped up.

Harry, Tariq and I started telling her the story of our arrest at the same time.

'Stop! One at a time,' Mandy said.

We took her through our tale of torture at the hands of the police. As I told them of being arrested at gunpoint, beaten and electrocuted, Mandy and Hibba's mouths fell open.

'This is not acceptable,' Mandy said. 'Do you remember which officers?'

I told them that it was a handful of the arresting officers while others just stood by and watched. Hibba had got a notepad out and was scribbling down everything we said.

'So have you been to the hospital for your hand?' she said.

'No.'

'How have you not been in hospital? You have been in jail for more than a week? We will make sure you are seen by a doctor.'

Hibba was looking at my arms and said, 'What are all of these thin scratches? Did they do this to you?'

I hadn't even noticed the lines that were all over my body. It was like dozens of paper cuts all over me.

'I guess so, they weren't there before,' I replied. I later discovered they were the evidence of the electrocution I'd suffered.

She told us to take our shirts off and started noticing bruising all over our bodies. I'm black and bruises don't usually show up on me but there were some massive ones I hadn't seen.

'This is unacceptable,' Hibba said.

'So what are you gonna do about it?' Tariq said.

'I am going to write a strongly worded letter.'

'A letter? Is that all you can do? A letter?' I said.

I was shocked that the British embassy could do nothing more than write to the police to complain. I thought they might be able to do more for us than express their annoyance at out treatment. Mandy explained we would be remanded in custody until our trial date and told us we would have to pay for our own legal representation. She said she could provide us with the details of lawyers later.

Mandy gave us a wad of paper with a list of charities that we could sign up to who could potentially help us.

'What do I have to lose?' I said, accepting them.

'Absolutely nothing,' she replied.

I signed all of the paperwork in five minutes. One of those organizations was Reprieve, a charity that helps those who have suffered human rights abuses. At that moment I had little faith that anyone would be able to rescue us.

As we walked back into the jail I started to descend into a black hole. The depression seemed to creep into my every pore, pulling a dark cloud over me. This feeling was to stay with me, shrouding my mind, for the length of my time in jail. I didn't give a fuck about anyone or anything. We were facing the death penalty so what mattered any more?

There was immediate tension between all three of us friends and we were at each other's throats.

'Why the fuck did you talk to Maz in the club, man? If you hadn't spoken to him none of this would have happened,' Tariq said.

'Fuck off, mate, you weren't complaining when you were driving a BMW 6 series around Dubai, were you? I've got more things to worry about than you. I've got a newborn baby at home while all you've got is some silly bird you've met a few times yet are supposedly going to marry.'

'Yeah, mate, and we should never have got that car,' Harry said, pointing at Tariq. 'You wanted to get a fucking Porsche so we ended up with the Beemer. It was too flash.'

None of it mattered, but there was so much anger inside us. We were hurting at the prospect of the nightmare ahead of us and we needed somebody else to blame. That meant taking it out on the people who were closest to us. It was totally irrational. We were looking for anything to fight over.

The first person we encountered back in the jail was Mohammed.

'Yo, boys. How are you doing? The embassy getting you out of here?' he said.

I handed over our charge sheet that said we had been accused of possession, facilitation and trafficking of around half a kilo of spice. Mohammed's face dropped.

'This is a big problem for you, my friends,' he said. 'You boys are in big trouble.'

Our normally jovial foreman's serious demeanour was worrying me even more. This was a man who was a hard-core drugs trafficker and he had a look of pity on his face. He took us into his room where the big black guy who seemed to know I had been in Dubai before was sitting.

'Yo, Baariq, check this out.'

Baariq read down the charge sheet and said, 'You boys are in trouble.'

These were people who were facing twenty-five years themselves and when I saw their reactions of pure shock and fear for us I started to panic.

The news was causing quite a stir in the jail and some of the other big bosses came into the cell to see us. Ayoop gave us his condolences while I was introduced to Russian Mafioso Rivas. He was the big bald Russian I had been so terrified of when we entered the jail, but at this moment he was full of sympathy for our plight. Along with him was another Russian called Andre, a slim blond guy who spoke as if he'd studied at Oxford. I was later to learn he was a master burglar who got kicks out of tickling his victims' feet as they slept and videoing it.

Mohammed tried to lighten the mood. 'Boys, you are going to be with me, but I am going to be out before you,' he tried to joke, but it wasn't funny. This was a guy caught with hundreds of kilos of hash yet he was saying we would be in jail longer than him. 'Seriously though, if you only get convicted of possession and get off the more serious charges you will get the minimum sentence of four years. If you manage that, then you'll be out at Ramadan, as that's when all the cases of four years or less get pardoned.'

During the previous week in jail we had only told Zain about the torture we had suffered at the hands of the police. We had pushed it to the back of our minds, our energies taken up with worrying about food, our friends and surviving the nightmare we were going through. Now I mentioned to Mohammed that the embassy officials were going to write a letter about our torture.

'What, what is this?' he said. 'You were tortured? What happened?'

We retold our story of being ambushed, beaten, driven into the desert and electrocuted. These guys, hardened prisoners who had been through the Dubai system, were in shock and disgusted by what had happened to us.

'This is not right,' Baariq said. 'Yeah, sure, you get a little slap or punch, but they electrocuted you?'

We were taken aback by their reaction. When I watched programmes where people got tortured abroad I always thought it was just how that police force, however wrongly, dealt with the people they arrested. Although we had been brutally tortured we merely thought this was the norm for Dubai police so there was no point in complaining.

'What did your embassy say?' Mohammed said. 'You guys are British so surely you can do something about this? On this side of the world when it comes to embassies the US and UK have power. You guys have power, you have a voice. You guys can change things in this country.'

'Mate, we don't have a voice.'

'You are British. Did you see an Arab or Pakistani embassy official out there? Exactly. Call your embassy every day. You can change things in this country.'

The other prisoners were giving us belief that we could fight this. They were saying that we could use what had happened to us as a tool. We already knew that the authorities wanted to fuck us because we had seen the charge sheet. If it wasn't for those handful of prisoners in Port Rashid, we would never have really believed we could fight the injustices that had happened to us.

I could sense that before our fellow inmates had seen our charge sheet they thought we were just like the other spice kids. To them we were spoilt little rich boys who had somehow managed to find themselves in jail with drug traffickers and murderers.

'You guys are big spice drug dealers,' Baariq said, sounding impressed. It turned out that the drugs were worth 100,000 dirhams (£20,000) – that was some serious cash. Like other inmates, he clearly disbelieved our claims to be innocent, but now we looked like players people started to sit up and take notice. We were bizarrely in a minority as most of the inmates were proud of the charges against them and would boast of the amount of drugs they had imported into Dubai. We all continued to reiterate that the drugs weren't ours but I knew we could play on this to make our life a bit easier inside. This was the chance I was looking for to distance ourselves from the other kids.

Slowly the others disappeared from the room, leaving me with Baariq. 'You still don't remember me, do you?' he said.

'No, I don't.'

'Do you remember the fight in the nightclub where you got into a brawl and a couple of police officers helped you? Well, one of them was me.'

I suddenly realized he was the cop who had dragged me away from the trouble when I was living in Dubai, and I apologized for not recognizing him sooner.

'Yeah, and you lied to me about not being to Dubai before!' he said, laughing.

'I'm sorry, brother, but when you came up to me and said you knew me I thought you wanted to bum me.'

'No, I'm not like that. That is *haram*.'

Baariq, who was from the Sudan, was a monster of pure muscle with a six-pack a world champion boxer would be proud of. As a former police officer he had been rewarded with a high position in the jail and was effectively number two behind Mohammed. Police officers, especially those who had been screwed by the authorities as I was later to learn that Baariq was, were given positions of authority by the jail bosses. Mohammed was a pure Emirati while Baariq was a former police officer so both had high standing in society – an all-important feature in Dubai. They were both also capable of keeping order as they commanded so much respect. It was an interesting, if slightly difficult, dynamic between Baariq the former cop and Mohammed the drug trafficker. It somehow worked, even though they clearly didn't like each other. It was a marriage of convenience.

Mohammed came back into the cell with a six-foot-tall and stocky, light-skinned Arab guy. He had black curly hair and a massive scar across his chest.

'Hey, Karl, this is good friend of mine, Arif,' Mohammed said. 'He lives in my cell.'

Arif nodded at me. I was to learn he didn't speak a word of English and was one of Mohammed's enforcers, who would break up fights and inflict punishment beatings on those who got out of line. He was a terrifying character and I made a mental note to avoid him.

It turned out Arif had been a close protection officer for the sheikh. His 'crime' was that he had the balls to arrest a high-powered official's son after he caught him with several kilos of heroin. But when he took him to the police station he was not commended for the arrest, but detained himself. One of his superiors said to him, 'No, the drugs belong to you. That's an official's son, are you crazy?' Arif was a higher rank than most of the guards who were in the jail and he didn't hide his disdain for them or the other inmates. Smoking may have been banned for the rest of us but he walked around with a cigarette in his hand. He knew he was untouchable because of his influence and would tell those guarding us what to do.

Arif's story opened my eyes to what the Dubai justice system could do to you. If you messed with the wrong people, or those in power wanted you out of the way, there was nothing you could do.

Once the buzz of the news about our charges died down I called home as I needed to hear Amy's voice. I felt exhausted and dazed. I had never been so low. When I told her the news she burst into tears and was inconsolable.

'Look, babe, calm down. It's going to be all right. They just say these things to scare you.'

'What happens if you are executed or get twenty-five years? What am I going to do with Faith? What are you going to do if you get jailed for that long?'

I understood Amy wanted answers but the barrage of questions was too much. I was the one facing twenty-five or death. Faith started to cry in the background and it broke my heart. I had to get used to the reality that I may never see my little girl growing up. If police officers had been fitted up and were in jail alongside me, what chance did I have? I felt like the embassy had washed their hands of us, basically telling us we would be lucky to avoid a firing squad.

I told Amy I had to go as there was a queue for the phone and made my way back to my cell. I lay down on my bed, my insides churning up with anger and fear. There was only one way to quell the pain and to try to avoid facing reality. I forced myself to go to sleep.

10

HIWAN

I can honestly say I wasn't a very nice person in the days after I heard I could be facing the death penalty. Tariq and Harry wanted to spend time with me the following day but I wasn't interested. All I wanted to do was sleep to quell the pain.

'Come chill with us, Ceaze,' Tariq said.

'I can't be fucked, man,' I said. 'We're gonna be in here a long time.'

'Fuck off then, you prick,' Harry said.

'And you can fuck off, mate,' I said. 'You're hanging around with all of these little rape candidates. What do you think is gonna happen to you if you're with them all the time? We're facing life in jail and we're gonna end up in a serious nick full of murderers and rapists. If you hang around with them you're gonna be a target.'

'I don't even give a shit, Ceaze, just fuck off.'

I knew we wouldn't be in Port Rashid for more than a few months before we were transferred to a top-security jail. Once we were charged we would be moved. I stormed off to my cell to sleep.

*

I woke up later that evening to the most glorious aroma wafting through my cell. It was as if my nostrils had been transported to heaven. When you are incarcerated in a cockroach-infested fleapit with an ubiquitous smell of rotting faeces and unwashed bodies, you learn the true value of something that smells good. I looked over the side of my bunk to see around 200 chicken, lamb and beef burgers spread out on the floor. Next to them were dozens of bottles of tropical juice. I pinched myself, but I wasn't dreaming.

It was illegal to bring food into the jail but there were enough burgers to feed a small army on the floor. After the disgusting food I had endured so far during my prison stay – slops that often consisted of gristly chicken with bones that splintered in your mouth, in a tasteless brown watery gravy – this was too exciting for words. I was ready to tuck in as I got down from my bed and made a move for one of the burgers.

I was quickly put in my place when Samir shouted, 'No, no, this we sell.'

'Come on, man, let me buy this now,' I said. 'I want this.'

'No, you wait.'

My mouth was watering so badly that I would happily have paid any price for one of the tasty smelling burgers. I sat on my bed staring at the delicious food until Mohammed came in to count the stock.

'Yo, man, you like the look of these?!' he said with a big smile on his face

'Listen, I will do anything for three of those hamburgers and a bottle of tropical juice.'

'Ah, you do *anything*, British?' He said it with a smile on his face, unsubtly suggesting I would pay for the burger with my body, which clearly wasn't going to happen.

'Nah, mate, how much cash will a burger cost me?'

'Each burger is five dirhams but you must wait.'

'So how the fuck is this allowed?'

'You see? This is what big drug dealers are allowed.'

He explained that the burgers were smuggled in once a week with the help of one of the guards. I was stunned.

'Fucking hell, is that what's really what's going on?'

'Yo, man, these jail guards are paid a pittance and there's money to be made from us. Money makes the world go round outside but inside everything is magnified. When things are wanted by the prisoners the price goes up. I have my sources and they can make thousands of dirhams out of us.'

Samir was running the crooked burger scam but it was over-seen by Mohammed.

'Yo, man, we have to bring this stuff in. You don't wanna be eating the food in here as it stops you getting hard, if you know what I mean, British?' he said smiling.

'What?'

'They put chemicals in the gravy to lower everybody's sex drive. They don't want all of the prisoners fucking each other,' he said.

I vowed to steer clear of the gravy. I was already avoiding the rice and now I would have to live on bread and cheese as I didn't think they could be pumped full of chemicals.

After the burgers were counted I was finally allowed to buy some and tuck in. As I sank my teeth into the heavenly meat I noticed there was a sudden movement of dozens of people outside my cell. The beautiful smell had permeated its way through the stinking jail and had excited the masses as much as it had me. I looked up to see the pleading eyes of hungry inmates looking through the cell door as I chomped into my burger. It was like feeding time at the zoo. There were hands coming through the cell bars trying to grab stuff off the floor so Samir ordered me to come down from my bunk and stop them from nicking everything.

The number of burgers each inmate could buy was rationed to two per person. But as always money talked in prison and most of the Bengalis couldn't afford to buy a single one. They looked on longingly but I wasn't in a position to help them.

Harry and Tariq came by to get their share of burgers but I ignored them after our row.

I wasn't a very easy person to deal with in those days as I was angry at the world, stressed out and depressed. My friends were an easy target. I tried to avoid them and spent a lot of time with Gary, who had been caught with Matt, in the next couple of days playing blackjack. Cards could be bought from the canteen. We wouldn't play for money as he was a Muslim and refused to gamble. I constantly beat him.

'Mate, I've got to introduce you to Ed,' he said. 'He's great at blackjack.' He took me into his cell and introduced me to him.

'So you're the blackjack guy?' he said in a cool Colorado accent.

Ed was a five-foot-eleven, stocky American in his early fifties. His hair was grey and white and was cut into a flat top. I immediately liked him and we were to become the best of friends.

'Come on then, show me what you got,' he said.

Ed shared a cell with the bald-headed Rivas who was sat on his bunk playing solitaire. Rivas, who was in his early thirties, had been arrested after a brawl. He was also charged with a high-level fraud. He was an enforcer for the Mafia, but didn't like to talk about his criminal enterprises on the outside.

'How's your little girl?' I asked.

Rivas had a daughter around the same age as Faith. The difference for him was that he was looking at about a year inside.

'She's all right, man, but I miss her.'

'I know, my friend.'

When you spoke to Rivas you'd never know that he used violence to make a living. He was the perfect example of first impressions being wrong. He may have looked like a tough Russian gangster, but he was a lovely guy.

I played with Ed for a while before I headed back to my cell to look at the papers the embassy had given us. I was feeling too depressed to sift through them before but now I was looking for any ray of hope that could potentially end this horrific saga. In one leaflet it said that British citizens arrested in a foreign country could be extradited back to the UK. This was great news. Serving a sentence in the UK would be a million times better than in the hellhole I was currently in. I would also be able to see Amy and Faith. I called the embassy and spoke to Hibba who was not able to offer much comfort.

'No, the substance you were caught with isn't illegal in the UK so as a result it's not an offence to possess or sell it here,' she said. 'Therefore there is no way of extraditing you back to Britain on your charges.'

This was like rubbing salt in a gaping wound. If we dodged a firing squad we could be stuck here for the next twenty-five years. I didn't know what to do so I called Amy. She was my emotional support, and without her I'm not sure I would have got through the experience alive. I told her about not being able to get extradited and she tried to get me to focus on what was really important.

'Karl, I know this is hard, but you will get through this. You have to. There is somebody here who needs you and wants you to speak to her.'

She held the phone up to Faith's ear and I told my little girl how much I loved her and that I would be home soon. She made baby gurgling noises on the phone. Tears welled up in my eyes.

Although it was one of the toughest things I had to endure I wanted her to hear my voice and know who I was.

My head was full of sadness and anger as I hung up the phone. I was desperately sad about missing out on my daughter's life and angry at the world for this injustice. From time to time I'd try to distract myself with cards or chatting to other inmates, but underneath I felt like I was shrouded in a constant shadow. Sometimes this manifested itself in me lashing out.

Every Sunday and Wednesday were 'chicken days' in the canteen and were a highlight. Other days were less appetizing as we were served chickpeas or dhal with impotence-inducing gravy. Chicken days created pandemonium as inmates fought to get to the front of the queue. Nobody wanted the spindly legs, they were all keen to get their hands on the only decent bit of meat, the breast.

My hand was bandaged but that didn't stop Urfan, a big Pakistani killer from Zain's room, from barging past me. He was in charge of the queue that day and was trying to get to the front to control the inmates. I felt a sudden pain in my hand. The better course of action would probably have been to ignore what had just happened. After all, it was normal behaviour in the jail on chicken days. But I was angry, thought I had nothing to lose and wasn't going to let anybody push me around.

I shoved him back. 'Get the fuck out of my way.'

'What you doing? Go to the back of the line now.'

'No, why would I go to the back? You just pushed past me. Can't you see my hand is in a sling?'

'Shut up and do what you're told.'

'Fuck you, you prick.'

'No, fuck you,' he snapped, walking up towards me and getting within a few inches of my face.

Mohammed had heard the commotion. 'What's going on, man?'

'This prick just barged past me.'

'So what do you want to do about it?'

'I'm going to have it out.'

'Okay, go on then.'

I started to rip off the bandage. As it came off I realized I had gone too far; challenging a hardened killer to a fight with a broken hand was not a good idea. Urfan and Mohammed were looking at me like I was insane. It probably wasn't too far from the truth. Mohammed suddenly grabbed me around the shoulders.

'No, you can't fight, man, come to my room.'

I was elated inside as I couldn't be seen to be backing down. The foreman marched me to his cell.

'Yo, man, what's wrong with you? You're crazy.'

'Mate, I don't give a shit. I'm not going to get pushed around by anybody while I'm here.'

'I know, but then there's acting insane. You need Allah. Why don't you come and pray with us?'

'Nah, man, I ain't doing that.'

'Okay, but you can't be squaring up to people like him as then you will have to fight all of the Pakistanis. Hundreds of them will come out of nowhere and they will stamp you to death.'

'Fuck it, if they kill me, they kill me.' I honestly didn't care any more.

I walked out of his cell and went to see Zain.

'What the fuck are you doing?' Zain said as I walked in. 'You can't be fighting all of these guys at once.'

'If I have to fight them then I have to fight them. I don't give a shit.'

'You're mental, mate, you're *hiwan*.'

The Indians in Zain's room started to laugh. '*Hiwan, hiwan,*' they chanted. The literal meaning was animal, and it stuck as my name in jail. Harry and Tariq came into the cell to see how I was. Like all good friends we argue, but within hours things are all right again. I told them about my conversation with Hibba.

'We're fucked then, ain't we?' Tariq said.

'Well you're gonna have to call off the wedding, aren't you?' I said with a smile on my face.

'Fuck off, man, I love her.'

'Yeah, course you do.'

'Seriously, what the fuck are we gonna do?' Tariq said.

I suddenly had an idea. 'You know, we're just gonna have to kill somebody and then we'll get extradited.'

'Mate, that's just fucking stupid,' Harry said.

'How else are we gonna get deported?'

'You're insane.'

Zain had heard enough. 'You lot are idiots,' he said as he walked out.

'So who shall we murder?' Tariq said with a serious look on his face. What about that dickhead Zain?'

'Nah, man, we can't kill him, let's just kill random.'

The twisted ideas that come to you when you're under extreme pressure show how the human mind can be affected by stress. To me at that moment in time it seemed like a completely rational plan. Why do twenty-five years here when we could get deported to the UK if we committed an offence that was also a crime there? I mentioned my idea to Ed.

'Hey, man, that's a fucking stupid idea,' he said. 'You'll get the death penalty for sure.'

Apart from the obvious downside of having to kill somebody he had spotted the other major flaw in our ridiculous plan. We were stuck here and there was nothing we could do about it.

We settled down for a few games of blackjack so I could try to forget reality. Within minutes there was loud commotion outside. I immediately assumed this was another fight – there seemed to be a couple of brawls a week – but then I realized that the tone in the shouting Indians' voices was one of panic rather than excitement.

'Ninjas! Ninjas! Ninjas!' they screamed.

'Aw, fuck, man,' Ed said. 'Boys, put all your tobacco in your balls as in a minute you're gonna see a bunch of ninjas running through here.'

'What do you mean ninjas?'

'Well, they're riot police but they look like ninjas and they have big riot shields, batons and tasers. They're gonna spin the whole jail.'

I could hear some of the inmates running towards the toilet to flush away contraband. Within seconds two cops wearing black commando trousers, long black T-shirts and balaclavas covering their faces stormed in. All you could see was their eyes.

'*Yallah! Yallah!* Go!'

All 350 inmates were herded towards the canteen. At the door stood two ninjas who took it in turns to frisk the prisoners. Alongside them was the main jail boss Captain Abbas. He was younger than I expected and had an immaculately preened moustache that curled upwards at the edges and a goatee beard. Another cop was filming the whole event. The ninja on the left looked at my sling and then barely touched me.

Baariq was stood behind me in the queue. 'Wow, they hardly even searched you,' he said. 'It must be because of your hand. They are scared to touch you in case they aggravate it.'

I didn't think anything more of it.

The noise in the canteen slowly built as more and more prisoners entered. Mohammed clambered onto a table and shouted,

'Everybody quiet!' When the room fell silent he said, 'Look, look, we have some rappers in the building. Stepping up we have Bobby, all the way from Sudan.'

It was like the precursor to a boxing match as Bobby stepped forward and performed for the jail, rapping about people getting shot in Sudan. I was impressed as I had no idea he could rap. When he finished there was a huge round of applause.

'And we have another rapper, all the way from London, England,' Mohammed shouted. 'Mr British Kerroll. Stand up! Stand up!'

I got onto the table and sang the song I had composed about the police called 'Blue Lights'. I sang:

'Last week chilling on them roads with my peeps them, weed spliff burning in the air what a fragrance. Money on the floor from blackjack on the pavement, strange cars coming, you know it's CID them.'

At the mention of CID the whole room erupted.

'Quiet! Quiet!' shouted Mohammed as he tried to control the crowds. 'Carry on, British, carry on.'

I sung the rest of the song and the crowd went mad. As I finished the ninjas left their posts and we were allowed back into the jail. Some mattresses had been ripped in half and people's possessions were scattered all over the floor. It looked like the prison had been burgled.

Qasim and Babar came into my cell. 'Pucka pucka CID, pucka pucka!' Qasim said in a strong Indian accent. It was his way of saying, 'Fucking good song, must sing again.' It's funny how something as simple as singing a song can break the ice. Performing for the jail while a bunch of ninja cops ransacked our cells made the inmates see me in a different light and dozens of prisoners came into my cell to congratulate me.

'Yo, man, that's cool shit, bro,' Bobby said as he walked through the door. 'We should work on a song together.'

Bobby was a good lad and I liked him. He told me he was originally from the Sudan but had been living in Brooklyn, New York, for years. He had travelled around as his dad was a diplomat but had been kicked out of the US when his father died. He did not want to go back to Africa as he would have had to do national service so he'd moved to Dubai.

After all that excitement I was tired so went for a nap. I was woken up by Baariq who looked animated.

'Karl, you write, don't you?' he said.

'Yeah, I can write.'

'Do you think you could write me a love poem? It's for a girl I love. I'll give you lots of *dokha*.'

'I don't write poems as such but I could write you a song.'

'Great, can you start now?'

'Yeah, mate, no problem.' Baariq walked off with a smile on his face. I had no intention of writing him a silly love song for a girl he was obsessed with right then. It would have to wait until I'd slept.

I laid back down and fell asleep. Ninjas, singing and requests to write a love song for a hardened criminal – it had been a strange day.

11

BLACK OPS ED

Ed was one of the main reasons I managed to maintain my sanity in Port Rashid. A few days after I'd rapped in the dining hall, Mohammed came to me with some good news.

'Black British, yo, man, I got you a westerners' cell. You can move in with Ed and Rivas.'

'Wicked, bruv, thank you so much.'

'You spend your whole time in here anyway, man, so that's cool,' Ed said as I brought my stuff in. Staying with the Syrians had been fine, but I'd formed a good relationship with Ed and Rivas so I was delighted to be moving in with them. Even more good news was to come a couple of days later when Tariq moved into our cell as well. As you walked into the room there were two sets of bunks along the wall. We were both on the top and Tariq's head was by my feet as the bunks were so close together.

'Behave in here, Tariq, or I'll kick you in the head while you sleep,' I joked.

'Fuck off, you Somalian pirate.'

Rivas came in the room looking stressed. 'Shit, I need to get my hands on a phone.'

'What's up, bruv?' I said.

'I need to get a phone to my boys in Central.'

'What's it like there?'

'Look, you really don't want to go there. There are lots of big fights, murders and rapes every week. It's nothing like this place. This place is like a walk in the park in comparison.'

'Yeah, man, I've heard about Central,' Ed said. 'It's real bad.'

Tariq and I looked at each other. 'Fuck that, we don't want to go there,' Tariq said. The thought of going to a jail where rape and murder were the norm filled me with fear.

'Anyway, I have friends in Central and they need a phone,' Rivas said. 'If I can get one, my wife will pick it up from here and take it to a guard who will smuggle the phone in for us.'

'Look, mate, I've got one in my property and you can have it,' I said.

'How are you going to get it?'

'I can just take it out of my property and put it in yours, mate, no problem.'

'You would do that for me?'

'Yeah, of course.'

Rivas thanked me profusely. He explained that he needed the phone sent to Central but the sim card brought back into the jail so he could contact his friends on a handset he had with Baariq.

I walked up to the hatch and saw the guard called Feroz, one of the good guards.

'British, what's up?'

I explained I needed to get my phone from the store cupboard and put it in Rivas's property as his wife needed it.

'No problem, my friend.' He opened the door and I walked into the reception area where the room to the storage cupboard was situated. While his back was turned I removed the sim card and slid it into my cast before putting the phone in Rivas's bag.

'*Shukran*,' I said, thanking Feroz for his kindness.

'Fuck, man, how did you do this?' Rivas said with a smile on his face as I handed him the sim.

'I just smuggled it in in my sling.'

Baariq came into the cell. 'So you got us a sim card?'

'Yes, mate.'

'Yeah, man, well done.'

It turned out Baariq had a Blackberry but did not have a sim for it, and I was happy to have done them a favour.

The days went faster when I was in good company and black-jack with Ed filled the hours. We kept track of the score in a little notepad I had. Ed would write 'Karl is a loser' as he won a tour-nament and I would jokingly call him a prick, even though something about him suggested he could have snapped me in two.

Harry, Tariq and I were sat around in our cell one morning while prayers were going on. The food and water were not agreeing with us and we all had terrible guts. It made me emit the highest pitched, squeakiest, stinkiest farts I have ever done. We decided to have some fun. While the whole jail was silent apart from the hum of prayer, Harry turned to me and said, 'Are we really going to do this?'

I looked at him and smiled as I let out the most almighty fart. It was like a plane taking off followed by an explosion. The noise echoed around the jail. Tariq, Harry and I were in stitches. We simply couldn't stop laughing. Minutes later when prayers had finished Baariq and Mohammed came storming into our cell while we were still struggling to keep it together.

'We know this was you!' Baariq shouted. He sounded angry but he was trying not to smile. 'You can't do this during prayers, have some respect.'

'Yeah, come on, guys, this isn't on,' Mohammed said. 'You'll get lynched if you do this again.'

We apologized while trying to keep straight faces.

The following day I was sat on Ed's bunk playing another hand when Baariq came running into the cell.

'Karl, take this and hide it in your sling,' he said, looking panicked as he handed me his phone. 'The ninjas are coming.'

I quickly concealed it as the officers dressed in black stormed into the cell. We went through the same process as we had before, but this time I was hiding an illegal mobile phone. I tried to look cool as I walked up to the guard by the canteen door but inside my heart was beating out of my chest. If I was caught, I was looking at another charge. But as before, he barely searched me and I was ushered through.

'I knew they wouldn't touch you,' Baariq said. 'I owe you one.'

I was happy to have helped Baariq again and to have him on side. I would happily have done it again as I knew he was a powerful ally.

Every three days the guards conducted a roll call when they counted the number of inmates. A guard would call out names one by one and that person would have to go into the dining room. Another guard would go and look for any stragglers who were lingering in their cells. One day I was in the shower when a guard was calling names, and Mo came in, looked over the door and stared at me as I was washing. He said, 'Come now, Mr Karl, it's time to get out of the shower.'

'All right, mate, give us a minute.'

'I will wait for you,' he said, looking intently at me. I was slightly freaked out that he was showing so much interest and quickly dressed as he continued to watch me. When I was ready

I went into the dining room and found Harry. He was standing with Baariq and I told them what had just happened.

'Yeah, mate, he's staring at me all the time too,' Harry said.

'Be careful with that one,' Baariq added. 'He likes young boys.'

The daily monotony was broken when a blond German called Christian was given a bed in our cell. Rivas had been moved into Mohammed and Baariq's room when Arif had been released a few days before. Christian, who was in his thirties, came into the jail wearing a German football shirt.

'Yo, boys, I've got another European for you,' Mohammed said as he brought him in.

Christian had a huge smile on his face. 'I from Germany, ja,' he said. We all laughed and welcomed him to the cell. He was in for drink-driving but was more concerned about the cops seizing his flash Hummer than being in jail. If anything he was excited about being inside.

'So who's boss in here?' he asked. 'All the guards seem really nice, especially that really tall guy Mo. He told me to come to him if I need a hand with anything. He told me he look after me if I get into any trouble.'

Tariq and I laughed. 'Mo's a batsman,' Tariq said.

'What is this? He play cricket?'

'Sort of, but he bats for the other team,' Tariq said.

'It's not that it's a problem him being gay,' I added, 'he just pervs on inmates so be careful, mate.'

When the Muslims were called to prayer and the strip outside filled with prayer mats I got out the *dokha* and explained what it was to Christian, who had never tried it. I handed him the biro that we used as a pipe. 'That's pretty good,' he said. Within a split second he made a horrific noise. 'Aaaaaaaaaaaaaaiiiiiiiiiiiiir!' he screamed at the top of his voice before quickly turning around on the spot several times. I laughed as I thought he was just being stupid but then he collapsed on a bottom bunk.

'Shit!' Ed shouted as he grabbed him, pulled his arms back and put his hand in his mouth to stop him swallowing his tongue.

Harry ran into our room. 'What the fuck are you doing, boys, making this noise during prayers?' he shouted. 'After the farting you're gonna get us all ironed out.'

'This guy's cracking out,' I said, meaning that he was tripping.

'No, he's having a seizure,' Ed said. 'You boys can be real immature sometimes.'

'I've never seen that happen before,' I said, my fear clearly coming across in my voice.

The praying Arabs were furious at the noise being made during their holy time and a small mob headed for our cell with Mohammed at the front. 'Shaytan! Shaytan!' the Arabs were screaming, meaning 'devil'. The inmates believed Christian was Satan who had been sent into the jail during their prayers.

'What the fuck are you lot doing, man?' Mohammed said. 'I've told you so many times you have to be quiet when people are praying. You have to stop doing this shit.' He was furious.

'These boys haven't done anything wrong. This guy has just had a seizure,' Ed said.

Mohammed calmed the situation down and sent the baying mob away.

Then Christian came to. 'Where am I?'

'What's your name?' Ed said. 'When's your birthday? Do you know why you're here? Take your time.'

Christian slowly came back to reality and Mohammed took him to the hatch near the phones saying he needed to go to hospital. The guards refused as they couldn't be bothered to call an ambulance and sent him back into the jail.

Within minutes Christian started fitting again. Ed jumped on him and again put his hand in his mouth. Christian was staring at the ceiling and looked like he was dead. I was terrified until he came round again. It was only when Mohammed took him to the hatch for the second time that he was taken to hospital.

Dokha briefly starves your brain of oxygen, and that caused him to have a seizure. Throughout the whole process Tariq and I were useless. I was so relieved Ed was there.

'So how did you know to do all of that shit and remain so calm?' I asked Ed.

'I was in the US army as a ranger.'

'What's that?'

'Well, you know *Call of Duty: Black Ops*? Well, that was me.'

I stared open mouthed at him. I had been playing blackjack with the guy for days but I had no idea he was a one-man killing machine. He told us how he had started in the US army as a medic before going into the infantry. He'd worked his way through several regiments, like his father before him. He was a crack sniper and had ended up in the US army rangers conducting black ops missions. He had been around the world killing people on top secret covert operations.

'I was in Iraq and I was one of the team who hunted down Saddam Hussein and his henchmen,' he said. 'I was there when we found him. He was hiding like a rat in a hole in the ground.'

What I respected so much about Ed was that when it got to the point where people were getting killed he just said, 'It got really heavy,' and wouldn't go into the detail. He told us the stories, but he wasn't proud of all of the people he had killed. He showed us his ranger tattoo and others from different regiments. Having Ed in my cell immediately made me feel safer. There's a lot to be said for having a man who could kill somebody with his little finger on your side when you're in a tinderbox jail that could kick off at any minute.

When Ed left the US army he became a mercenary and was training the Dubai army. He was arrested after being set upon by a group of Arabs who he had then beaten to a pulp.

'What you boys went through with your torture was pretty full on,' he said, trying to steer the conversation away from himself. 'The kind of stuff they did to you I would only expect to see in war zones like Afghanistan or Iraq. You boys should tell people about this.'

'Tell who, though?'

'The embassy.'

'We already have but they just said they were going to send a letter.'

'What the fuck? Get onto them every day and don't give up. You are just sitting back. This is your life now. Do you want to be in here forever?'

He was right. We needed to take action and I resolved to harass the consulate until they took notice. Spending time with Ed was helping me get through the horrors of jail life and I appreciated his support.

'So what's happening with your friend Harry, man?' Ed said. 'Why's he hanging around with all those spice kids?'

Harry was living in a cell with Sharia, Maroon and Danny. There was constant childish banter in that room. They acted like a group of teenagers on their first school trip and would do things like covering each other's faces with toothpaste while they were asleep. One kid called Farhan was always masturbating, so Harry crept up on him and threw talcum powder all over him.

'I think he just wants to be in control of the room and have a laugh,' I said.

'He can have a laugh in here with us, man.'

'I know, but I just think it's his way of coping. He likes to have the childish banter with the kids.'

'Look, man, I know he's your friend but you need to get him away from them. If anything happens to Harry you're going to be the first one there, correct?'

'Yeah.'

'And if anything happens to you I'm going to be the first one there. If anything happens to me then the Russians are going to come as well. You can't have Harry in a situation where things could go wrong. Also, if you all end up in Central the last thing you want is to be with a load of kids who are the most likely to be raped.'

'No, I'm all right and they're fine,' Harry said when I tried to get him to move. 'I don't want to be in a cell with Ed, he's too regimented.'

I didn't see what Harry meant. Ed had always been cool and never moaned about anything. I realized I had to let Harry do his time in his own way. As long as he was happy, that was fine by me.

One thing that I found when I was in jail was that the smallest things can change people immeasurably. I was always a big fan of Monopoly and wanted to see if it was possible to get a board to pass the time.

'You mean Mayfair monopoly?' Mohammed said when I approached him. 'I'll kick your ass, man. I *own* London. I own an apartment in Knightsbridge, man, next to Harrods, and other houses. I'm the boss!'

'So how can we get hold of one?'

'There's an inspection of the jail tomorrow so ask Captain Abbas in front of everyone. He won't be able to refuse.'

The next day captains Abbas and Aziz came into the jail with the inspector and went into the cells, asking us to take our curtains down. When they were walking down the corridor I stepped forward and said, 'Excuse me, sir, but is there any chance we would be allowed to have a Monopoly board?'

'What is this?'

'It's a board game.'

'Gambling?'

'No, no.'

'You promise?'

'Absolutely.'

Mohammed joined us and started to talk to the captain in Arabic, explaining that it was a British game and it would be good for prison morale as it would bring the prisoners together. Captain Abbas agreed.

My brother Ross had recently returned from his trip abroad so I got him to bring in a copy of the game. The box was searched by Captain Abbas before it was brought down to the jail.

'Black British! Black British! Come, come!'

When I was handed the simple game I was like a child on Christmas morning. I never thought I could so much pleasure out of a humble Monopoly set.

I walked along the strip and saw Mohammed.

'We play now!' he said.

'Nah, mate, you ain't playing,' I joked.

He scowled. 'What? I helped you get this!'

'Only joking, mate, let's go.'

We spent hours playing with Harry, Tariq, Rivas, Ed and Maroon. The gangsters in the other cells were queuing up to borrow the board. The game transformed killers and drug dealers into children desperate to play with a new toy. Mohammed would offer bribes of more food to anyone who would give him

Mayfair or Park Lane. 'I got Mayfair, man,' he would delight in shouting. It was to be our staple pastime for many months.

When it was quiet I watched telly in a bid to escape the humdrum. Mohammed had bought the forty-two-inch flat screen for the jail, as well as a cable subscription. He had been allowed to do this as long as he bought a TV for the guards as well. As there were hundreds of Indian and Pakistani workers in the jail we were always outnumbered when choosing the channel. They always wanted to watch the Indian channel Zee Aflam which I couldn't stand. Ed, Baariq and I were watching MTV one day, but when the former cop left the room one of the Indians immediately grabbed the remote and turned the TV over. I was furious.

'What the fuck are you doing?' I said, squaring up to him.

'Baariq gone, we want TV,' he said in broken English.

'We're watching a programme and you can't just change it.'

'Yes, we change. If we no watch, nobody watch,' and he turned off the telly.

I jumped up on a marble table and ran across it towards the TV, pressing the on switch. Ed swiftly followed me and we were faced with the angry group screaming at us. There were about forty Indians at the start but the number grew quickly as they heard the row. The TV kept getting switched on and off as we screamed at each other. Harry had run into the room when he heard me shouting.

'What's going on, bruv?'

'TV dramas, mate, but it's getting out of hand,' I said, glaring out at the crowd.

'Look, I'll take out the big two and you two cover this side. I can take most of them,' Ed said coolly.

'Yeah, yeah, fuck it, let's do it,' I said. We were so hyped up that it seemed like a good idea.

'What is this?!' shouted Mohammed as he walked into the room with Baariq. He spoke rapidly in Hindi to the Indians before turning to us. 'You guys are crazy! You can't fight everyone.'

'They can't just change the TV channel, man,' I protested.

Mohammed laughed. 'You *hiwan*! There are a lot of them. Do you want to get yourself killed? Come, let's play Monopoly and I'll beat you.'

I had been getting paid regularly by Baariq in *dokha* for the love songs I was writing for him. It was a simple arrangement and worked for me. At the same time Rivas would give Tariq some of the special tobacco as they had got close. I didn't think anything of it until Mohammed started going around and searching everyone's cells.

'What's going on, Mohammed?' I said.

'Yo, man, don't say anything but a load of *dokha* has been stolen.' Mohammed was the one who controlled tobacco in the jail.

Tariq and I looked at each other. We currently had a large stash of the stuff hidden in our pants. It didn't take a rocket scientist to work out that Baariq and Rivas had probably stolen Mohammed's goods. Later that day Zain was walking down the wing past a group of local gangsters playing Monopoly when a large lump of *dokha* fell out of his pocket. Ayoop and the gangsters went mad, screaming and shouting as they grabbed Zain.

'Where did you get this from?!'

'I, I, got it on a visit.'

'Liar!' Ayoop shouted as he gave him a slap around the face. 'You a thief!'

Zain was in tears, pleading his innocence. Baariq was next to Ayoop and joined in.

'You lie!' he thundered.

I didn't know what to do. I didn't want to see my friend get beaten up by a bunch of gangsters, but if I got involved I could be in trouble. Luckily Mohammed came to the rescue and pulled Zain into his cell and Harry and I went for a smoke in the hoosh. Some bed sheets were hanging on a line and we hid behind them to avoid being spotted by the camera.

'Baariq, slap me now!' I heard Zain cry. 'I would prefer for you to beat me rather than everyone else beat me, I haven't stolen *dokha*, it wasn't me, I promise you. I swear on Allah's life.'

We hadn't heard my friend come out with Mohammed and Baariq and they didn't realize we were there. Mohammed was trying to calm him down.

'Okay, okay, don't worry, I believe you and will tell the others.'

When Mohammed left, Baariq turned to Zain and said, 'Thank you very much for not saying it was me who stole the *dokha*.'

Then they both walked back into the jail. Everything made sense. Baariq had stolen the dokha and given bits to Zain, yet had accused him of lying in front of the others. I was impressed by Zain's loyalty and his refusal to snitch, but I resolved to be wary of Baariq as he had shown his true colours. More than anything I was relieved that the stolen dokha in mine and Tariq's pants had not been discovered, as we could have been the ones on the end of a beating.

12

BUYING YOUR WAY OUT

The TV room incident had hammered home the fact that we were always going to be outnumbered by the Arabs and the Bengali immigrant workers. We needed to somehow gain a foothold in the prison governing committee to gain some influence.

'Mohammed, I'm sick of being pushed around in the queues,' I said to him one day.

'You think you can do any better? *Yallah*, go, you do the lunchtime shift.'

This was the opportunity I had been looking for.

'Okay, Mohammed, no problem,' I said with a smile on my face.

I walked back into the cell and told Tariq and Ed about our new role.

'Look, we need to do this to try and gain a bit of power as otherwise we'll be stuck as normal guys, having to queue up and let the Indians push past us,' I said. 'We can get pushed around or we can climb the ranks and have a better time.'

'That's good thinking,' Ed said. 'I was okay just kicking back as I'm not gonna be here as long as you, but I'm happy to help out. You're gonna need some manpower on this one.'

Ed sat down and drew the canteen on a piece of paper. 'Right, boys, this is how it's gonna go.' It was like he was planning a military operation. I laughed, but I was delighted he was on our team.

'This is the plan,' Ed continued. 'Tariq, you speak the language of the savages so you can be handing out the trays here.'

'Yeah, bruv, I speak Urdu,' Tariq said. 'It's my dad's language. I got that.'

I hadn't heard Tariq speaking any Urdu since we arrived in the jail but let it slide. I was on the door and Ed was on the strip. The plan was set. A slight flaw in our game plan was that we didn't account for how annoyed the Pakistanis who previously ran the canteen would be.

It all started so well, with inmates calmly queueing and walking through. I even thought Tariq could speak the language as he appeared to be interacting with the other prisoners. I was just starting to relax when, in a split second, everything changed.

Around 200 Pakistanis and Bengalis forced their way through, surging past Ed and then me, screaming at the top of their lungs, 'Canna! Canna! Canna!' meaning they wanted canteen food. The sheer weight of inmates was like a tidal wave knocking over a straw hut. Tariq was sent flying and was knocked on his backside. Even Ed, with all of his military expertise, was brushed aside, despite trying to hold back the tide. Harry, thinking the situation was hilarious, joined in, pushing me in the face as he ran past shouting, 'Canna!' People were jumping on the tables and screaming. It was anarchy. Unable to deal with such extreme chaos, the Indian jail workers in the kitchen closed the hatch and refused to serve anybody. Nobody was getting any food today and our bid for power had been an unmitigated disaster.

Mohammed came storming into the dining room.

'Shut up!' he shouted, and the room fell silent. He walked up to us and pointed at us each in the face.

'You wanted this? Now you see what happens? This is my jail. I put people in positions for a reason. You don't even speak the language. You have this Indian,' he jabbed his finger at Tariq, 'this Indian who doesn't even speak his own language. What kind of Indian are you? I thought you would speak this jungle language.'

'Tariq, you useless prick,' I said. 'You told us you could speak Urdu.'

'No, mate, I speak Punjabi.'

Mohammed started speaking Punjabi while Tariq just looked blankly at him.

'Mate, you're backwards. You can just about speak English.'

'No, their Punjabi's different to what I know.'

'Whatever, mate.'

Mohammed gave us a complete dressing down in front of the whole jail and it was humiliating. We felt like children. We skulked off with our tails between our legs. Later that day he came into our room.

'You learn your lesson now?' he said. 'I've got a job for you guys. Why don't you boys look after the burgers? You boys are going to be here a long time. If you boys want to be big boss in jail like me, you can control the burgers. Let's see how that goes.'

Despite our catastrophic effort in the canteen we had landed the plumb job. We couldn't believe our ears. The Syrians were leaving the jail soon so in Mohammed's head it made sense to give us a try.

It was quite a simple system. Mohammed had a contact in a certain restaurant who delivered the food discreetly, and he paid off one of the police who allowed the burgers to come through. We would order hundreds of items every week direct from the restaurant using a payphone. The order arrived in large plastic bags. Mohammed went to the hatch, grabbed the food and gave us the goods.

The burgers cost 3D (60p) a piece for Mohammed to buy and each would cost 5D (£1) to prisoners. Each plastic cup of tropical juice was 5D (£1). It was a seller's market and everything came at a price. We put everything into piles. Ed did the stock check as he was the brains. I handed out the food and took the money, while Tariq wrote down what had been sold. When the order came we basically took what we wanted from the bags for ourselves before the general sale began. One person from each room came to our door with the whole cell's order before the Indians and Bengalis descended on us.

I always tried to look after Harry by sneaking him extra burgers, but we had to be subtle about it as others wouldn't have been happy. I would put aside an extra little tray of treats for him hidden under my bed.

After our first burger sale, Ed and I took the cash to Mohammed's cell.

'Wow! You guys are good,' he said, delighted. 'Those Syrians lost me money, as they claimed they didn't get enough money for the burgers. How have you boys made me money off this?'

We handed Mohammed his money back and a 200D profit.

'Thank you, man. All I want is my money back. The Syrians always gave me back less than the burgers cost me in the first place. Here you go.' He handed me back the cash we had made. I couldn't believe our luck.

'This money is nothing to me,' he went on. 'I am a big drug dealer. I am rich. I'm a boss, I have iPhone,' he said, as he got the latest model out of his pocket. My mouth fell open.

'How do you have a brand-new iPhone in jail?'

'When you are a big drug dealer like me you can get every-thing.'

It was totally illegal to have a phone inside and he, like Baariq with his, would have faced further criminal charges if it was found. Cops could walk in at any point and there were cameras looking up and down the strip, but Mohammed was happy to brazenly get his phone out. He showed us pictures of his apart-ment in Knightsbridge, next to Harrods, of him skiing in Austria and of his Lamborghini.

When you enter prison you expect people to be fundamen-tally bad and rotten to the core. More than any other inmate, Mohammed shattered that belief. He was an international drugs baron but was one of the kindest people you could meet. He would mix with everyone, playing cards with the poor Bengalis despite them stinking after not washing for months. He ran the jail for love, not profit, and it made everybody's lives there more bearable. We were all very lucky to have him.

It turned out Mohammed had been caught after he was tar-geted in an undercover sting. He was in the lobby of a hotel conducting a high level drug deal with a buyer while his driver waited with hundreds of kilos of hash.

'Yo, man, I thought this could have been a bit dodgy so there was no way I was gonna hand over the drugs myself,' he said. 'I would always just leave a package on the floor and get the buyer to pick it up.'

He was right to be cautious as the buyer was from the Dubai police. When officers carry out a sting they try to get the target to hand over the drugs himself as it results in a greater charge. Mohammed was too cunning for this and refused. When he real-ized the game was up he tried to run away. I could only imagine how funny it would have looked as he tried to waddle out of the hotel as fast as his fat little legs would carry him. Needless to say there was only one outcome and he was apprehended pretty quickly.

Tariq piped up, 'So, Mohammed, man, I've been wanting to ask for a while. What happened to your little finger?'

He laughed, 'This is what happens in drug dealing if you don't play the game properly, man.'

He told us that another drugs baron had cut off his little finger as a punishment for a deal that went wrong. He had given his drugs to a street dealer who was subsequently arrested. Mohammed never got paid and therefore couldn't pay the drugs baron. His men chopped off his finger as punishment.

The burger business went well for us and we made a steady profit. But there were always those who couldn't afford to buy any, even though they were just £1 each. I'm no Good Samaritan, but I realized I could actually make a difference to these guys' lives with a bit of generosity. When there were burgers left over I would make sure they would get into the hands of those most in need.

As well as the marathon Monopoly games we spent a lot of our time playing poker tournaments. Gambling was illegal so we would play with cotton buds and little bits of card to represent the chips. We would all put 20D in the pot and the winner of the tournament would take the cash.

Maroon and Bobby spent a lot of time with us and had become my friends. Neither of them particularly got on with the rest of the spoilt spice kids and had been living in a room with a bunch of Iranians who were in for people trafficking. The boss of their room was called Captain, as he had a fishing boat he used to smuggle the illegals into Dubai. Unfortunately for him his boat had caught fire while on a run and he had to be rescued by the coastguard, along with a boat full of illegal workers, when it sank.

During a poker game one night Maroon said, 'Hey, man,' in his lazy Californian drool, 'I can't handle living in that room any more. It's so dirty. It's full of bed bugs and they're all squashed up the wall. Can I come and stay with you, man?'

'Yeah, man, let me ask Ed.'

Ed was happy for Maroon to join us and he moved in the next day.

We had room as Christian had recently been released. Bobby didn't seem to care about the squalor, even though it resulted in an aroma that followed him around. 'You stink, man,' I used to joke. We had been showing each other lyrics and rapping together ever since the canteen incident. I thought he was a cool guy.

Time can drag when you're inside and we all dealt with it in different ways. Maroon started to spend a lot of time asleep.

'Why does your friend keep sleeping?' Baariq said. 'Has he been drinking the tea?'

'What do you mean, man?'

'Don't you know? They fill the tea with chemicals and tran quillizers to knock you out. It helps kill your sex drive and stops you getting hard. They don't want the men fucking each other.'

This was ridiculous but not surprising. It was more evidence of the hypocrisy of the Dubai justice system. Despite painkillers such as codeine being illegal on the outside, in jail the authorities drugged both the gravy and the tea with tranquillizers. The stark irony was not lost on us. We dubbed it 'crack tea'. Despite it killing the pain of being inside by knocking you out, I avoided it after trying it once anyway. It tasted like a cross between coffee and tea with no milk, and smelt of rancid perfume with a slight hint of bleach. As you got to the bottom of the cup there were black bits that hadn't dissolved.

'Why you lot don't drink this stuff?' Maroon said after I repeated Baariq's news. 'It makes me sleep like a baby.'

I wasn't interested. It looked like sludge, tasted like shit, and would stop me from getting a hard-on. What was the point of that?

Tariq decided to try it as well and fell into a deep sleep for hours, allowing us to have some fun. Maroon and I got some talcum powder and covered him from head to toe in it. He looked like Casper the Friendly Ghost. When he woke up he went mad.

'Karl, you are the grumpiest prick in the world when you're woken from your sleep,' he screamed at me. 'How would you like it?'

Our behaviour may have been juvenile but it was hilarious. He stomped off to the bathroom and washed his face. When Tariq returned he petulantly pulled my sheets and blanket off.

'Tariq, come on, man,' I said, struggling to hold back my laughter. I just let him do it for his own revenge. It was just too funny.

After the talcum powder episode Maroon seemed less keen on the tea.

I couldn't sleep one night when I heard the sound of police boots walking down the strip. Fear and a natural instinct to survive sharpened my senses in jail and I learnt the smell of blood and how to sense danger. I got to know how people walked so when I heard boots coming into the jail in the middle of the night I knew it was a guard – and likely to be something dodgy. I moved my curtain slightly and saw Feroz walk into Baariq's cell with two big bags. I went to see him after the officer had left and he was sat there with all these new clothes and trainers.

'Yeah, I have a new phone,' he said.

'Fuck me, mate, how did you do that?'

'If you know the right people anything is possible.'

I was about to ask him how I would go about smuggling a phone in when I heard somebody walking down the strip. One of the inmates was making his way back from the hatch, carrying a big bottle of juice.

'How has he got hold of that?' I said.

'Haven't you heard? Mo likes boys sucking him off and if you do you get little treats.'

'Jesus, that kid's never using one of my pipes again.'

Baariq laughed but this was serious. I had been concerned about how Mo had acted before but didn't know the guard was actually grooming and fucking young lads.

I went back to my cell for some sleep as I was finally being allowed to go to hospital to get my hand seen to the next day. I had been constantly on to the guards about my injury but nobody had done a thing. I'd tried the embassy but despite saying they would chase it up, it felt to me that little had been done.

In the end Mohammed told me the best way of getting things done.

'What you have to do is call the British embassy in Dubai after it's closed and you'll be put through to England. They'll call the Dubai embassy the next day and lodge the complaint. Then they'll have to do something about it.'

It seemed like a good plan and it worked like a dream. Within a couple of days I heard from the embassy. They said they had followed up my call to the Foreign Office and had got me an appointment at hospital. I had been living with a dull ache in my hand for three weeks and it had become my normality, but it wasn't fun.

*

The next day, an Indian man came to get me and told me I was wanted at the hatch, and then I was shown into the police seating area, where two officers called Salem and Mussa from Jebel Ali Police Station were waiting. I was surprised that they allowed me to walk to the car without cuffing me and I stayed that way for the whole journey.

As I walked out of the jail I felt the sun on my skin properly for the first time in weeks. The taste of freedom made me want it even more. As we got into the car P Diddy's 'I'll be Missing You' was playing on the radio and I started to dance in the back.

'You like this stuff, yeah?' Salem said. 'I'm a big fan of Puff Daddy.'

'Me too, man.'

'Where you from, man?'

'England.'

'Ah, yes, I have been to England. You must know my friend?'

It never failed to amaze me how Arabs thought we would all know the people they knew in the UK. 'He lives in Birmingham. You know?'

'Yeah, I've been there a few times.'

'You must know him then. His name is Michael.'

'It's not ringing any bells, mate.'

Mussa then asked what it was like in Port Rashid. I told him it was dirty and that we weren't allowed to smoke.

'You no smoke? I heard this but I thought it was just a rumour. You want to smoke?'

'Yeah, mate, I'd love one.'

'Okay, at the hospital I let you smoke.'

We arrived at the hospital, which was ultra-modern and clean, and I was shown into a waiting room where I was booked in. Salem had warned me that I would have to be handcuffed to the bed as the doctors were scared when dealing with prisoners. An Indian doctor came in and looked at my hand and said I had a broken fifth metacarpal and that I would need to have it set back into place.

He injected me with local anaesthetic but before it had a chance to work he started going at my right hand, trying to push the bone around. I was screaming in agony but unable to move properly as my left hand was handcuffed to the bed. As he was moving my hand there was a sudden crack as the bone realigned, and pain shot through my body. I yelped and tears ran down my face. I thought the pain from when the cops broke my hand originally was bad, but this was a whole new level. It was excruciating.

The doctor put a cast on my hand and told me to be careful as the bone needed time to heal.

After that I was desperate for a cigarette and Salem was happy to give me one on the way out.

'Go the other side of the car and have a smoke,' he said as he took off my handcuffs. 'But don't run away!'

My instant reaction was to flee, but I thought better of it. I had no plan and I would have been caught in minutes. I thanked the two police officers for their kindness and they asked me if I was hungry.

'We know nice little burger place. We get you some food.'

I couldn't believe my ears. I didn't think they would take me for a meal but within minutes we had pulled up outside a small burger restaurant. We went inside and sat near the back.

'Just act normal,' Mussa said.

I ordered a turkey bacon cheeseburger and wolfed it down in a couple of minutes. I couldn't believe my luck.

'You want more?' Mussa said.

This was crazy, but I was happy to accept the offer. It reminded me that most people in Dubai are inherently good. The burger was good, but being outside the jail for the first time in months made it one of the best meals I have ever had.

After I was shown back into Port Rashid I told Harry and Tariq what had happened.

'What, you didn't bring any back for us?' Harry said. I explained that I had to eat everything there and then. Tariq was more interested in whether I had seen any women.

Meanwhile, Zain was still being treated as an outcast by a lot of the inmates after Matt's claims that he had snitched. I tried to spend time with him but he was starting to do my head in. He was constantly asking whether he could get in on the burger scam but no matter how many times we told him he couldn't, as Mohammed wouldn't let him, he still kept on bugging me. On the outside I was happy to put up with Zain's occasional eccentricities but inside, when there's no escape from each other, small annoyances got blown out of proportion. It was easy to feel paranoid when you were locked away from the world, and he couldn't stop worrying that his girlfriend was cheating on him.

'Look, man, there's no way she'd fuck you over. It's only been a couple of months.'

'How do you know?'

'She seems to be a good girl.'

'How the fuck do you know her so well? You probably fucked her, didn't you?' he shouted.

I suddenly snapped and said, 'Yeah, I did fuck her,' even though I hadn't.

'You cunt, you're meant to be my friend,' he screamed. 'I knew you'd fucked her. Watch when you get to Central, I'm gonna make sure all the Pakistani boys come and cut you up.'

This was too much. Ed overheard what had been said, 'Woah, man. Zain, you need to fuck off, you annoying little shit.'

Zain looked like he was going to say something but thought better of taking on Ed. 'You're fucking gonna get it, Ceaze,' he snarled as he stormed off towards his cell.

Things did not get any better over the next few days. Zain would mutter 'Karl is a prick' under his breath, just loud enough to hear, whenever he walked past my cell. Zain was always after extra burgers so whenever I heard the sound of his slippers I would say to Tariq 'These lamb burgers are real good' and suggest we add an extra fifty on the order to keep for ourselves, just to wind him up. People react in different ways to being inside, but it just made Zain angry, which in turn meant he was hard to be around. Later on people would say the same thing about me!

Apart from the dramas with my old friend I'd noticed that Baariq and a new Italian guy in the jail called Arman were spending a lot of time having secret meetings. Arman was a slim, olive-skinned bloke who was in for fraud. He didn't socialize with us, keeping himself to himself, but he seemed to have a lot of time for Baariq. A few days later Arman walked down the strip and gave Baariq a huge hug. The jail number two had a big smile on his face. I was sat with Matt and said, 'What's that all about?'

'That greedy bastard's just happy as he's made a shitload of money.'

'What do you mean?'

'Don't you know? Baariq can get people out of jail for the right price.'

My head started to spin. Could this be the chance we had been looking for to get out of this hell?

'Yeah, mate, it's crazy,' Matt said. 'Baariq has people in the prosecution in his pocket and if you pay enough, sometimes he can get people bail. That gets you out of Port Rashid, but you're still stuck in the country awaiting trial. You can't leave the country as you're on a no-fly list. But you know he used to be a cop?'

'Yeah.'

'Well, he worked at the airport as an immigration cop. He used to be involved in a human-trafficking scam where he would let loads of illegals into the country. Now he's using his contacts there to get inmates out of Dubai. Once you get bail he calls his old mates and you get taken off the no-fly list. That allows you to get on a plane home, never to return again.'

This sounded too good to be true, but I wanted it to be reality more than anything. It turned out that 150,000D (£30,000) in Baariq's pocket was enough for Arman's freedom.

'Do you think he'd be able to do that for me, Tariq and Harry?' I said, my heart beating hard with excitement.

'I can ask,' Matt said. 'But don't speak directly to Baariq about this. He gets funny about that sort of thing.'

I thought this was strange as I had a decent relationship with Baariq. I'd hidden a phone for him and thought he trusted me. I decided to let it slide, though, as I didn't want to jeopardize the chance of us getting out. I went to find Tariq and Harry, who were hanging around outside in the hoosh and explained what Matt had said to me.

'So, if we raise enough cash we can get out of here,' I said.

Tariq's eyes looked like they would pop out of his little head. 'That's fucking awesome, mate.'

Harry wasn't so sure. 'If he can get people out of jail, why he's he still here?'

'I'm not too sure, but I'm willing to give it a go as long as it doesn't cost too much.'

'Whatever, bruv.'

I walked back into the jail, buoyed by the gold-plated chance we had been given to escape a life in prison. Matt walked up to me and dragged me to one side.

'Look, bruv, Baariq reckons he can get one of you out at a time and it's gonna cost 25,000D (£5,000) each.'

I was elated. 'Thank you so much, man, I will get onto my family to raise the cash.'

In our desperation to get away from our living nightmare it seemed Baariq held the key to our release. I could almost taste freedom. The dream of getting home to see my little girl looked like it may just become reality.

13

A CRUEL TWIST

I immediately called my brother.

'Ross, I can't really talk too much but I need you to get some money together. I think I may have found a way to get out of here pretty sharpish.'

'How?'

'Let me go and use another phone.'

I went into Baariq's cell. 'Mate, can I use your phone?'

I was sat there with the fixer having a conversation about how he was going to get me out. It was twisted.

'Can you trust him?' Ross asked.

'Look, at the end of the day it will be all blessed and if it ain't all blessed I'll move him up when he's akip.' I was using street slang for 'it will be all right and if it's not I will attack him when he is asleep'.

'If you're sure, bruv. How do you want to do it?'

'I reckon we should only pay half the money upfront and half when I get out.'

Ross agreed. The plan was to get the cash to Matt's girlfriend on the outside and then Baariq would put the wheels in motion. I hung up.

'So how long does the process take?' I asked Baariq.

'It's going to take a few weeks.'

'How come so long? Arman was only in the jail for a couple of weeks.'

'Your case is a lot more complicated and it's a drugs case. A lot more paperwork has to go missing for it all to be possible.'

It seemed fair enough but I was still suspicious. I walked out of the cell and went to find Mohammed. I wanted to check I wasn't being done over as Baariq was clearly a slippery character.

'What's up, man? How's everything in my jail, my man? Anyone tried to fuck you?'

'No.'

'Can I fuck you?'

'No!'

Mohammed would always intimate he would like to have sex with one of us. 'Joking, joking,' he added.

'Look, I'm gonna do this thing with Baariq where he's gonna get me out. I'm gonna pay half now and half when I get out. What do you think?'

'Yeah, man, it could work out for you.'

'What do you mean "it could"?'

'It could work, but you have to be careful with these Sudanese. They're very slippery.'

'Wouldn't you trust him?'

'No.'

This confirmed my fears that the dream of release had serious potential to go wrong. But still, I couldn't pass over the chance for freedom. I had been in jail a month and I knew I wouldn't be able to handle being here for the rest of my life. It was worth the risk.

My brother met up with Matt's girlfriend to give her the

money. She later met one of Baariq's people on the outside and handed over what I hoped would pay for my ticket to freedom.

When inmates got pardoned the guards would shout out '*Afraj! Afraj!*' and Mohammed would read out the lucky prisoners' names. Four days after I'd paid, Baariq came to my cell and showed me a bit of paper with Arabic writing on it and said, 'Look, that's you there! You are going to be a free man.' My heart almost skipped a beat. I was going home. And when my name came out of Mohammed's chubby lips, my insides almost exploded with excitement. Harry, Tariq and I were all high fiving and hugging each other.

'Go get your stuff, my man, you're going home,' Mohammed said.

'Wow, you're going home, man,' Tariq said. 'What you gonna do?'

'I'm gonna see my little girl, fuck my missus and have a beer!'

'Fucking hell, mate, you're actually going?!' Harry said with a massive smile on his face.

We knew the payment had worked and we would all be going home. Most importantly I was going to see my little girl. I was told it would take a couple of weeks to process me before I was allowed to leave the country.

'Look, boys, while I'm waiting to leave I'll sort out the cash for you both,' I promised.

'Go on, hurry up, you cunt,' Tariq said.

'Yeah, mate, get out of here,' Harry added.

Maroon and Bobby came to say goodbye, both looking shocked I was leaving.

'How have you managed that?' Bobby asked.

'I dunno, maybe they're starting to release people,' I said. I didn't want to jeopardize my release by telling anyone else about how I'd managed it, not even my jail friends.

Ed came into the cell, walked up to me and gave me a huge hug. 'Well done, my man, I'm so happy for you.'

I walked out of my cell and down the strip for the final time towards the phone room. I was on the biggest high ever. No drug would ever match that feeling of pure adrenaline mixed with the relief that the living nightmare was about to end. But despite my elation I tried to remain calm and humble. There were many others who were not so lucky.

All of the jail bosses were standing by the phones with massive smiles on their faces. Their smiles swiftly broke and they burst into laughter. It took me a second to realize what was happening. The whole thing had been a cruel joke. I was going nowhere.

Despite my crushing disappointment I just smiled and called them a bunch of wankers. They came over and started hugging me.

'You big drug dealer, man, you here with me,' Mohammed said.

It was like my insides were being torn apart but I knew I couldn't show any weakness. Baariq had a cheeky look on his face.

'Don't worry, mate, you'll be going home soon,' he said as he gave me a big hug.

I had paid the money so I figured it had to happen at some point. But to have it dangled in front of my face and then snatched away so cruelly as a joke was brutal. Even though my head was in serious turmoil I told myself they didn't want to humiliate me. I tried to think it was good that they felt comfortable enough with me to have this extreme joke. I looked on it like an acceptance and I tried to supress my true feelings. Inside I was fuming and devastated at the same time. But, as I walked back to my bed

I realized there was no point in being sad for things that you can't have.

'You silly prick,' Tariq said as I walked into the cell. He always did have the most tact.

The one real positive that came out of the 'joke' was the change in how the bosses treated me. It was like all of the players in the jail had a new-found respect for me now I'd I shown them I could take a prank in the most extreme circumstances. I became an accepted member of the jail hierarchy. I noticed that if I was standing with a group of people speaking Arabic, they would all try to teach me the Arabic words. But the biggest bonus of all was about to happen. Prison life was about to become a whole lot easier.

One night Baariq came into my cell to wake me up. I immediately thought he wanted me to write another song. Instead he said, 'Come, come.' I went to his and Mohammed's cell and was greeted with a truly glorious sight that I could only have dreamt of. All of the jail bosses were sat around one of the most magnificent feasts I had ever seen. I had been invited to the top table. The aroma of fillet steak, shrimps and chicken permeated the room. There was a banquet of TGI Fridays, KFC, chicken, rice and lamb. Mohammed gave me a massive smile.

'Yo, man. You see who the bosses are now, bitch?!' he said. I burst out laughing. 'You want to sit with the bosses now, yeah?!' he added, before stuffing a KFC burger in his face.

I loved him for inviting me into the inner sanctum. I sat down next to Ayoop, the other local gangsters and Rivas. Samir was also there, along with Babar. My favourite dish was mashed potato with cheese in the middle and greens on top. The meal was their way of letting me know I had been accepted. I was working my way up the prison hierarchy. I stuffed my face with food before saying that I needed to take some bits back for Tariq and Harry.

'Fuck, man, where did you get this?' Tariq said. 'I'm gonna go in there and get some food.'

'You can't do that, man,' I said, pulling him back. 'They'll think you're a little Indian beggar.'

I also didn't want to jeopardize the position I had got myself into. If we had to stay in jail for a while, we had to be in a position of influence.

The next person to leave was a big blow to me as I had grown to love this guy like a brother. I had no idea anything was afoot, even though Ed was in my cell. He never said a word to me, in true Black Ops style. Then one day his name was called out by Mohammed.

Ed turned to us and said, 'Guys, I'm gonna have to meet you all in Las Vegas.'

I was delighted for him but I was scared at the same time. Ed had been like the daddy of the cell and I knew I would have to take on that role now.

'Good luck, man, and see you on the other side,' I said, as I gave him a big hug. I couldn't believe he was going. He got his stuff together and walked out to freedom.

The only bonus of Ed leaving was that it meant Harry could move into our cell. It was the first time we had all shared a room together in jail and it was like old times as we would wind each other up constantly. Tariq's mum had sent him a Gordon Ramsay cookbook. Not even he really knew why but he would delight in reading out the recipes to us and it sent Harry crazy.

'Shut the fuck up, man,' he would say as Tariq read out a lasagne recipe for the twentieth time.

I would read out the lyrics to my songs in a really posh English accent and Tariq thought it was hilarious.

'It's myself C's and I do what I want, say what I want C's, and I live how I live cos I gotta make peas,' I said in my best Queen's English.

'Fuck off Ceaze, you know this does my head in,' Harry said.

'On the street it's deep, we might creep in your sleep. Do what we do when we wanna get down. Strong heads on our shoulders, feet on the ground, if there's a mic in the room just pass it round. Let me spray a couple bars and show you how.'

It sent him insane but Tariq and I found it ridiculously funny.

Apart from getting amazing food with the bosses I started to become more involved in the politics of the jail. Babar and Qasim got into a fairly standard fight in the TV room with a couple of the Bengalis and it was all kicking off when Mohammed came in and tried to break it up. But in the ensuing melee the jail foreman was punched in the nose by one of the Bengalis. When they realized what they had done they sensibly ran away. Mohammed came onto the strip with Babar and Qasim, who were screaming like the Queen had just been shot.

'The foreman's been punched! The foreman's been punched!' they shouted, waving their hands around.

Instant panic set in in the jail, with dozens of people running around screaming. Mohammed was followed into his cell by the crowd and an intense debate in Arabic kicked off before Babar and Qasim went running back out the room. They grabbed a random little Indian guy and dragged him back into the cell. I heard the sound of him being slapped and I went into the room to see Babar and Qasim on top of the innocent man, attacking him and shouting, 'Who hit Mohammed?!'

'I don't know, I don't know!' whimpered the Indian guy on

the floor. 'All I know is that it was one of the people who sleep outside.' The jail was so rammed that dozens of Indians slept in the hoosh.

'Take us to who it is!' Babar shouted.

'I don't know!' he cried.

Babar and Qasim started to go crazy, running around slapping anybody of Indian extraction. After the sixth person had received a beating, Baariq decided enough was enough.

'Right! If you're Indian, Bengali or Pakistani, in the hoosh!' he shouted.

'Come, British, come.'

I was amazed to be roped in to help out. This was a real jail drama that could only be resolved by the prison bosses. Neither Babar nor Qasim could remember which of the many Bengalis they had got into a fight with so in a warped sense of justice all of the Bengalis were lined up outside. I went and grabbed Harry. This was too good to miss.

People who lived on the strip were excused as they had already been told that the attackers slept outside. Of the sixty Indians who lived in the hoosh, Babar and Qasim whittled it down to thirty possibles. They were all lined up and Babar and Qasim moved down the line beating people one by one. Some of these Indians were huge grown men but were reduced to tears, cowering on the floor. It was one of the most messed-up things I have seen. Bengali after Bengali wailed that it wasn't him as he got beaten around the face.

Baariq turned to me and said, 'You do that one.'

'I ain't doing that, man,' I said. I appreciated being involved in prison decision-making but I wasn't going to attack some poor innocent Indian for the privilege. Baariq respected my decision.

Babar and Qasim carried on their mission of abuse and were

halfway through before Rivas appeared in the hoosh dragging a small Indian guy.

'He was hiding in the toilets, I thought you might want to talk to him.'

'That's him! That's the one!' Babar cried.

The whole crowd of Indians and Pakistanis, along with Babar and Qasim, ran towards him. They started to slap and beat him until he was a quivering wreck on the floor. The beaten guy summoned enough strength to point at one of the other Indians and said something in Hindi, at which point the crowd rushed the new target and started to kick and beat him instead. The second victim had about as much loyalty as the first as he too pointed at another man. He was grassing on the third guy. The crowd rushed him, slapping and kicking him into submission.

Harry and I couldn't help laughing at the sight of a huge Indian crying as little Qasim and Babar gave him a slap. It didn't matter how big you were if you didn't have any authority in Port Rashid, and it showed me just how important it was to be part of the jail hierarchy. It was the first time I had been invited to help deal with an important jail incident and although I didn't do much it cemented my position.

Unfortunately, things hadn't got any better with Zain. It pained me that the one person in jail who I should be closest too had become an enemy. I tried to avoid him but he made a point of coming by and muttering threats under his breath. I had enough to deal with without Zain's dramas, being full of pent-up aggression and anger with the world because of my situation. So, when Zain walked past again and again said I was going to get stabbed up by all of the Pakistanis in Central, I lost it. I stormed after him and into his cell.

'Right, Zain, I've had enough,' I shouted. 'Let's have this out.'

I lunged forwards and punched him in the face. I still had my cast on but I didn't care. I was furious. Zain started to scream and within seconds a group of a dozen Pakistanis ran into his cell.

'I'm gonna cut you, I'm gonna fucking cut you,' Zain wailed as I took another swing.

The next moment I was being pulled off Zain by Feroz the guard. It was probably just as well because the Pakistanis were going crazy and looked like they were about to attack me. I was pushed outside into the hoosh, with Mohammed and Baariq following behind.

Feroz turned to me and said, 'So what happened, British?'

'Nothing really,' I said, trying to play down what had happened. I knew I could be in serious trouble now.

'What do you mean nothing really? Keep him here,' Feroz said to Mohammed and Baariq before walking off to see Zain.

'Yo, man, I know Zain has been on your case but you can't just be going around punching people,' Mohammed said. 'This is more *hiwan* behaviour.'

'I'm sorry, Mohammed, but I just snapped.'

Feroz returned and said, 'He told me you punched him in the face.'

'What? Is he snitching on me?'

'What is this snitching?'

'Giddy giddy,' I said, slang for he's talking.

'Of course. This isn't nothing, British. You can't be punching people and expect to get away with it. What do you say happened?'

'Well, I walked into his cell and punched him and everyone started screaming.'

'Why did you do that?'

'Because he kept telling me he was going to stab me up when I go to Central, so I lost it.'

Feroz laughed. He spoke to Baariq in Arabic before walking off. Baariq turned to me and said, 'Give him 500D and this goes away.'

I was stunned. 'I thought I'd get an extra charge,' I said.

'No, you're okay. Feroz's on the payroll. He's a normal person trying to make some extra money and that's where I come in. How high you can get in the police force in Dubai depends on where you're from. If you're not an Arab you can't get promoted and their pay is terrible. He has to earn some extra money, which is good for us.'

I could understand where he was coming from. Poor pay and no promotion prospects because of the racist culture of Dubai created a situation where corruption was rife. I made sure I paid Feroz the 500D and never heard about the incident again. Fortunately for me, Zain kept quiet and didn't bring it up again. Despite us falling out I honestly believed he wouldn't try to get me into trouble, so stayed silent.

My new-found position of authority in the jail came with the added benefit that I got more time in control of the TV remote. I was sitting in front of MTV one morning when Baariq came and joined me. It appeared he now trusted me enough to tell me why he was in prison. I already knew this from Matt but I wasn't going to let on, and listened while he told me how he'd been a police officer working at the airport.

'And I got your friend Ed out as well,' he said. I'd suspected as much and was pleased to have confirmation. It gave me hope that my release could still be on the cards. 'But the bastard has skipped the country without paying me what he owes me,' he added.

Ed had paid half of the fee upfront but before Baariq's people had been able to get to him he had jumped on a flight and flown back to the US. I suppressed a smile when Baariq told me this. Nobody, not even the conniving Baariq, could get the better of Ed.

As well as being an immigration cop, Baariq ran an events company on the outside and that was why he had been in the club when he dragged me away from the baying mob the year before. He got out his phone and showed me pictures of him and rapper 50 Cent. I couldn't help thinking how similar they looked but kept this to myself. He even said he hired Beyoncé for one gig. Nothing really surprised me about Dubai. It was all for show, and all designed to make money. Baariq explained how he had been dating a girl who was the daughter of a top-ranking official. She and her family wanted them to marry but he refused.

'My life would've been so controlled,' he said. 'They even put a tracker on my phone. One night after leaving a club two cars with tinted windows pulled up and tried to get me to go with them. I told them to fuck off and I ended up beating the shit out of them. They were my girl's dad's security. Anyway, when I got home there were cops crawling all over my house. They said I didn't have a licence for my gun and they threw me in here. It was bullshit but there was nothing I could do. I've been told if I marry her I'll go free, but I can't do it, man. That's why I can get other people out, but me? I'm fucked.'

You hear some bizarre things in jail but this was seriously crazy. It at least answered the niggling doubt I had about why, if he had as much influence as he claimed, he couldn't get himself out. I waited until Mohammed and I were alone to check the veracity of Baariq's story.

'Yeah, man, it's true,' he said. 'But be careful with Baariq. He's slippery.'

I had a deep down feeling that I couldn't trust Baariq, and Mohammed's comments just added weight to that. But I also knew that if I wanted to keep on rising up the jail chain, or get out through one of his scams, I would have to align myself with Baariq, for better or for worse.

14

US AGAINST THE WORLD

Cash was not the only way to corrupt the justice system of Dubai. Knowing the right people was even more valuable. *Wasta*, or influence, resulted in people accused of offences that would see a normal person jailed for twenty-five years getting out in weeks. Maroon and the other spice kids had been kicking up a fuss and their parents had met to pool their resources. Maroon's dad was a US satellite expert who was working for the Dubai government while the others' parents worked in the oil industry.

'Hey, man, do you have anyone who can go to the meeting?' Maroon asked.

'My brother or his missus might be able to go along.'

'No worries, man, I'll make sure they get in.'

At the meeting all of the spice kids' representatives, along with my brother's wife Diana, agreed to join together to pressurize the authorities. They argued that we had been in Port Rashid for five weeks and it wasn't fit for habitation. They said they would use their positions of authority to get a meeting with the sheikh's office. It was agreed they would write a letter to the sheikh demanding we all be released.

'Yo, man, they're gonna see what they can do,' Maroon said

afterwards. I didn't hold out much hope. What could a bunch of parents do to get us out?

'Seriously, man, my dad works for the Dubai government and he'll be able to use that position to try and get us out. Don't underestimate the power of *wasta* in this country, man.'

I wasn't so sure but anything that could help was worth a try.

I'd been spending a lot of time with Bobby, playing poker and putting songs together, and had asked him about his case a couple of times but he had always been quite vague. Some people in jail are just like that and don't want to talk about their charges, but I started to get a little suspicious that there may be more to it when I spoke to Baariq.

'You need to be careful who you're hanging around with,' he said.

'Why?'

'Because there's talk that Bobby's a snitch who grassed on a few sons of Russian Mafiosos he had sold spice to. They want to get him.'

'That's fucked up, mate, but how does that affect me?'

'Because you're his boy and you know how it goes.'

I couldn't believe that my friend would be a grass. I just couldn't comprehend it. I went to see Bobby to ask him.

'Mate, there's shit being said about you that you grassed on people. Tell me it ain't true.'

'Nah, man, course not. I wouldn't do that.'

That was good enough for me. We had become close friends and I'd believe him above Baariq any day. I went to see the jail number two and told him.

'Man, I don't believe him,' he said. 'You have to be careful.'

Baariq was getting worked up and he clearly thought something was amiss, although I didn't care as I didn't think it could be true. But then Bobby started to become a bit aloof with me. He was obviously annoyed that I had doubted him. I was stuck with Baariq playing detective and being weird with me while Bobby was avoiding me.

The irritation of jail politics was briefly set aside when there was a sudden furore during morning prayers. The tranquil silence that enveloped the jail, as it always did during prayers, was shattered when a Somalian guy came into the jail and started walking on people's prayer mats. I was in my cell when I heard the Muslims screaming at him and came out in time to see a big black guy standing six foot seven inches tall starting to undress as the Muslims ran around shouting.

When he was naked he began to grind his cock against the bars. He was making grunting noises and whimpering as he made love to the dirty steel poles, and ignored the Arabs who were trying to pull him away so they could attack him for gyrating while they prayed. Mohammed got to the front of the mob and grabbed him, dragging him out of the jail while other inmates were trying to drag him back in so they could give him a slap. It was a game of tug of war with the naked man. Harry, Tariq and I were wetting ourselves.

'He can't be in here,' Mohammed said to the guard, once he'd got the Somalian to the hatch, 'he crazy man.'

The guard shrugged and opened the door and the naked giant disappeared from view. Within minutes he was kicked back into the jail. The guards clearly couldn't be bothered to deal with him. 'I wanna fuck!' he shouted, as he started to repeat his performance, pole dancing. He paused for a moment and walked up to me. The look on this guy's face was deranged. He said, 'You don't need this,' referring to my cast and started to take it off.

'Get off me, mate,' I said, trying to contain my laughter.

'I fix, no problem.'

I ran down the strip to try and escape the madman, but he quickly followed, while Mohammed and Baariq told him to stop and tried to block him so he couldn't get to me.

'I must fuck,' he said suddenly and started grinding the bars again.

'Yo, man, you've gone too far,' Mohammed said, and he man-handled him towards the hatch again.

The Bar Grinder, as he became known in Port Rashid folklore, was never seen again after being thrown into solitary confine-ment, a room with white tiles, no bed and bright lights, that was kept perpetually cold. Baariq told us he had originally been arrested after he was found running along a beach naked.

Of course, some of the humour in jail was down to our own making. When I was putting in the food order Baariq said he wanted to get a cake. He gave me the measurements and I read them out to the restaurant. I'm not sure exactly what went wrong but I clearly messed up, as three enormous cakes, each three feet in diameter, were delivered to the jail. The food order was supposed to be a subtle affair, but I had just blown the lid off it.

Captain Aziz came storming into the jail, shouting, 'Where's Black British?!' I walked up towards the entrance and he yelled, 'You insane?'

'Why, what's up?'

'In office we have three cakes the size of small tables!'

'Can we have one then?'

Captain Aziz laughed at my audacity. 'No, we must send back. *Yallah, yallah.* Go.'

It wasn't only the cake that caused problems. The bosses had been using their midnight feasts as an opportunity to get phones and other contraband into the jail. One day some guards who weren't on the payroll intercepted the orders, finding not just the food but a new Blackberry in amongst the KFC. Captain Abbas came down on the whole jail and stopped all orders coming through. That meant no cigarettes or *dokha* coming into the prison. Unless the ban on food could somehow be bypassed a jail drought would kick in.

That would be a disaster but would at least be a distraction from the main issue that seemed to have gripped the jail – the on-going gossip over whether Bobby was a snitch. I was defending him to everyone, saying it couldn't be true.

The apparent truth was soon to come to light. I was in our cell with Baariq one day as he was on the phone to one of his contacts.

'So that was one of my old police colleagues and he confirmed to me Bobby snitched on a Mafia boss's son.'

I couldn't believe my ears. Every part of my being wanted to believe it wasn't true.

'I told you to steer clear of him,' Baariq added.

'I don't believe it, Baariq. Show me some proof.'

'Okay, you want proof, I will show you.'

Baariq wasn't happy that I was doubting him, and within a couple of days he walked into the cell holding a piece of paper.

'Look, you see. Bobby's a snitch,' he said as he passed over Bobby's case papers.

It was there in black and white. Bobby had grassed on another guy to get the charges against him reduced. A sudden wave of pure rage swept through me and I stormed out of the cell, oblivious to the fact prayers were ongoing and the strip was full of Arabs bowing to Allah. I ran down the strip, treading on prayer mats as I went, with Baariq following swiftly behind. Bursting into the spice kids' room, where Bobby was now staying, I saw he was asleep on a top bunk. I ran up the ladder and jumped on him, repeatedly punching him in the face.

Bobby screamed out in alarm and Danny, who was also in the room at the time, cried out for help as I continued to hit him. Within seconds Mohammed and Baariq grabbed me to pull me off. I kept hold of a struggling Bobby so our battle continued in mid-air as the foreman and Baariq held us up. Then they pulled me back to the ground and separated us. In the meantime around thirty Arabs were going mad outside as I had trodden on their prayer mats.

'You're a fucking snitch! A fucking rat!' I screamed, tears flowing down my face. I was crushed from the betrayal from my friend and had completely lost it.

'No, I'm not, man. I ain't a snitch. It ain't so.'

I was going crazy, screaming and shouting as Mohammed and Baariq ushered me out of the room and pushed me into Zain's cell. Baariq tried to calm me down.

'Man, you didn't have to go and do that.'

'That geezer's a rat and hanging around with him could've caused me a lot of trouble.'

'Yeah, but we could've done it a lot smarter.'

'I just saw red. The geezer's been lying to me for weeks.'

Harry and Tariq had come into the room, concerned for me – Harry in his boxer shorts as he had just woken up, a confused look on his face.

'Look, you fucked up,' Baariq went on. 'You ran through a lot of people when they were praying. They are all unhappy with you. Not only have you disrespected them but you have also beaten up a Muslim in his sleep and didn't ask Mohammed's permission. Don't be surprised if you get jumped.'

'Fuck that,' Harry said. 'Let them try.'

We walked back to our cell and I apologized to a few of the Arabs but within minutes it was clear that this was not enough. Mohammed and Baariq came into my cell.

'Look, guys, I love you and I do everything for you, but you can't be doing this shit,' Mohammed said. 'We are all family here but you have disrespected my authority in front of everyone. What can I do? There has to be something, I have to save face. Look outside.'

Around thirty Arabs were gathered outside my room with Bobby in the forefront. They tried to get into the cell and Harry slammed the door shut. Maroon and Matt were with us and they stood barricading the door. It was us against the world. Tariq was hiding underneath the covers on his bed. Mohammed and Baariq were still in the cell and were shouting at the Arabs outside to try and calm them down.

I said to Maroon, who was overweight and as athletic as a sloth, 'You might want to get out of here and keep your head down as we are about to get a beating.'

But Maroon said, 'No, man, we ride together, we die together.'

Harry wasn't quite so happy. 'Well done, mate, we're fucked now,' he said as he struggled to keep the door shut.

I knew I was screwed. I said, 'Look, lads, don't stand with me, just let me take my beating. I'm not ready for it, but I'm just going to have to take it.'

I opened the door and there was a gaggle of angry faces. They were all shouting in Arabic.

'Yo, bro, why'd you do me like that?' Bobby said.

'You ain't my brother, you're a snitch. But I shouldn't have hit you like that so I'm going to put my hands behind my back and let you have a free shot.'

'Yeah, man, hit him,' Mohammed said encouragingly.

Bobby stepped forward and threw the slowest, weakest punch imaginable. Unfortunately my instincts kicked in and I dodged it, but as I did I slipped, and fell to the floor. I scrambled back up as the other Arabs went mad again, trying to get in. They were only prevented by Maroon, Harry and Matt blocking the entrance to the cell as the throng of Arabs pushed forward, trying to get to me. Mohammed jumped in the way and told everyone to leave.

'*Yallah!* Go! I will sort this out!' he said. The Arabs were not happy but they weren't going to challenge his authority.

After things had calmed down Mohammed said, 'All right, man, this is how you sort this out. When he is outside playing cards you have to go up to him and make a sincere apology in front of everyone. Then it may be okay.'

The Arabs have a weird sense of respect. I went to find Bobby, who was sitting with all of the local gangsters. We had been getting on so well with these guys and I had just screwed it up in one foul swoop.

'Bobby, I'm so sorry,' I said. 'That was so wrong of me to do that. I felt so hurt to hear what I found out about you as I loved you like a brother.'

'All right, cool,' he said with a strange smile on his face. Although he accepted my apology things didn't seem quite right.

That night I didn't sleep a wink. I knew I had messed up and feared being knifed as I slept. The next day I was out in the hoosh with Baariq and he warned me that the Arabs still wanted my blood. I thought I was going to get beaten to a pulp.

'Make sure you apologize to the locals for disrespecting them and take Ayoop a little present of *dokha*,' Baariq said. Ayoop was a big seller of *dokha* and the drought was going to affect him badly. At that moment Bobby walked out and I approached him.

'Look, Bobby, I'm so sorry for what happened,' I said. 'Let me put my hands behind my back and you can take a swing properly this time.'

'Nah, man, it's all cool. Maybe next time just wake me up first.'

I've always been passionate about music.
My first time performing after a few years.

The marina area in Dubai, where we were arrested.

Far left In hospital when the hand broken during my torture was eventually treated.

Centre Not the most stylish outfit. I wore those trousers for months before I could be persuaded to part with them!

Left The crowded cell in Port Rashid, with bunks for six.

Slops! Prison food was disgusting.

Some smuggled doha, a new phone and snacks.

A couple of inmates in Central, in white prison garb.

Below, clockwise from left Souvenirs from Central. Clothes made for me by one of the inmates out of bed sheets and towels; a wallet made from a cigarette carton; some beads made from date seeds.

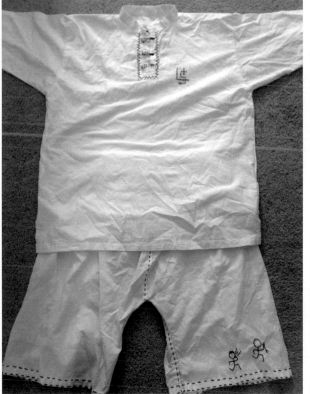

David Cameron met the Sheikh of Dubai in London in May 2013.
Thanks to the publicity campaign carried out by Reprieve,
the prime minister used his influence to get us released.

Two days after I came out of prison I was with my
good friends on stage watching Plan B.

On stage with my friend of fifteen years, Sammy Porter.

Maverick Sabre, Liam Bailey and myself on tour.

With Justin on the day we finished the book.

Modelling for Gabicci, with Mr Jack Manhood.

Although I felt things were now okay between Bobby and me, I was conscious of the potential repercussions and hardly slept for several nights. When you are surrounded by gangsters you think want to cut you up, sleep isn't easy to come by. When I did pass out I slept with my feet where my head usually was. Despite Bobby now having a rep as a snitch, me punching him had ingratiated him with the local gangsters and the rest of the Arabs. For now he was safe, but I knew when he moved to Central the threat of the Russians coming after him would put him in real danger.

Punching Bobby had another unfortunate repercussion. I had seriously hurt my hand again and was in constant pain. I went to the guard at the hatch and he arranged for me to see a doctor who was based at the jail to treat inmates' minor injuries. He confirmed I had broken the hand again and organized a transfer to hospital. It turned out that I was going to be staying for a while, as they needed to operate on my hand again and reset it, so I gave my last bit of *dokha* to Tariq and Harry. The mood in the jail was getting quite intense as the *dokha* drought kicked in. You don't know the meaning of stress until you've been locked up with a bunch of criminals all denied their one pleasure.

Just before I left, Baariq came up to me and said, 'Look, when you get to the hospital call me and put the police officer there on the phone.'

This sounded a bit weird but Baariq said it would be for my benefit.

Salem and Mussa were the guards on duty again for ferrying me to the hospital.

'Black British, how you doing, my man?' Salem said, beaming.

'I'm good, bruv.'

'You going to the hospital again? Didn't you fix your hand already?'

'Yeah, yeah, but I fell out of bed.'

They both laughed. 'Crazy British.'

When I arrived at the hospital I asked the guards if I could use the phone on the front desk. I called Baariq's mobile and handed the phone to the guard. A look of recognition crossed the guard's face as soon as Baariq started talking and he smiled broadly. The other cop at the desk then grabbed the phone and started having what sounded like a jovial conversation in Arabic. He eventually handed me back the phone and Baariq said, 'Don't worry, this lot will look after you. They're on my payroll and I've told them you're a friend of mine.'

I was amazed Baariq's influence could stretch so far and thanked him before putting the phone down.

The first guard said, 'Okay, you want to smoke, no problem, go to the toilet. You can have what you want whenever you want. You can have visitors and whatever food you want.'

This seemed like it was too good to be true, so I thought I would test it out and ordered a McDonald's. Within minutes I was being presented with a beautiful Big Mac, large fries and chocolate milkshake. I was also delivered twenty Marlboro Lights. It was like I was in a five-star hotel. The most beautiful thing was that I didn't even need to pay for it. I called my brother and asked him to bring me some *dokha*. I told him he had nothing to worry about as all of the police were on side.

It turned out that the recent fight had shattered the bone again and I needed a titanium plate in my hand. I was taken down for my operation the following day. When I woke up from the anaesthetic I thought I was dreaming as I heard a cockney voice say, 'Jimmy, Jimmy, wake up.'

Zain was by the bed and chucked a bottle of *dokha* at me, saying, 'There's a little gift.' I swiftly hid it in my bed.

'What the fuck are you doing here?' I said. Despite falling out with my old friend I was delighted to see him.

It turned out most of the spice kids had been freed six weeks into their jail time. Zain told me that several of them, including Maroon, had been pardoned after the meeting at the sheikh's office. All of those whose parents' had any *wasta* had simply been let go. Zain's brother was a powerful banker and had gone to the meeting, so that's why he was out. I was happy for Maroon, but devastated that all of the kids whose parents had lower level jobs such as electricians, like Danny and Bobby, were still languishing inside Port Rashid.

Zain tried to reassure me. 'Look, bruv, they're releasing everyone so you need to get yourself back there sharpish as your name's probably on the list.'

It was true, it did improve our chances. If there was a movement towards releasing spice cases then we might be out soon. But after my past disappointments I wasn't going to get my hopes up.

My time in hospital was a brief but happy taste of freedom. Seeing Zain and my brother was, on one hand, the best thing in the world but on the other made me really sad. It brought home the reality of the horrific situation I was in. For the benefit of the guards I made sure I didn't take the mick, though, and whenever they came to visit we would go and sit in front of the officers to give them peace of mind. When Ross came to visit I asked the guards if they were hungry and offered to treat them to a meal. We ordered a massive spread from Hardee's, a food chain like TGIs, for us all. Ross slipped me a couple of thousand dirhams while Zain let me use his phone to call Amy and go on Face-book.

After three days of living the high life I called Harry and Tariq, who had one of Baariq's phones.

'Bruv, there's a serious drought here,' Tariq said. 'We're shar-ing one cigarette between five or six people. It's ridiculous. You've got to bring some in your balls. Most of the spice kids have gone and we're stuck here with no smokes.'

I said I'd see what I could do, but I wasn't in any rush to get back to Port Rashid as I was having too good a time in hospital. Ross came to visit every day after work and we would play Monopoly. Life was good.

Every night the cops just fell asleep at their desk, meaning that it would have been easy for me to escape. The exit to the ward was not locked and I could have been outside the hospital in minutes. I seriously thought about the possibilities, but I knew if I escaped I would look guilty and would have no chance of ever getting out of jail if I was caught.

I started to plan for my return to jail instead. I collected cling film from the hospital lunches and wrapped cigarettes and *dokha* in separate packages.

On the day I was being taken back I put the cigarettes in my cast and a big package of *dokha* under my balls. As I entered the jail Feroz and his colleague searched me. Feroz would've been tipped off that I was carrying contraband by Baariq, but he needed to make it look like the search was real. I acted drowsy, trying to make them think I was sick so they didn't search me properly. It was surreal coming back into jail. I was disconsolate that I was walking back into incarceration in this stench-filled prison after experiencing a degree of freedom for a few days. On the flip side, I was excited to see my friends again and give them a gift I knew they would love.

When I got into my cell I said to Harry and Tariq, 'Come here, boys, I've got it all.'

They looked like little kids on Christmas morning as I pulled out two packets' worth of cigarettes wrapped up and a big ball of *dokha*.

'Fucking hell, bruv, how'd you manage that?' Tariq said, awed. They hadn't had a proper smoke for four days and I was like Father Christmas and the Easter Bunny all come at once.

After a smoke I went to see Ayoop. I needed to get rid of this fear that I was going to be attacked by the local gangsters and the best way of doing that during a drought was a gift that could be smoked. I gave him a large ball of *dokha*.

I said, 'Look, my brother, here is a gift for you. Do you mind if we sell some on the side?'

'Listen, my brother, you are good boys and you can do whatever you want. For this gift here, thank you from the bottom of my heart.'

'Thank you, bruv. Look, Baariq has more for you.'

The *dokha* had come in big chunks and I had told Baariq he would have to hand more over to Ayoop as he was letting us sell it in jail. Unfortunately Baariq didn't hold up his side of the bargain and Ayoop came to me four days later to complain.

'That man moves like a crab,' he said.

I eventually gave Ayoop more out of our stash. The last thing I wanted to do was upset the local gangsters again.

Now we had supplied the local gangsters we were real players in the jail. I would always give the gangsters big tickets of *dokha* which garnered us extra respect. We knew they knew we were playing on their turf, but they couldn't get anything else into the jail and this put us in a powerful position.

Although we had *wasta* in the enclosed world of the prison, the real power lay in the hands of the authorities and we were about to be brutally reminded of how little we could control our fate. It came without warning, like a bolt from the blue.

'Jamal Tariq Patel! *Yallah! Yallah!* Central!'

Tariq was off to Central, and he was all alone.

15

TARIQ GOES TO CENTRAL

A few days earlier I'd been standing by the phones with Harry and Tariq after a few inmates had been taken to Central. The thought of the place sent shivers down my spine. A dark-haired Arab called Shekai was nearby. We called him Crazy Hair (for obvious reasons) and his brother Abra we called Crazy Beard.

'Fucking hell, I don't want to go to Central,' I'd said with feeling.

'Why not, man? Central's fine,' Crazy Hair said in a soft voice with a slight Arabic accent. 'If you come to Central with me, you have no problem. My brother was a very big gangster in Central and ran the place.'

This alone made the hair on my neck stand on end but was nothing compared to what I was about to hear.

'I'm not scared of it,' Crazy Hair went on, shrugging. 'I have many cousins and brothers inside who are there for me. My brother Abdul was killed in there. He ran the place but there was a group who wanted to get rid of him. They paid off the guards and got them to call his name on the speaker to say he had a visit. On his way there he was ambushed and they cut off his fingers, ears, nose, sliced up his face and stabbed him to death.'

He said this all in a matter-of-fact way, as if it was completely normal.

I looked at Tariq and Harry. Our stunned silence and the expressions on our faces spoke volumes. We all knew for sure we did not want to go to Central.

'People get taken out of the jail and never come back, but not because they've been released,' he went on. 'People are brought out in body bags most days. Guards don't come inside and it's run by the prisoners.'

And then days later Tariq received the call, along with Danny, Bobby and a small teenage lad called Farhan. Tariq had a look of sheer terror on his face. 'I don't wanna go, I don't wanna go,' he kept saying over and over. Harry and I were trying to calm him down and help him get his stuff together. He only had minutes before he would be leaving.

Rivas the Russian came into our cell after he had heard the news. Thanks to the phone I'd given him he was in constant contact with his Mafia pals inside Central.

'Don't worry, I'll put in a call to my boys. The Russians run the place and they will look after him.'

A small act of kindness in giving a phone that I didn't need to Rivas could effectively save my little friend's life. Tariq was going to be protected by the Russian Mafia, the very group that ran the jail.

Baariq came running in and said, 'Go to the hatch and say you don't want to go.'

Tariq got to his feet and ran up to the hatch. 'I don't want to go to Central!' He said.

'No, you go or you go in solitary,' the guard said.

Tariq had no choice. There was no way he would have lasted in solitary for a couple of days let alone for the rest of his sentence. He ran back into the room. 'Shit! I haven't even got much money,' he said. He'd given most of his cash to Baariq to get a Blackberry smuggled in. Harry and I got together a load of our money and gave him some clothes as we didn't know what he would be allowed to wear in Central. It was like a lamb being thrown to the wolves. We wrote down Baariq and my brother's numbers for him.

Bobby came into the cell. 'Hey, man, I'm off too. Guess I'll see you down there.'

I hugged him. 'Good getting to know you, man. Sorry about the shit that went down.' I genuinely meant it. I didn't like attacking people and losing it, prison was just sending me mad and made me snap when I normally wouldn't.

'No problem, man, look after yourself.'

Danny came to speak to Harry and handed over his parents' details so they could stay in touch. He looked like he was about to burst into tears. Tariq wasn't faring much better.

'Central now!' One of the guards shouted.

Harry and I walked them to the door along with Mohammed and Baariq. As Tariq left Port Rashid on that day at the end of August he glanced back one last time, a sad look in his eye. I felt deflated by the whole episode but I have to admit I was pleased that it wasn't me going to Central. Prison is all about survival and we had a much greater chance in Port Rashid than in Central.

It was a couple of days before we heard anything from Tariq and we were pleased to hear his voice but he sounded terrified. What he said did not shatter the horrific legend of Central, but only lived up to the sheer brutal image of the place. We realized we were in a holiday camp compared to the hell of where Tariq was.

'Bruv, you won't believe the shit that's gone on in here,' he said. 'I got talking to this guy on my corridor and the next thing I knew, he'd been raped. He had his drink spiked by this one geezer called Salim, who fucked him. Now he's been taken off by a load of Arabs and they're taking it in turns with him. It's so gross.'

'Fuck, mate, are you okay?' I said.

'Yeah, mate, but it's horrific. I can hear blokes getting raped at night. Sometimes I can hear screams, other times I can hear guys having sex. I can hear people sharpening their knives at night-time. I've met a few of Rivas's mates and I'm just hanging around with them.'

Rivas had been as good as his word and got in touch with his Mafia pals who vowed to look after our friend. But Tariq had clearly had a lot of time to think and had got paranoid about Harry and me.

'Did you snitch on me and say it was all mine to get out early?' he demanded. Given that it was only him who had been transferred to Central it was an understandable thought, but he knew us better than that to even ask.

'No, bruv, of course not,' I said. 'None of us have any idea why you were transferred and we weren't.' I tried to make a joke of it. 'Look, Tariq, just tell us if you've been bummed.'

'Fuck off, Ceaze, it's not even funny.'

I passed the phone onto Harry who spoke to him for several minutes before hanging up. Harry and I sat there in silence for a few seconds.

'Fuck that, I'm not going to Central,' I said at last. 'I'm not a rape victim.'

'Yeah, fuck that.'

'But, Harry, you look like a battery candidate, you'd fit right in.'

We were being stupid and trying to make a joke of it but it was serious, and we knew we could be transferred at any time without warning. Tariq was evidence of that.

A few days later Harry spoke to Tariq again. We knew murder was rife in Central but what he relayed to us was pure evil. Two rival gang members were fighting and the loser promised to come back and sort the other out. He enlisted his friends from the HIV wing to chase his enemy down, cut him open, cut themselves and then mix their blood. He was infected as a sick punishment.

'It was barbaric, bruv,' he said. 'How am I going to survive this?'

We didn't have the answers but told him to stay with the Russians and to keep his head down. We feared for Tariq, but we realized how lucky we had been to avoid being transferred with him. Port Rashid was starting to thin out as the immigration cases left as part of an amnesty and more and more people went to Central.

I couldn't see any light at the end of the tunnel or a way out of our current situation. Money was also getting short. Being inside and calling home every day was costing me hundreds of pounds a week. I needed cash to keep in touch with my girlfriend and little girl. Baariq had gone quiet about his plan to get me out and the pardons had dried up so I had to do something to earn money.

Baariq said Harry and I needed to get our own phone as we were always fighting over whose turn it was to use his. He told us he could help us smuggle in a Blackberry through one of the guards. I had seen stuff going on but I was a little dubious. He told us to arrange for Zain to get a tracksuit and some trainers along with the phone. He was told to cut a hole in the back of one of the trainers and put the phone in the sole. Zain would then seal the hole back up with superglue. He was told to put *dokha* in the other trainer.

'If you do this you can get more involved with the smuggling business,' Baariq said.

I was in Baariq's cell that same day when his phone rang. 'That's Feroz on the phone,' he said.

I looked at him in disbelief. Surely this wasn't possible? 'You're kidding me,' I said.

'You answer it, I don't want to speak to him.'

I picked up the phone.

'British, it's Feroz. Put Baariq on the phone.'

I looked at him, my mouth falling open.

'See?' Baariq said, a smile spreading across his face.

'Erm, he's in the hoosh, Feroz.'

'No he's not, he's stood beside you. I'm looking at the camera now.'

I handed over the phone.

'Feroz, what's up?' Baariq said coolly.

'I need 3,000D today,' I could hear Feroz saying. 'If you want the parcel it needs to be in here within the hour. Make sure it's here sharp.'

'I told you,' Baariq said as he hung up the phone.

I was in shock. Baariq and prison in Dubai never failed to amaze me.

Later that day Zain brought the package to the jail and handed it to Feroz, who brought it onto a table in the visitors' area and made out that he was searching it. It was all show for the cameras. When he was finished he called my name and I came to collect my parcel. The mission had been a success and my eyes had been opened to a whole new area of smuggling.

Every now and then there were people who came into the jail who lifted the mood. Time can go slowly when you're facing twenty-five to death, so any interesting personalities who passed through were welcomed. One of the funniest people I met during my time inside was Said. He was a six-foot-four Arab with a long ponytail who was as camp as a drag queen. The reason we loved him so much was that he set a prison record for seventeen fights in a single week, chasing after other inmates with his slipper for anything that even slightly annoyed him. When he entered the jail he was carried into our cell catatonic and dumped on a free bunk.

'What the fuck, Mohammed?' I said as he was carried in. 'Why have we got this guy in our cell?'

'Yo, boys, sorry about this but he has to have a bed. He's a pure-blood Emirati.'

We didn't have a choice. It was several hours before he woke up, and when he did it was worth the wait. For such a big man his voice was remarkably high pitched and gentle.

'I want tramadol,' he said in a dreamy, angelic voice. Harry and I wet ourselves laughing. When he came to he explained he had been arrested with his wife after a car crash. He had necked a load of tramadol and had passed out at the wheel. The problem was that there were thousands of the tablets in his car.

'But I really miss tramadol, man,' he said. 'Has anyone got any?'

'Nah, bruv, none of that in here, mate, but you might want to try the tea,' Harry said.

Said was an instantly likable guy, but Baariq and Mohammed had their reservations.

'Watch that guy. He might be police,' Baariq said.

'What? Said? You've gotta be joking, right?'

'No, no joke. The police do this all the time. They spy inside jails and land you with extra charges when you walk out.'

'Yeah, man, we have phones and shit in our cell,' Mohammed said. 'He might be a sleeper. If he is, you need to find out.'

That the police would do this was news to me, but I promised to keep an eye on him. It was soon pretty clear that Baariq and Mohammed's fears were unfounded. Quite simply put, Said was too hilariously crazy to be an undercover cop. If a little Indian looked at him strangely he would take off his slipper and run after him. If someone said something he didn't like it was the same reaction. I was constantly woken up to the sound of Said screaming as he chased another poor inmate down the strip. Despite his huge bulk Said was like a child, and Harry and I were his disapproving parents.

'Said, get here now!' we'd shout whenever he kicked off. He would look at us with his big puppy dog eyes, shoulders slumped, like a child who had just been berated.

'That guy, he said something wrong to me and I just had to slap him,' he said one time as he shuffled towards us. I was laughing so hard my sides were hurting.

'Said, please, no more,' I said, tears streaming down my cheeks.

'I'm sorry Mr Karl, but he disrespected me.'

It was so funny that here was this huge guy but he was scared shitless of Harry and me. As soon as we shouted his name he would start cowering like a little girl.

How anybody managed to get into so many scraps is beyond me, but he did. In truth, we loved him for it as he brought so much light to our dark situation.

After a couple of weeks Ayoop, Baariq and Mohammed adopted the same parental tone with him. In the four months he was inside with us I rarely went a day without hearing him getting told off.

A couple of lads who breezed in and immediately made themselves known were two Saudis called Mushari and Abu. They came into the jail wearing top-line designer clothes, laughing and joking. Everything seemed like one big game to them. I was watching TV when they first entered the jail. They walked in and grabbed the TV control before changing the channel.

'What the fuck are you doing?' I said. I was grumpy most of the time and not great to be around.

'Hey, sorry, man. We're new here.'

'Oh, okay,' I said, changing my tune. I remembered how horrific it was entering the jail for the first time. 'What are you in for?'

'We were outside a club, having a spliff, when this guy came up and asked for some,' Mushari said. 'Of course I handed it to him and then we got arrested for dealing as he was an undercover police officer. But you know what, man, it's okay, we won't be here long.'

'Yeah, all right, mate,' I said, laughing. 'Better make yourselves comfortable. You're gonna be in here for a while.'

Their hopes of getting out any time soon seemed a little unlikely as they were looking at twenty-five years for dealing. I got the pair a tea each and handed them some chocolate milk from my supply to help them settle in.

Not long after this I was called to the hatch for another trip to the hospital to check how my hand was. As I walked into the visitors' area I saw Mushari and Abu with a man dressed in the finest Arab dress. He was carrying their bags.

'What? You boys are going home?' I said, amazed.

'Yes, we're going,' Mushari said. 'I told you we wouldn't be here long.'

It turned out they worked for the Saudi royal family as wedding planners. The *wasta* their employers' possessed meant they were free, while others in less privileged positions continued their incarceration. I was put into a van with them and they were buzzing. They were being taken to police headquarters where they would sign their paperwork before walking out to continue their lives.

'Hey, Karl, check this out,' Mushari said.

They showed me pictures of their Lamborghinis, except they had somehow managed to put a goat on the bonnet.

'That's killing it, man,' I said.

They had so much cash that damaging their super car with goat hooves didn't matter to them. Despite being in a police van the officers let them smoke away. They were above the laws of normal inmates.

The trip to hospital was uneventful. My hand was healing but I was feeling depressed. We had committed no crime yet we were inside facing the death penalty. The Saudis had been facing twenty-five years for a crime they did commit but were now free.

Meanwhile Rivas had recently discovered that his wife had run off with one of his friends. He was in bits. In my depressed state I started thinking how I could possibly cope if I found out Amy had done the same to me. When I got back to jail I called her.

'Look, Amy, I think it's time you left me,' I said. 'It's not looking good for me here. It's not fair on you and you need to move on.'

'No, I'm not gonna leave you,' she said as she started to cry. 'You'll be home soon.'

'If there's anybody else, just say and you can walk away. I'd rather know.'

'Don't be stupid. I don't even have the time. I have Faith 24/7, and I wouldn't do that to you.'

I believed her as I knew how much she loved me. She also spent a lot of time with my mum. But I thought it was unfair for her and I was worried something would happen that would send me over the edge. Tariq had gone to Central and there seemed little hope of Harry and me avoiding the same fate. We didn't have *wasta* and buying our way out seemed to have failed. I saw my life stretching out in front of me, banged up in a Dubai jail, and I didn't know if I could cope.

16

ROLLING THE DICE
ON OUR FUTURE

Just when I started to give up, there was a sudden ray of hope. Harry and I were called to the guard's phone near the visiting area where a lawyer called Marc was on the other end. Marc explained he worked for a charity called Reprieve who provided aid to British prisoners around the world. We had filled out several forms for charities two months ago, when we were first told we faced twenty-five to death, and Reprieve was one of those.

I explained how we'd been arrested and tortured in the desert, how my hand had been broken and I had been electrocuted in the balls.

'Oh my God, that is terrible,' he said in a posh English accent. 'Are you okay?'

'Yeah, we're all right. We just want to get out of here.'

'Well, I can't promise you anything but we might be able to help you.'

'Look, we'd be grateful for anything. The British embassy have a lot more notes on our case.'

'Okay, let me look into it and I will get back to you.'

'Whatever,' Harry said to me, as Marc hung up.

'Yeah, not worth getting too excited about,' I said.

An hour later we received another call to the office.

'There are quite a few questions I want to ask you,' Marc said. 'Is there a safe number I can call you on?'

I was a bit reticent about giving out my mobile number, simply because it was illegal for prisoners to have handsets inside. How would it look to a lawyer if we were breaking the law in jail? But I realized that if he was to help us I had to trust that telling him about the phone was the right thing to do.

'Yeah, I've got a number I can call you on.'

Marc gave me his mobile number for me to send him a message, so he could call me back, and I hung up.

I went to get my Blackberry from our hiding place inside a drain in the hoosh. Phones belonging to the local gangsters and Baariq were also hidden here and were wrapped in plastic bags.

Marc asked me to go through exactly what happened to me and the more I explained the more shocked he became. I took him step by step through the torture and for some reason talking about it to Marc really affected me. It was only then that I realized how horrendous an ordeal it had been. Even when we had told the other inmates I had been normalizing what had happened in my head.

I told him that Tariq had been arrested with us and had suffered the same fate but he was now in Central. After I had finished, Harry told Marc his own side of things then handed the phone back to me.

'Karl, this is unbelievable,' Marc said. 'What have the British embassy done about it?'

'Well, they say there isn't much they can do. They said they were going to write a strongly worded letter.'

'That's disgusting! This is an absolute disgrace. Do you mind if I share your notes with some journalists and try to get some exposure?'

'Yeah, sure, no problem.'

'Look, I can't promise you anything as sometimes Reprieve don't take on cases, but this is definitely worth exposing. Press coverage could really help your case. I can assure you we will get anything cleared with yourselves first before it goes to print or is aired, so you can make sure it's okay and tell your families.'

'Okay, great. Look, thank you so much. Anything that could help us is really appreciated.' I figured we needed as much help we could get.

I gave him my brother's number and Harry gave his dad's. Marc asked if we had legal representation and we said we hadn't appointed anyone yet as it wasn't clear if our case was going to court.

'Keep your heads up, chaps. We might be able to help you out. At least you have one more person fighting your corner now.'

I put the phone down grateful at Marc's interest but still sceptical he could really do anything to help. If the Dubai authorities wanted us inside, there was little we could do about it. However, Marc immediately contacted my brother who then called Amy. I phoned home later that day to be greeted by my girlfriend in tears.

'Why didn't you tell me about the torture?' she said.

I'd completely forgotten that I hadn't told her. I hadn't wanted to say anything at the time as I didn't want to upset her unnecessarily. The fact I had been arrested was enough for her to deal with. Now I told her exactly what had happened.

'So that's why you had to go to the hospital. I thought you were just fighting inside.'

'No, the police did it. Well, I have had a couple of fights too,' I admitted.

'You poor thing, I'm so sorry. Are you sure you're okay? How's Harry?'

'We're fine. We suffered a few scratches and bruises at the time but now we're okay.'

Talking about the horror of a couple of months ago was messing with my head so I promised to call Amy soon and hung up.

It was a two days before we heard from Marc again on our mobile.

'I've spoken to a few people and we are trying to get your case on a radio show, is that all right?'

'Yeah, that's no problem.'

'I've been speaking to your brother and he said he'd be happy to talk on the radio and so are Harry's mum and dad and Tariq's sister. I need you both to write down full statements of what happened as we want to get your case in the papers. Have you got any medical proof?'

'There are X-rays and I can try to get hold of them but it might be a bit difficult. I think they're in the medical cabinet in the doctor's office so I'll ask them if I can have them.'

'Okay, great. Well, I'm going to try to come and see you in about a month or so.'

Despite the interest in our case on the outside, life continued as normal for us. The sinister guard Mo had been lurking around and was starting to show an unhealthy interest in me. I was sickened by the guy and as a result revelled in taking the mick out of him.

'Mo, you look lovely today,' I said. 'Your hair looks really nice.'

Mo blushed and said, 'Thank you, British. If you ever want to come outside for a cigarette, let me know. Do you like me? If you do, I can get things for you and make life better for you.'

My ribbing had gone too far. 'Nah, man, you're all right.' I said before walking off.

A couple of times in the ensuing days I woke up to find my blanket being lifted by Mo. He had clearly been staring at my half-naked body.

'What the fuck?' I said, half asleep.

'Sorry, British, I was just trying to wake you to search.'

Nine weeks into our stay Matt had moved into our cell, but had started to become quite insular because he was missing his wife. Being in a cell with us, where we constantly wound each other up, probably wasn't the best place for him to be. Harry and I covered him in talcum powder as he slept and he went crazy when he woke up. He would smoke copious amounts of *dokha* before speaking to his wife on the phone for hours. He was always arguing with other inmates over the fact he was hogging the phones. He was getting particular grief from Yahir, one of Mohammed's minions who was in charge of the phone area. One day Matt came stomping back into our cell.

'I'm fucking sick of that Yahir. He's always kicking me off the phone.'

'You're not gonna take that shit from them, are you?' Harry, said. 'They obviously don't respect you.'

Matt stormed off to find Gary to continue his moan.

Unusually, it was Harry's turn to start a drama. One of the hardest things to get into the jail was the humble lighter. The guards were willing to turn a blind eye to cigarettes and phones, but lighters were a definite no-no as somebody could start a fire. As a result we ended up paying 300D (£60) for a basic Bic lighter. Harry had been smoking with Qasim and had left his lighter on the bed. When he returned it was nowhere to be seen.

'Have you picked up my lighter?' he asked the group.

'No, mate, we wouldn't steal your lighter,' Gary said.

Harry immediately suspected Qasim as he had been sitting next to him. He came back into our cell, saying, 'I think Qasim has jacked me for the lighter.'

I started laughing.

'Nah, mate, it's the one we bought,' he protested.

'We can't have that,' I said. 'Go and ask for it back.'

Harry went back in and demanded the lighter be given back to him. Suddenly he lost it, starting to shout. This was remarkable as Harry had remained calm the whole time we were in jail.

'Is it really about to go off?' I said to Matt.

'Yeah, mate, sounds like it.'

We went running into Gary's cell in time to see Harry grab hold of Qasim. Babar stood up and was about to get involved but Matt and I jumped on him and held him back.

'Give me my lighter! Give me my fucking lighter!' Harry screamed as he shook Qasim. Harry pushed him over and the Pakistani murderer smashed his head on the edge of the bed.

Mohammed came running in. 'What's going on, man?'

'Qasim's stolen my lighter,' Harry said.

'Okay, boys, leave it to me.'

Harry, Matt and I went back to our cell. A few minutes later Mohammed came in with our lighter.

'I knew he had it!' Harry shouted. 'He's a thieving cunt and I'm gonna smash him.'

'Mate, it's fine. You've got it back, don't worry about it,' I said.

'No, Ceaze, if this was you it would be a big deal and you'd go fucking mental.'

He had a point. I had got into scrapes over less. At that moment Qasim appeared at the door. 'I'm sorry, Harry,' he said.

'Fuck off, you prick, I'm gonna iron you out.'

Qasim looked at Mohammed and walked off.

'Hey, man, I've spoken to him and he said he won't do it

again,' Mohammed said. 'But you should know better than to leave it lying around. People want lighters.'

I managed to calm Harry down with the suggestion of a game of Monopoly.

It wasn't just Harry who was close to boiling point. Tensions were running high in the jail as a result of Captain Abbas's continued crackdown. The prison canteen food was becoming almost inedible. Even the remaining Bengalis were complaining, and they would eat pretty anything.

'Hey, man, this is too much,' Mohammed said one day as he looked at the slops on his plate. 'I have to do something about this.'

In a moment of madness he ran back to his cell and called his uncle at the police headquarters. His uncle promised to do something about the conditions but I couldn't help thinking that using an illegal mobile phone to call a police officer from jail wasn't the best idea.

'Hey, boys, we have to stand up if we're gonna do something about this,' he said after the call. 'You British should stand up for the cause.'

We all agreed something needed to be done, so around forty people crammed into the small space by the hatch. 'Captain Abbas! Captain Abbas!' we all chanted as we started to bang on the hatch and door. Within a couple of minutes Captain Abbas came into the jail and he looked furious. Matt was at the front with a Qur'an in his hand. He opened up the Muslim's holy book and started reading out passages about looking after others and the sharing of food. Captain Abbas screamed at him in Arabic before slapping him once hard around the face.

The crowd went crazy, screaming, 'Yaaaaaar!'

Captain Abbas pulled Matt through the door without realizing that, in a moment of impeccable timing, some of the families of the inmates were coming into the jail for a visit. He quickly shoved Matt back into the phone area where the baying mob of prisoners was still going crazy.

'Fuck this place! I'm gonna fuck this place now!' Matt screamed, a red mark emblazoned on his cheek.

Captain Abbas tried to calm the situation down. 'Look, I am sorry for just now. I will order burgers for everyone and then you can have burgers and *shawarmas* for the next three days.'

The inmates all erupted in joy. We lived on KFC, Pizza Hut and Hardee's for the next few days. Baariq put his hand in his pocket to pay for extras for everybody.

Soon after that one of the guards told Baariq he'd found a way to get the burgers back in. This meant we could eat properly again and smuggle tobacco and *dokha* in. It improved everyone's mood.

Not long after Matt was slapped by Captain Abbas he got into some more serious trouble. He was still spending too long on the phone and Yahir, a quiet and unassuming Arab who was one of Mohammed's sidekicks, had asked him to end another call. Matt told him to 'fuck off' and when Yahir hung up the phone, disconnecting Matt's call, Matt went mad and punched him, laying him clean out. Unfortunately for Matt, Ayoop and his brother Mansoor, who were friends with Yahir, were behind him at the time and started to beat Matt. I ran out of my cell to see my friend being laid into by several local gangsters.

'Stop! Stop!' Mohammed shouted as he got in the way of the group attack. Mohammed took several blows to the face before the local gangsters realized the foreman was in the way.

'Matt, get in the visitors' area now!' Mohammed shouted. The guard opened the door and they disappeared.

The whole incident illustrated again what an amazing person Mohammed was. His own sidekick had been punched by Matt, but Mohammed stepped in to stop him from getting a beating. Gary, who was arrested at the same time as Matt, came into my cell looking frustrated.

'This guy is just crazy,' Gary said.

'I know, man, Matt keeps losing it,' I replied. 'We can see something's eating him up. What's wrong with him?'

'I don't know, mate.'

I saw this as my opportunity to find out the truth of whether Zain had snitched or not.

'So what's the story with Matt and Zain then?' I said. 'Did Zain snitch on you two?'

'No, Zain didn't snitch.'

'So was it the other way round?' I said. 'Did Matt snitch on Zain?'

'I don't really want to talk about it. I don't want to drop Matt in it but take it from me, Zain is no snitch,' Gary said before getting up and walking out.

I knew all along that Zain wasn't the snitch. I just felt sad Zain had been an outcast when it appeared that Matt had been the real grass.

In September, the time for Mohammed to face trial had come and we all saw him off to court every day for a week, hugging him and wishing him luck. From his jovial demeanour you would never know he was facing twenty-five years in jail.

'These police officers are fucking stupid, man, they couldn't catch a fish,' he said after one hearing.

But the day he was found guilty of drug trafficking a dark atmosphere cloaked the jail. On the day before his sentencing

Mohammed was quiet and contemplative. It was strange to see this larger than life character subdued for the first time. When he returned he had regained his swagger.

'Yo, boys, I got ten years,' he said with a smile on his face. 'I should've got twenty-five. I'll be out if here in no time. My family have got connections.'

The biggest implication for us all was that now he had been sentenced he would be on his way to Central. The foreman had become like a father figure to the whole jail, caring for rich and poor, privileged and abused. We were all devastated that he would soon be leaving us.

When criminals are sentenced in Dubai they are usually immediately transferred to the country's most notorious jail. But Mohammed had so much clout he was able to string out his stay in Port Rashid for a few days more.

'I've got *wasta*, man,' he explained. 'When you are big drug dealer like me the cops listen when I speak.'

We all loved him for his bravado, but even more for how he looked after us all. This feeling of affection from every inmate was most apparent two days later, when he received the tragic news that his dad had died. He had heard he was seriously ill an hour after the 5 a.m. morning prayer and had dressed up in his traditional Arab silk clothes to show he was an important and wealthy man. I came out of my cell to see him reading from the Qur'an and all of the Muslims in the jail joining in prayer for his sick relative. It was a moving sight.

Later that day Mohammed heard the news that his dad had passed away. Tears flowed down the great man's face as each prisoner in turn walked up to him to pay their respects.

'Mohammed, I am so sorry to hear about your dad,' I said. 'If there is anything I can do for you, please say.'

'Thank you, British, it means a lot.'

When everyone had finished paying their respects the inmates joined together again in prayer. A low hum filled the jail and the pain we were all feeling for our friend was tangible. Despite fighting constantly, all of the prisoners came together in solidarity. For better or worse, it felt like we were members of one pretty messed-up family.

The following day Marc came to see us for the first time. I'd told him to say he was our lawyer and then he would be able to come into the jail during visiting hours.

'Black British, other British, your lawyer is here,' one of the guards shouted, and Harry and I were ushered into the visiting room. Feroz had agreed for us to be able to see Marc on a separate side table, rather than having to speak to each other over the phone through the glass. Marc stood as we entered. He was a six-foot-two white guy in his forties, with dark brown hair in a side parting. We both shook his hand and sat down. We thanked him for coming to see us and handed over our written statements detailing what had happened to us.

'Were you able to get the hospital reports?' Marc asked me.

'I can get them now,' I said, heading over to the doctor's office which was just off the visiting area. I told the doctor I needed my X-rays for my lawyer and to my surprise he handed them over. Marc looked through the reports.

'Wow, this is horrendous. I can't believe these people have done this to you and they're getting away with it. We will do everything we can to help you and try to get you out of here. What's the jail like?'

'It's filthy and you wouldn't even want a dog to live in these conditions,' Harry said. 'There are people sleeping on the floors, bed bugs infesting everything, people coughing and spitting on the floor, and the stink of shit from the toilet can be smelt all over the jail.'

'Oh my God, that's inhumane. You poor boys.'

'Are you going to get the chance to see Tariq as well?' I said.

'I'm going to try to do my best, but Central Prison isn't as accommodating as Port Rashid is. I've been speaking to him on the phone and he seems to be doing okay. Look, we are going to try and get you on a few TV stations. My contact at the BBC is interested in highlighting your case. I've spoken to your brother Alex and he is going to help doing press. We've also spoken to some of your friends to get character references. Can I take this report and these X-rays with me?'

'I don't mind,' I said.

'Won't you get in trouble?'

'I'm looking at twenty-five to death, what can they do to me?'

'That's a fair point. Okay, I will take them out.'

He risked his own safety smuggling those reports out of jail and it was at that point we knew he was truly on our side.

'The other thing is that you need to get a lawyer. Here is a list of good lawyers in Dubai and we would recommend you use one of these, although you probably won't need one until you go to court.

We thanked him and promised to stay in touch.

When I called my mum she wasn't happy about the potential media attention and didn't want us to do it. My nan was very ill, after my granddad died, and Mum hadn't told any of my extended family about the arrest. Harry wasn't sure either as he thought he'd put his family through enough. There was also the fact we hadn't been charged or been to court and still had a hope that we wouldn't be jailed and would get a pardon as the spice kids and Zain had done.

'Look, at the end of the day, bruv, they're trying to fuck us with the charges they are accusing us of, so we haven't got anything to lose,' I said to Harry, and he agreed. We spoke to Tariq and he was also on board.

When the media campaign began in October 2012 it was like the blue touchpaper had been lit.

I called my brother Alex and he said he had just been interviewed by BBC radio and was in the car with Marc. As I was talking, Alex said, 'One sec, bruv, my other phone's going off,' and it was ITV. He passed me on to Marc, but no sooner had I started to talk to him than the Press Association was on the other line. They were passing me back and forth as media outlets from across the UK called them to hear about our story.

While I was on the phone Mohammed shouted out, 'Hey, you two, get in here, you're on the news!'

Our faces were on Dubai One, the country's premier TV channel. The report said: 'Three British men claim they were tortured by Dubai Police. Dubai Police said these allegations are untrue.'

Some of the inmates looked at us with real venom and anger after that report. We were disrespecting their country by making apparently untrue accusations. People we were close to, like Mohammed, Baariq and Rivas, warned us of the dangers we faced now we had embarked on our media campaign.

'Hey, boys, you're big celebrities now!' Mohammed said. 'But you have to be careful, my friends. If you make noise in this country, they fuck you. They don't like noise. But you boys have to go all the way. Nobody has ever stood up to the Dubai authorities and won.'

When I called home later and spoke to my friend Al he told me we were across all of the TV channels. I also spoke to Tariq in Central where they were able to watch BBC News.

'Bruv, I'm famous in jail,' Tariq said. But he was more than aware that he had to watch his back even more. The haters were out to get us and he was in a much more precarious position than us.

I joked, 'Cover your bumhole, mate.' He laughed, but knew it was serious.

Spice kid Danny's mum came to visit Harry the next day. She had lived in Dubai for twenty years and said nobody had ever spoken out against the authorities in the country and not suffered as a result.

'She said we were idiots for doing this media stuff,' Harry said. 'She said if we said anything more we would guarantee being landed with a twenty-five-year sentence. She said they'll make our lives hell, bruv, as they don't like noise. She thinks they'll turn it around on us. Anyone who has ever tried to do anything has failed. Bruv, do you think we've done the right thing?'

I wasn't sure but I did know we didn't have a choice – even if we were gambling with our lives.

17

BUYING AND SELLING
IN PORT RASHID

'Mohammed! Central!' came the call from the guards. We all gathered round to give the foreman a hug. It was only a few days after our friend had heard the news about his dad. He had been sentenced to ten years, lost a close relative and transferred to one of the world's worst prisons in less than a week.

'Don't worry, man, I'll be fine in Central,' he said. 'Now I can eat as much chocolate as I like.'

It was ironic that, despite being a top-security jail, you could get many more luxuries from the canteen in Central compared to Port Rashid.

'Hey, Mohammed, can I have that Ralphey?' Harry said. The Great Britain Ralph Lauren shirt was what Mohammed was wearing when we first met him.

'Of course, man,' he said, handing it over.

He turned to me. 'Black British, I'm leaving you now. I know you're gonna miss me but you have to try and get along with everyone. You are a good guy and don't need to keep on getting into fights. Be careful of that Baariq, he can't be trusted. I think you should have my bed. Baariq is going to be foreman now and I know you're doing a lot of things in here so why don't you move in as you'll have access to the phone? You can have all of my extra blankets and pillows. You need to start living like big drug dealer like me.'

With that he made his way to the door and waved goodbye. Without Mohammed there was a big void in the jail that couldn't be filled. The only plus was that I was brought into all of the smuggling scams and was looked on as Baariq's number two. I could spend as much time as I liked on the phone and could walk straight to the front of the queue. I had been upgraded to the level of prison boss and life was much easier – at first.

Baariq explained how things worked.

'We have two guards on the payroll who will near enough do whatever we want for a bit of money. You know Feroz is a good guy. He'll let you into the visiting area at night and go right up to the entrance of the jail. You'll see a hatch to the outside. He'll open it up for you and let you get in whatever. And there's another guy who's recently started who I've got on side, a good lad. But all this comes at a cost.'

There were two deliveries a week whenever Feroz was on duty. We would call Zain or other ex-inmates who had offered to help us out by bringing contraband to us. The tried and tested method – as I'd already seen with Zain – was to hide the contraband, such as phones, tobacco or *dokha*, in the heels of shoes. Feroz would pretend to search the package for the benefit of the cameras but knew what was happening.

At other times I would walk up to the hatch and Zain would be outside. He would chuck the tobacco down my top and I would walk back into the prison.

Because she knew how desperately I was missing my little girl, Amy sent Zain some pictures of Faith to pass on to me. Faith was now six months old and I had missed three months of her growing up, half her life so far. Those pictures were more valuable than any mobile phone or tobacco. I approached Feroz when nobody else was around and told him I had a delivery coming in.

'No problem, give me 500D, but no mobile phones. You guys already have too many phones in there.'

I called Zain and within an hour he was at the outside hatch. 'Black British!' I heard from the inside hatch and made my way to the phone area. Feroz let me through into the visitation area and Zain was waiting outside. He put the cigarettes and *dokha* down my top before handing me my letter. Feroz opened it on the table in front of the camera.

'You have baby?' he said, looking through my pictures. 'Why your baby brown? Why is this?'

'Because my girlfriend's white,' I replied.

'Ah, I see, I see. You are married?'

'No.'

'What?! How you have baby? You definitely *hiwan*!'

The Arabs could not understand the concept of a black man and a white woman together. The fact we weren't married blew his little mind.

Other times Zain would come in and see us on a regular visit, go to the toilet and hide a package underneath the sink. I would then go to the toilet and retrieve it. Baariq didn't need to lift a finger to get stuff from the outside. His guards would come into the cell at night-time and drop packages by Baariq's bed.

On average I was making about £200 a day from my illicit enterprises. But phone credit was expensive, as were the little luxuries that make life in jail comfortable. We paid the guys in the canteen to bring us this stuff called Tang which is like Kool-Aid. Then we started paying Feroz to bring us Lanimaid, which is a thick sour cream. I put it with jam or chicken and it tasted great. On chicken days I would pay other inmates 50D for the best pieces. But most of my cash went home to Amy. I was unable to be there for her so the least I could do was send her the money I was able to earn. Zain would come and collect it and wire it back to her.

While prison life was getting more comfortable physically as the weeks passed, mentally it was taking its toll. Harry and I started to row again as time was dragging and we were frustrated. We had no idea what was going on with our case. We had been inside for five months yet nothing had happened. It felt like I had been inside forever and I was climbing the walls. I was impatient, fidgety and short-tempered. I felt like I was losing my mind.

Harry had got himself a lawyer through his dad, but I didn't see the point as there was nothing they could do until our case went to court. Marc had given me the list but I'd been told that it was a waste of money instructing anybody until we knew what was happening with the legal process.

'Bruv, my lawyer says it's because you haven't got representation that our case has been delayed,' Harry said.

'That's bollocks, mate. How can you blame me for our case taking longer? It's just a long-winded process. Look at Baariq, he's not been to court the whole time we've been here.'

'Well, we're waiting on you, mate, sort it out.'

I gave in and got in touch with a firm on Marc's list. A representative from the firm came to see me so I could sign over power of attorney. It was a brief meeting with a male secretary and I was told the firm would now be working on my case.

Later that month, a couple of weeks before Christmas, we were called to the hatch for our first court appearance. Harry and I were handcuffed together with Said and a few of the locals. We were marched into the back of a prison van that once again was so hot it burnt when we sat on the metal seats. It reminded me of the time we had all been arrested those months before. I was happy that things were finally moving on our case after months of being inside.

When we arrived we were ferried in through a back entrance and shown into a huge holding cell that was split into four smaller cells. You could go into any of the four cells as the doors were open. Our handcuffs were taken off and I looked up to see prisoners from Central with huge scars on their faces staring at us. Massive Russians with shaved heads and tattoos were sat around looking menacing. An Arab with bloodshot eyes and dozens of weeping cuts on his arms sat in the corner. All of the Central prisoners were dressed in white T-shirts and trousers.

The inner doors to the four cells were open, allowing the bunch of psychotic-looking criminals we were in there with to wander around freely. It was freezing, but my blood also ran cold from the people around us who were scoping us out. I suddenly noticed Tariq, who was already in the cell, sat on a bench.

'Hey, Tariq!' Harry and I shouted. We went over and gave him a big hug. It was the first time we'd seen him in three months.

'What's happening in Port Rashid, bruv?'

'Same old, just smoking loads of *dokha*.' Harry said.

'Ah, man, I'd love to have some *dokha*. We don't get any of that shit in Central.'

Tariq looked really well as he had been out in the sun, eating good food and had been working out with weights.

'Look at you, man, you're almost as dark as me!' I joked.

'Yeah, mate, you look like a little Sri Lankan,' Harry said.

'Fuck off, you pricks,' he laughed.

'Look, Tariq, if you've been bummed it doesn't make you any less of a man,' I said, as I put an arm around him.

'Don't make any jokes about that, bruv,' he said. 'It's not funny.'

It was good to see how well he was doing and that he was interacting with the others from Central, laughing and joking with a few lads he had come in with. He introduced us to them and we introduced him to Said.

Harry had spoken to Tariq on the phone before our court appearance and had arranged for him to bring us some tobacco. Smoking was allowed in Central so he could simply buy tobacco from the canteen. Tariq had brought us some cigarettes hidden in his pants. But where he had sellotaped them to himself they were covered in his pubes.

He had also cut out a hole in his slippers and wedged cigarettes in each side before sewing them back up. Said had agreed to wear the counterfeit-laden pair and swiftly swapped slippers with Tariq.

Our names were called and we were taken up to court by a guard. The room resembled a Crown Court in the UK and had dark wood panels on the walls with green carpet everywhere. A judge was sat at the front of the court but said nothing during the time we were there. We were pushed into the dock where we confirmed our names. Our lawyers were stood behind a bench but weren't allowed to say a thing. It was just a prosecutor talking but we didn't understand a word. The next minute we were taken back to the cells. The whole process had taken two minutes and we had no idea what was going on. We eventually said our goodbyes to Tariq before we were taken back to Port Rashid.

*

Back in the jail, Matt was becoming more and more irate with life. He had been to court a couple of weeks before with Gary and they had both been sentenced to four years with deportation. As spice was not illegal when we were arrested, the courts had ruled that anyone sentenced to four years for possession would be immediately released. Two weeks on and Matt was still inside. He had continued to get more and more psychotic after the Captain Abbas and Yahir incidents but the latest development seemed to be tipping him over the edge. I would often hear him slamming down the phone after rowing with his wife.

'Did they say anything about any of the other spice cases?' he asked, as I walked past him on the strip.

'No, mate, I have no idea what they said. Look, you've got to chill and stop stressing about it. You're going to go home.'

He stormed off and I went back to my cell. Moments later I heard a commotion outside. I could hear people shouting his name and we all ran out to see Matt being carried along the strip by Baariq. His eyes were rolling back in his head and he was frothing at the mouth. He was making a horrific choking noise that I will never forget. Baariq carried him back into Harry's cell.

'He's tried to hang himself with the phone cord,' Baariq said, bringing him into Harry's cell.

All of the Arabs were going crazy, trying to attack him. Suicide is seen as a shameful death in Islam and in their eyes he had brought shame on the religion.

Baariq laid Matt out on Harry's bed.

Arabs were outside the cell screaming, 'Bring him out. We beat him.'

Harry and I held them back before Baariq told them to leave.

'No one talk to me, why ain't I gone home yet?' Matt said as he came round. 'I need to call my wife.'

We made sure he stayed lying where he was until he regained his composure.

Within days Matt had received his wish and he was on his way out. I heard his name being read out and realized this was my last opportunity to ask him about the cash I had paid him and Baariq to get released.

'What about my money?' I asked.

'You need to speak to Baariq, mate,' Matt said, and swiftly walked off to get his stuff. I went to see Baariq.

'So where's my money?' It was the first time I had spoken directly to him about the bid to buy my way out.

'What money?'

'The money I paid to you to get my release. It's been four months and I'm still here.'

'I'll have a word with my guys and see what's happening. But realistically your case is too high profile now for me to get you released.'

I had realized I was unlikely to get out through Baariq's methods but to have it confirmed to me was a blow. I felt like I had been done over by Matt and Baariq. As I walked out of the cell I saw Matt heading towards the exit. He looked back and I gave him the finger as he slipped out the door.

I found out that the authorities weren't happy about us going to the media when I got an unexpected call to the hatch. I was ushered into the visitors' area by Mo the guard and the door was slammed shut behind me.

'Go with these men, British,' he said.

I looked over and froze on the spot. A shiver went down my spine when I saw two of the cops who had tortured us. Rooncy cop and Ferrari hat were stood in front of me with smug looks on their faces.

'Where are we going?'

'To the station,' Rooney said.

'I ain't going anywhere with you until I've spoken to my lawyer.'

'You can do that at the station.'

'No fucking way, mate,' I said and ran back to the door and banged on it with all my might. The hatch opened and I shouted to Baariq, 'Get Harry! Get Harry!' Within seconds Harry had appeared.

'The police officers who tortured us are trying to take me back to their headquarters. Get on to Marc as they won't let me call my lawyer.'

'All right, bruv,' he said as I got dragged away by the cops, who handcuffed me and took me to an unmarked car.

'You still here?' Rooney said. 'Why you no go home?'

'Ah, yes, it is because you make noise,' Ferrari cop said. 'You make noise and they fuck you.'

I was confused and terrified. I knew that now I was going through the court system the cops couldn't legally drag me out of prison and question me again. Adrenaline raced through my body. Was I going to get tortured again or worse? Surely they wouldn't risk that after what had happened to us had been exposed in the media? But they could easily be making an example of me and it wouldn't be hard for them to make me disappear. Both the cops seemed to be enjoying themselves as they laughed and joked in Arabic.

A few minutes later we arrived at the police station. It brought memories of the abuse we had seen in this place flooding back to me. They walked me down to the cell block where Tariq, Harry and I had spent three days fearing for our lives, and put me in the same cell. I was terrified, as I was by myself with no protection and had the horrific recollections of when we were here previously. But when I walked into the cell there were only two Arab guys and an Indian sitting on the floor. The whole cell block seemed more serene, with no haunting cries coming down the wing.

I was wearing my prison slippers and my hair had grown into a big afro. One of the Arabs looked at me and said, 'What's your case?'

'I'm in for spice.'

'Oh, man, I know hundreds of people who have been arrested for spice,' he said in a faux American accent.

'How do you know hundreds?'

'Bro, haven't you heard? Someone in the Royal family's son took a lot of spice and thought he could fly and jumped off a balcony. He died, man. That's why the sheikh has sent his police force out arresting everyone for it.'

That answered a lot of questions. It hadn't made sense why people were being arrested for a substance that wasn't even illegal.

'What are you guys in for?' I said.

'We were doing heroin.'

'Really?' I said.

'It's not so bad, man. All the kids are doing heroin these days.'

At that moment a huge light-skinned ogre of a man, towering six foot four, was thrown into our cell. He had massive arms adorned in dozens of tattoos. A cut on his head dripped blood down his face and he had psychotic wide eyes.

'Let me out! Let me out!' he screamed as he punched, kicked and shook the bars. 'Yaaaaaaaar!'

It was an old trick, I realized, but it was still as terrifying as when we had first been arrested. If the police officers wanted to kill me, what better way than putting a crazed madman in my cell? The Arabs looked petrified as well and we stayed sitting on the floor, trying to keep out of his way and avoiding eye contact. After a few minutes of ranting he calmed down and only started again when a police officer walked past.

While I was in the cell the police officers kept walking past, whispering to each other. All I heard was 'British'. They were trying to freak me out and it worked. The uncertainty, not knowing whether I was about to be tortured, was a horrific feeling. It was almost worse than the pain of the abuse itself.

Around an hour later I was collected by a guard who showed me into a small office. Sat behind a desk was the prosecutor I had seen several months before. A senior police officer with several stars on his lapels was sitting on a sofa.

'Just tell me what happened,' the prosecutor said.

'I already told you months ago when I was arrested.'

'Okay, tell us again,' the police general said.

'I'm not going to say anything without a lawyer.'

'Don't worry, you don't need a lawyer for this,' the prosecutor said. 'We're just asking you some questions.'

'That's why I need a lawyer.'

'Come now, just tell us what happened.'

I decided it would be better to cooperate and went through the whole arrest experience and torture including how my hand had been broken.

'Where did they take you?' the cop said. 'Was it to a deserted area or the desert?'

'Look, mate, Dubai is the desert. You turn one road you are in the desert. The buildings I could see were a long way in the distance and there was sand everywhere.'

The cop drew a diagram of a series of roads. 'Was it here?' he said.

This was ridiculous. 'I have no idea, mate. I was tortured and I was in shock. There were sand dunes rising above my head. It looked like the desert to me.'

After that I was taken back to the cell. The two Arab heroin takers were still there, but the psychotic guy had gone. The first heroin kid asked what had happened. I told him my tale.

'Look, you have to be careful, my friend, as the Arabs don't like noise,' he said. 'They want an easy life and don't like headaches.'

I barely had enough time to respond before I was collected and marched to see another police officer. He was a short bald-headed, weasel-faced guy who introduced himself as the chief of Dubai police.

'Why am I still here?' I said.

'We have to ask you a few more questions.'

'No, why am I still here when all of the other spice cases have gone home?'

'Maybe it's because you're making some noise.'

My heart sank. It had always been a gamble going to the media but it appeared our roll of the dice had cost us. I could have kicked myself for getting into this situation and felt sick to my stomach.

'Look, we don't like a lot of noise over here. Why not forget about this and maybe things go away?'

'I'm not going to just drop it. What they did was wrong.'

'Okay, tell me what happened.'

I went through the whole ordeal again, and as I did I noticed that a red light was flashing on the police chief's phone and the screen showed it was recording. To get it on record I said, 'This is illegal, I am not meant to be talking to you without legal representation.'

'Don't worry about that legal stuff,' he said. 'It doesn't matter here. I'm just asking you a few questions because I'm concerned about you.'

'Look, can I go now?'

'Of course, we're not holding you here.'

I was taken back to the cell before Rooney and Ferrari cop came to get me and put me back in the car.

'Do you remember me then?' I said. I knew they knew who I was and I was goading them. I was fuming and was desperate to get a reaction from them, pushing my knee into the passenger seat to try and make it uncomfortable. It may sound crazy, but I just wanted to regain a little bit of control.

'No, no, we've never seen you before,' Rooney lied.

'You were the ones who kept hitting me, weren't you? You were both hitting me outside the car. I remember you and your friends. You must've had good fun. I think I must've made a good punchbag.'

'I don't know what you're talking about,' said Ferrari cop.

When I got back to Port Rashid Harry came to see me. I told him what happened.

'Mate, I can't believe they're doing this. Why didn't they call me? Did we do the wrong thing by going to the media?'

'All I know is that we've got to fuck them now. It's all or nothing.'

'Right, well, I've spoken to Marc and a lady from Reprieve called Kate. Marc said you should give them a call. I also called the embassy to let them know what happened.'

When I spoke to Marc he introduced Kate, who dealt with the charity's PR. It seemed Marc was excited by the development.

'This is fantastic! They've given us more ammunition. This is exactly what we needed. We've got them by the balls now.'

I wasn't so sure. We were playing a dangerous game of chess

212

with the Dubai authorities and the outcome would decide if we would walk to freedom, or be incarcerated for the rest of our lives.

18

THE JEBILLALLY ZONE

When a group of African bank robbers and a gang of Pakistani murderers entered Port Rashid it marked a seismic shift in the balance of power. The Pakistanis came in first. I was in my cell with Harry when I heard noise outside that sounded like a reunion of long-lost friends. A group of huge men from the Pashtun tribe were being greeted by Babar and Qasim like long-lost brothers.

The new inmates were covered in bruises from the torture they had endured. They had burns from the hand and ankle cuffs that had been applied too tightly for days on end. One had huge bulbous eyes that were bloodshot from where he had tried to hang himself in the holding cell. Even though he had tried to commit suicide the other inmates did not give him grief for it, probably because of the torture he had endured. Despite their beaten appearance, the group had smiles on their faces and were clearly delighted to be in Port Rashid with Qasim and Babar.

Within a minute of the Pakistanis entering, five dark-skinned black guys sauntered into the jail and immediately started acting like they owned the place. Three were short and stocky, one was tall and had white blotches on his skin, while the fifth, the leader of the group, was broad and about six foot two inches tall. He had an air of authority about him that suggested he shouldn't be messed with.

The Africans and the Pakistanis all knew each other, having been in the police headquarters together. They had witnessed some of the barbarity that was inflicted on each group by the police.

The leader of the Africans, who were all from Kenya, introduced himself as Jebillally. He spoke in a soft African accent and was an affable guy. He mentioned that his gang had been caught after they carried out a big robbery.

'Yeah, man, we robbed a cash van and we got caught. But these Arabs can't even do torture properly,' he said.

'Really?'

'Yeah, they handcuffed our hands above our heads so we lost all feeling in them and they made us stand for days after they caned our feet. But it was nothing compared to what I've had in other parts of the world. What happened to you?'

I told him our experiences.

'Shit, man, that's pretty brutal,' Jebillally said 'Have you done anything about it?'

'Yeah, we've got in touch with a charity who are fighting our case.'

'Good, I hope you guys fuck these people.'

The whole atmosphere seemed to have changed in a matter of minutes. Two powerful groups of people had come in and immediately stamped their mark on things. But it wasn't in a bad way. Over the next few days the mood in prison seemed lighter. The Africans had started to make themselves at home and almost overnight the jail was transformed into a nightclub, an African disco and a poker den. The sounds of people laughing and Africans drumming on water barrels became ubiquitous. Baariq allotted the new inmates cells but didn't seem bothered by the potential challenge to his authority.

I was walking down the strip when I heard noise coming from one of the Pakistani cells. One of the African robbers was screaming and shouting at the other inmates with a huge smile on his face. I laughed when I saw they were getting so heated over the kids' game Uno. He was dubbed Uno forever more.

We invited the robbers to play poker as a way of welcoming them to the jail. We had been renting out the Indians' cell near the toilet for our card sessions as Baariq didn't want a game of poker going on in his room. Two of the stocky robbers were keenest and came along. Harry dubbed them Chuckoo Boy and Medesdos after two TV characters.

The remaining robber was a bit of an outcast as he smelt like he hadn't washed in a year. His stench was the worst body odour you could ever imagine. Even the other Africans didn't want him with them.

The Pakistani murderers also became a serious force within the jail. One of the group, a large psychotic hulk of a man called Nayeeda, was in for a double murder. He'd got drunk and thrown a man off a building before stabbing the victim's pal and throwing him off as well. He had fled to Pakistan where the Dubai cops tracked him down to an opium den and extradited him back for trial. Knowing he was a psychotic murderer, I would give him *dokha*. He couldn't speak English but knew the words 'no money' which he constantly repeated; I thought I had better keep this guy on side. You never know when a double murderer might snap. The three others had acted together when they killed a man.

I had been trying to persuade Harry to move into my cell with Baariq for a while but he was comfortable where he was. But now that the jail was starting to fill up with random people I finally persuaded Harry that moving into the foreman's room was a good idea. It also meant he could get involved in our smuggling business. Nayeeda was constantly asking for *dokha* and we decided to draw the line under our charity after he asked both Harry and me for a small packet within minutes of each other. I didn't want to make enemies of the Pakistani murderer crowd, but in jail you can't be pushed around, no matter who is doing the pushing.

Although it was important to appear tough in prison it didn't stop me wanting to protect the innocent and show humanity for those who were subjected to injustices. A slight, young lad called Culavalley showed me just how tragic life can be for those who had nothing. This little Indian lad with piercing green eyes came into the jail with a load of visa cases, but he stood out from the crowd straight away. He came into our cell and asked if anybody wanted a massage.

'No, man, we're all right,' I said.

'I can dance for you?' he said hopefully.

Harry and I looked at each other. 'Go on then,' he said.

'You hum Michael Jackson?'

Harry and I started doing the backbeat to 'Billie Jean' and Culavalley started to dance in the campest way I have ever seen. Harry and I were in hysterics and I cheered him on as he danced away. It was funny, but a little weird at the same time.

'Any time you want me to dance and I will come.'

'What's your name, man?'

He started to sing, 'Why this Culavalley, Culavalley this,' and danced at the same time.

'So your name's Culavalley?'

'Yes, you can call me that.'

Later Culavalley persuaded us to let him give us a massage for

10D. I passed out in minutes. After that I employed Culavalley to clean my room and bring me tea made from my own powder bought from the canteen, and always paid him above the going rate. I sensed an air of slight desperation about him and wanted to help. He became a regular visitor to our cell, but there were times when we couldn't find him anywhere. One day I went to the local gangsters' room to see if he was around.

'Black British, how are you doing?' Ayoop said as I walked in.

'Cool, man, I'm just looking for Culavalley. Have you seen him?'

'No, my friend, he might be out in the hoosh?'

I looked down and saw five pairs of slippers by the bed. There were only three local gangsters in the room and the curtain of one of the bottom bunks was pulled across. I walked out of the cell, worried that Culavalley was being taken advantage of or raped. My fears for his safety were confirmed the following day when I was hanging out in the local gangsters' room with Mansoor and Culavalley. The little Indian started to dance and I banged away on a water drum to make a beat. I thought we were just playing a bit of music and messing about but Mansoor appeared to be getting excited by my friend's moves.

'Strip! Strip!' he said.

'No, no, this is wrong,' I said.

'Just drum.'

'No, man, this *haram*,' I said.

'This no *haram*. This party, party!'

I realized I couldn't stop what was going on, and that Culavalley seemed complicit in what was happening, so I walked out of the room, feeling sad for my friend.

'Culavalley, why do you let these guys do this to you?' I asked when I caught up with him later that day.

'They are paying for my flight home when my sentence is done and I must do whatever they want,' he said, looking at me with his big eyes which had ridiculously long eyelashes.

Culavalley told me how he was a chauffeur on the outside but had got drunk with a friend, crashed the car and run away from the scene. He had been handed a six-month sentence.

'I need the money, I have no job, I can't do anything as I'm in jail. It cost my family so much money to get me here and I have let them down. I have shamed myself and my family.'

Although Culavalley consented to what was happening to him it was effectively rape. He had no choice. He was the local gangsters' sex toy, a mere plaything for them to abuse. No matter how bad things got for me I had to remember it was nothing compared to what was happening to him.

'Culavalley, I will pay for your flight,' I said.

'Really, you would do that?'

'Yeah, me and Harry will pay for it.' I knew Harry would be more than willing to help out our friend. A tear dropped down his cheek.

'Thank you so much. If you guys want more than massages tell me.'

'No, man, it's cool, just bring us tea and stuff.'

Despite the offer of the flight Culavalley still couldn't be found some days. He needed more money and would do anything for it.

As I thought, Harry was happy to help out Culavalley but his kindness, and the fact he'd been my best friend for years, didn't stop our relationship from deteriorating after he'd moved into my cell. The problems started with Baariq, who was being weird with me. I assumed it was because I had called him out on the cash he owed me after he failed to get me out. We started to argue about silly little things, like an old married couple. I was annoyed with him about the cash and that meant I was obnoxious and argumentative with him. At the same time, I had been looking at the pictures of Faith a lot and the fact I was missing my little girl growing up was killing me inside.

I was angry with the world and went further and further into self-destruct mode. I didn't care about anything and was difficult to be around. It sounds ridiculous, but Baariq hated it when I farted so I made sure I did it as much as I could.

One time I did a particularly loud fart and Baariq lost it.

'What's wrong with you? You've turned into a cunt,' he said.

'Bruv, you don't know me. You can't judge me.'

'Why do you act like this all the time? You have to sort yourself out. I can't be around you when you are being this difficult.'

'Yeah, mate, you are being a bit of a prick,' Harry piped up. I didn't need my old friend turning on me and I was annoyed with him for it. While my relationship with Baariq was slowly falling apart Harry was getting close to him. I noticed they were spending more time talking, laughing and joking.

As Harry was now involved with the smuggling business it meant he had access to the guards and was getting to know Feroz well through various smuggling missions. Harry's mum had come to see him and he had paid Feroz to let him through at night to spend some time alone with her in the visitors' area.

Although Harry and I were now having some run ins he always maintained his humanity in jail towards others. A Sri Lankan guy called Mohammed Islam came into the jail for theft just after he'd had a child. Harry sent his wife money as they had no other way of surviving.

'Your friend Harry is a good man,' Feroz said to me one day. 'He looks after Mohammed Islam and he doesn't have to.'

Harry's kindness was testament to what a decent person he

was. And his good relationship with Feroz opened up a whole new hiding place for our contraband. We had been putting everything in a drain in the hoosh but there was always the risk that another inmate could steal our stash or there would be a ninja raid and it would be discovered.

'Why don't we hide it in the ceiling panel in the kitchen?' Harry suggested. 'That way nobody can get to our stuff and when we need it Feroz can get it for us.'

It was a good plan. When we ran out of tobacco we would just call Feroz and he would bring us some from our stash. Other times he would leave the door to the kitchen open so we could access our contraband.

I received a call from him on my mobile one day.

'Look, the ninjas are coming later on today. Make sure you tell Baariq.'

It gave us enough time to hide our stuff in the ceiling panel and the raid went off without a hitch.

With Baariq taking Harry under his wing more, he decided he could trust my friend with a delicate mission. One day the foreman asked Harry if he could get somebody on the outside to make a credit card payment. The following day Harry came up to me with a big smile on his face.

'Bruv, you'll never guess what.'

'What's up?'

'You know Baariq asked me to get a payment made for him? Well, my mate called me to say it was a subscription for a website called Muslima. It turns out it's a dating site to meet Muslim women.'

I burst out laughing. This was so typically Baariq.

'I'm guessing things aren't going too well with his missus then?' I said. I decided it wouldn't be a good idea to bring up the website with him, no matter how tempting it was.

When Baariq was out of the cell, Jebillally would come in to see us. He was a good guy and easy to talk to. After he'd got to know us a bit better he told me about how he and his gang had got caught. Uno worked as a van driver for the security company the gang was planning to rob. On a routine stop, Uno went into the back of the van, grabbed a load of the cash bags, and ran out clasping the loot. Chuckoo Boy was waiting in the getaway car. It wasn't exactly a master plan.

When the cash was delivered to the hideout the gang split the money and all went out partying. Things started to go wrong when Jebillally (who dabbled in the illicit gold trade) got into a fight the following day. He saw a man who owed him cash for a gold bullion deal and went to forcibly remind the guy to pay up. The big African was arrested and then released on bail. Meanwhile the police officers investigating the security van robbery already knew Uno was involved as he had disappeared from the scene. The cops pulled his phone records which linked him to Jebillally. Now all the cops had to do was follow Jebillally and wait until he led them to the rest of the gang.

Our friend unwittingly led the police to Chuckoo Boy. The officers knew he was likely to be one of the gang when they looked at his feet and saw he was wearing new Gucci shoes yet supposedly had no money. They followed him to Uno and they swooped on the gang.

'We tried to keep our mouths shut but they tortured us until we screamed,' Jebillally said.

Uno was the first to crack but I respected him for what he said to police. He told the officers who tortured him, 'It doesn't matter what you do to me. I've sent the money back to my village and now I am seen as a king there. They have never seen so much money in all of their lives.' At least he'd made all of his family and friends' lives better.

Jebillally had managed to get some of the cash into jail and was constantly asking Harry and me to change up $100 bills. My eyes widened when he produced a wodge of notes from his underpants and coolly pulled one off the top.

'Mate, why have you got so much cash on you?' I asked. There was easily $10,000 in his hand.

'I can't trust these police officers. They'd probably steal my money. They'd say it was money I stole and seize it or put it in their own pockets.'

Jebillally was a career criminal who had travelled the globe robbing banks. His father had been a general in Kenya, so as a result he had a diplomatic passport that allowed him to go wherever he pleased until his father died. Unfortunately for him he was caught doing a bank heist in Mexico when his diplomatic immunity had run out and he was sentenced to four years inside. He had a bullet wound in his arm from his time there.

'This is how you say sorry in Mexico,' he explained. 'I was in jail and doing some stuff for the cartel, selling weed inside. One of my guys was caught and the stuff was confiscated. The boss of the cartel wasn't happy and he said to me, "We either shoot your guy dead or we wound you."'

'Fucking hell, they have guns in jail in Mexico?' Harry said.

'Yes, my friend. In Mexican prisons you can get anything.'

I supposed we should be thankful for small mercies.

'Anyway, I said I would take a bullet as they were going to kill my friend. I'd prefer to take one on the arm than him lose his life.'

Jebillally was a tough guy and not one to be intimidated by Baariq, who was annoying him by moving random inmates into his cell. I was walking down the strip when I heard Jebillally suddenly shout, 'From now on this side of the jail is the Jebillally zone. I control this area now.'

Baariq returned a few minutes later after hearing what had happened. 'Hey, Jebillally, what's this about the Jebillally zone?'

'Yeah, man, I don't like how you've been running the prison so this half is mine.'

'Fine, do as you please. Have the toilet half.' Baariq knew that he wasn't able to stand up to Jebillally. The power in the jail had shifted.

The Petans had an impact too, though less directly. As a result of them bugging Harry and me for *dokha* whenever we were smoking, we ended up saving a life. It was difficult to say no to them when we knew they had no money to pay for the tobacco and they would just follow us around looking hopeful. Harry and I ended up sneaking off to the toilet, just to have a smoke. We were trying to work out where best to have a puff to avoid the camera when we heard one of the four cubicle doors close. There was the whoosh of something dropping and then a loud bang as something struck the toilet door. I crouched to look under the door to see what had happened.

'What the fuck are you doing, bruv?' Harry said. 'They'll think you're trying to look at their balls.'

Some of the inmates had been known to look under the toilet doors in hope of catching a glimpse of bollocks.

Babar was slumped on the floor with a noose tightly around his neck. His bloodshot, bulbous eyes were open but he looked dead. The cold look in his eyes will haunt me forever.

'Fuuuuuuck!' I shouted in blind panic. 'Babar's dying!'

Harry scrabbled to look over the top. 'Shit, we need to get inside.'

I tried to reach down and open the door but couldn't get to the handle. The next second Nayeeda ran into the toilet.

'Babar's in there dying!' I screamed.

Nayeeda ran into the door with all his might and it went flying off its hinges, the door and Nayeeda toppling onto the life-less body of Babar. A horrible 'Sssssssssssssssssss', like a tyre letting out air, came from Babar's mouth and filled the toilet block. It didn't sound human and made me freeze.

Harry and Nayeeda dived straight in and tried desperately to release the noose, but it was so tight it was cutting into his skin. After a few seconds of vigorously tugging at the makeshift rope, which was made out of the thick cotton edging from the sheets, they managed to pull it free from his neck. His eyes were rolling back in his head and we were all shouting his name and slapping his face to try and get him to come back to us. Qasim and Baariq came running in and Baariq tried to perform mouth-to-mouth resuscitation before carrying Babar back to his cell. I quickly dis-posed of the noose in the bin. If he had been caught trying to commit suicide he would have faced another charge.

Harry and I had saved his life because we couldn't decide which toilet cubicle to go into. I waited a couple of hours and went into Babar's room.

'Why, Babar?' I said. 'Why did you want to do this?'

Babar couldn't speak great English but looked at me and said, 'Too much tension.' Babar was due to go to court the next day for sentencing and the pressure had got too much. He came up to me and gave me kiss on the cheek and hugged me. 'You my brother, I love you, *Allah Karim*, God is with you. Me and you always tension, tension, tension but no more. This finish.'

It sent a shiver down my spine. We had always argued over petty things but his near-death experience had brought us together.

Babar's suicide attempt brought home to every single inmate that we would all be facing our destiny in court one day. Babar was looking at the same penalty as Harry and I, and had buckled at the prospect of confronting what was going to happen to him. Although the Arabs disapproved of suicide he didn't get any comeback from the other inmates as they all had sympathy with his plight. Babar's suicide bid hammered it home to me that, while we could laugh and joke and try to make our lives better by making money, time was speeding towards a moment when we too would have to face reality. Twenty-five years or death by firing squad.

19

NUTS

The days leading up to Christmas were some of the hardest I have ever experienced and the closest I have come to ending my own life. I was desperately missing my little girl and the thought of not being there for her first Christmas was tearing me apart. Once I called Amy and she was out shopping, Christmas music playing in the background. I dreamt of being with them.

To make matters worse things had gone quiet on the media front. Marc had warned us this would happen, but it made us feel like we had been forgotten. I was scared we had put everything on the line and would be screwed by the authorities for our gamble. I was getting more and more depressed and angry as Christmas approached, snapping at people and becoming hard to be around. I'd given up on my appearance, no longer bothering to shave and letting my hair grow long until it was in such a mess that I got Chuckoo Boy to braid it.

Harry was also worried about the lack of media interest in our case, but because I was feeling angry and depressed I even lashed out at him when he brought it up.

'Bruv, do you think we did the right thing?' Harry said to me a couple of days before Christmas. 'We should've kept our mouths shut.'

'It's too late, mate. We have to ride it out.'

'Yeah, mate, but I wanna go home. I've had enough of this shit.'

'Look, mate, I'm the one who's got a little kid at home. You act like it's you that's suffering the most here, and I know you've left your family, but I'm not seeing Faith grow up.'

'I've got a missus as well, you know.'

'Ah, fuck off, mate.'

'You're just a prick, why are you arguing over this shit?'

'I know you wanna go home. We all wanna go home.' I stormed off in a rage.

It was a ridiculous argument but we were both feeling the pressure. We had nobody else to take it out on. The only person who really helped me through that time was Amy. Speaking to her always gave me strength to survive the ordeal and get to the other side so I could see Faith again.

Harry and I made up as we always did. Our arguments never really lasted more than a couple of hours.

'Oi, bullet head, are you willing to stop acting like a Somali pirate and act like a normal human?' Harry said.

'All right, sorry, Mr Simpson.' Harry had been going a pale shade of yellow, from the lack of sunlight. He looked like a character from *The Simpsons*.

'Come on then, let's go and smoke some *dokha*.'

Baariq never let us smoke in his cell so we wandered down the strip to another room, where we agreed we needed something to lift our spirits. We decided that if we could get the captain to allow us to have a TGI Fridays on Christmas Day then things would at least be a little better.

'Come on, Captain Aziz, Christmas is like a Christian version of Ramadan,' Harry said persuasively after we'd approached the captain.

'Yeah, we pray, we eat and celebrate Christ's life,' I added. We weren't going to pray, but we had to ham it up.

'If you get more than ten people, then it will be okay,' he said in the end.

There was a slight snag. There were no other Christians in the whole jail. I went to see Jebillally and the Africans.

'Look, if you say you're Christians for a day we can get a feast in.'

'Sounds good, my friend.'

The Africans were on board but we were still three short. Harry and I ran around and dragged three Punjabi inmates into our plan.

'If anybody asks you, you're Christian,' Harry said, 'and we'll give you some chicken.'

We went to see a surprised and slightly suspicious Captain Aziz.

'You sure these people are Christian?'

'Of course, Captain Aziz,' we said.

'Okay, get a menu and bring your order to me.'

We were delighted. We called TGI Fridays and wrote down the entire menu before going back to him with our order of king prawns, steaks, burgers and platters.

'No, no. You have to go and see Captain Abbas now,' he said, as we walked into his office.

He had grassed on us and I knew the top captain wouldn't be so accommodating. Baariq agreed to come with us to argue our cause.

At first Abbas turned us down flat.

'Come on, Captain, Aziz said we could get TGI for Christmas,' I pleaded. 'How's this even fair? This is our culture.' After

229

Mohammed left the feasts had dwindled so I was looking forward to some proper food.

'It's not your culture now, you're in Dubai.'

In the end he let us order ten chicken *mendhi*, an Arabic rice dish from a local restaurant. It was the best we were going to get so we accepted.

The evidence proving that the authorities were trying to fuck us again for making noise came on Christmas Day.

We were woken by a guard calling us to the hatch. We were taken to the booking-in area where we were faced by two police officers who announced they were from the court. They handed us several bits of paper.

'What are these?' Harry said.

'These are the court papers and you must sign them,' the first officer replied.

'We ain't signing anything until we get it translated.'

I went back to the hatch and called for Baariq who joined us and read out the charge sheet. But as he read the paper his face dropped. It turned out they had added a further, equally serious charge of intent to supply. Not only were we supposedly traffickers but we were also dealing in Dubai. In addition they had inexplicably trebled the amount of spice they had found in our hire car to 1.7 kilograms. To finish us off they added a further charge to Harry's sheet of having cannabis in his blood. The blood tests had obviously been a farce as I had been smoking with Harry the day before we had flown out together, but I just hadn't admitted it upfront and now I hadn't been charged with the same offence.

The timing was aimed at screwing with our heads in an attempt to break us. The Dubai authorities were letting us know they were not going to stand for us complaining to the media and refusing to drop our case against the police.

'I'm not signing this and you're a bunch of cunts,' I screamed in the police officers' faces.

'We need you to sign your paperwork so we can process the case to court.'

Harry went mad, 'Fuck off, we're not signing it. Fuck off, you pricks.'

We were risking another charge as it was a criminal offence to swear at a police officer, but we didn't care. We hammered on the hatch and when the guard came to let us back in Harry and I pushed past him, swiftly followed by Baariq. I stormed to my bunk and sat there in a rage. I honestly believed my life as I had once known it, as a free man, was over. I was never going to see my friends, family, Amy or Faith ever again. My future was in a Dubai hellhole jail. The authorities had won and their plan of fucking with our heads had worked. I was broken and it was Christmas Day. Harry and I sat on our beds, shell-shocked.

'I'm not sure I can do this, you know, bruv?' Harry said.

'Bruv, I'm feeling exactly the same way. I'm not sure how much longer I can hold out for but all I know is we have to stay strong.'

I somehow managed to pass out and the next thing I knew Baariq was opening my curtains telling me the food had arrived. The captain had stuck to the agreement and we were delivered ten chicken *mendhis*. We gave the Africans and Punjabis their food but didn't eat with them. Harry and I wanted to be by ourselves, though Baariq stayed with us in our cell.

After a couple of mouthfuls I was amazed at how spicy the food was. My lips started to tingle. I could feel something large and solid in my mouth and spat it out. Harry looked at me, an alarmed expression on his face. In my hand was a single cashew nut.

'No!' Harry said. 'Fuck!'

'What's wrong?' Baariq said, alarm in his voice.

'I'm allergic to nuts.'

'How bad?'

'Mate, I could die. I'm real bad.'

I had ended up in hospital several times before, but I knew this was the worst possible situation to be in. In a jail, in Dubai, with no EpiPen. Harry and Baariq were flapping around. Harry put his arm round me.

'Are you all right, mate?'

'I'm all right now but I won't be in a few minutes. Calm down, it's going to be all right. Go and get one of the officers and tell them to call an ambulance for me.'

I was trying to keep my friends calm but I could feel my mouth filling with saliva. As I staggered to the toilet I was getting weaker and weaker. I had to make myself sick, and fast. Leaning over the putrid toilet, I tried to make myself vomit. Considering the smell was enough to make you heave it was remarkable that my body wouldn't let me puke up. I could hear Harry and Baariq banging on the hatch on the other side of the jail. Despite Christmas being a Christian festival, there were barely any guards on duty.

Giving up on trying to be sick, I made my unsteady way to the front door.

'What do you want?' the guard at the hatch said scathingly.

'I need an ambulance as I've eaten a cashew nut and I could die.'

'Why?'

'Because I'm allergic.'

'What is this allergic?'

Baariq translated and he finally let me through to the nurses' room. The jail nurse was a small Filipino guy called Andrew who had long hair and a high-pitched, squeaky voice.

'Mr Karl, how are you?'

'I'm not in a good way. I have an allergy to nuts and I just had one.'

'Oh my God, sit down, sit down.' He took my blood pressure. 'You need to try and relax, Mr Karl.'

There was a large clock on the wall and I saw that it was just after twelve noon. The guard came into the room.

'You need to call an ambulance for him before he goes into anaphylactic shock,' Andrew said.

The guard had a bemused look on his face as he sauntered off. 'Yes, I will sort it out.'

Half an hour passed. My lips started to swell and sweat was pouring off my body. It was becoming difficult to swallow. Harry came in to check on me and was shocked.

'Oh, mate, you look like the Nutty Professor,' he said.

'Harry, I really need to go to the hospital now.'

Harry went to get help and a few minutes later the guard returned to the room. He looked at me and smiled. 'I don't think you're sick enough to go,' he said.

'Look, he needs to have an ambulance now,' Andrew said. 'You need to call an ambulance before this guy dies here.'

'Yes, I'm going to do so.'

'Don't do so, do it now,' Andrew said.

The guard looked annoyed before stomping off melodramatically. I could feel the poison running around my body and knew that I was in a bad way. I couldn't move and my face was so bloated I looked like I had been beaten by Mike Tyson. My eyes were swollen and I was struggling to see; I could only just make out the face of the clock which told me I had been in the room for an hour.

I was getting drowsy and I felt like my body wanted to give up, but a part of me knew I had to fight to stay alive. Harry came in to keep me company. He was rubbing my shoulders saying, 'Come on, man, you're gonna be okay.' Something in his voice gave away how scared he was for me.

Enough was enough. I staggered out of the door.

'Get me a fucking ambulance now. I need an ambulance now!' I screamed. Adrenaline was the only thing that got me up out of my seat.

'I have ordered it already,' the guard said, in a stroppy tone.

'I bet if I was sucking your cock you would've ordered it an hour ago.'

'So you're being rude now. Do you want to wait a bit longer?'

'Look, just sort this out for me.'

'I've done all I can do. Go and wait in the nurses' room.'

'Fuck this, I'm going back into the jail.'

Harry helped me in. 'Mate, call the British embassy and Marc from Reprieve,' I said. 'Tell them what's happening and how long I've been waiting to see if they can do anything about it.'

I went back to my cell and found Baariq in the room.

'Man, you okay? Let me get you some water.'

I sat on my bunk and had a cigarette. Baariq didn't even complain as he could see what a terrible state I was in. I felt like I smoked it in three seconds flat and suddenly Harry was shaking me as the ambulance had arrived.

'Come on, bruv.'

I could barely walk and Harry was helping me to the door, I was shown to where two paramedics were waiting.

'Woah, come, come,' the first said. 'You allergic to anything?'

'Yeah, nuts and penicillin.'

The guard came out moments after the paramedics started checking me over.

'Look, we have to get him to a hospital now. He is going to die,' the first paramedic said. The second was taking my pulse and it was off the scale.

'This man is seriously ill and we need to get him out of here now,' the second ambulance man said.

'I have to wait for an escort to come from Jebel Ali,' the guard insisted.

'This man cannot wait. If we wait, he will die.'

'I've done everything I can.'

'We are not having this death on our hands. You will have to give us one of your guards.'

'It still won't be enough,' the guard said. 'Prisoners must be escorted by two officers.'

'Right, well, we're taking him now.'

As they helped me to the ambulance they warned me that I was about to go into anaphylactic shock. I took my first step into the back of the vehicle and everything went black.

When I came to I was in a hospital bed. I was drenched in sweat and as I looked down at my arm I thought I was hallucinating. It had trebled in size. I had rashes all over my face and had crazy hives or prickly heat all over my body. I started screaming as I genuinely thought I was going to die. Salem, one of the police officers who'd escorted me before, was at my bedside and tried to calm me down.

'Come on, man, you'll be okay, calm down,' he said.

'Raaaaar! Raaaaaaar!' I screamed. I was freaking out so much and writhing around that Salem had to handcuff both my hands to the bed. Then I saw my little five-year-old nephew walk in and at that point I thought I was dead. It didn't make any sense that he would be here.

He walked up to me and said, 'Uncle Karl, Uncle Karl.' Was this what I would see after I died? Had Ross's boy died as well? I reached out and touched what I thought was a heavenly vision and felt his skin. He was standing in front of me.

'You're here?' I said.

'Yeah,' he replied, looking freaked out.

'Oh my God, I thought I was dead,' I said.

Harry had called my brother to tell him what had happened and he had rushed to the hospital to see me. When Ross came in I started to relax. The realization I wasn't dead made me feel somewhat better.

The first thing I said to Ross was, 'How much money have you got on you and do you have any cigarettes?'

'You crazy fucker,' he said as he chucked me 600D and a couple of packets of cigarettes.

Ross had to go when the doctors came in to assess me. My swelling was going down and I could see properly again.

Salem came in. 'Ah, Mr Karl, I was scared for a minute there. You were very sick.'

'Hey, Salem. Yeah, mate, I wasn't good. I'm sorry for swearing man.'

'Yeah, man, I understand. That other police officer, I'm going to report him.'

Within a few hours the swelling all over my body had gone down. I felt physically drained but a million times better than I had a few hours before. I had survived the Christmas Day from hell. Salem and Mussa came to the hospital to pick me up.

'Ah, Mr Karl, you look much better,' Salem said, patting me on the back for good measure.

'We're going to buy you a KFC to celebrate,' Mussa said with a smile on his face. 'It's our Christmas present to you.'

'Thank you so much, you two, I really appreciate it,' I said, genuinely touched by their concern and generosity towards me. I was starving after my ordeal and stuffed down my food before being taken back to Port Rashid.

'Remember, Mr Karl, don't do anything silly with that officer,' Mussa said. 'We will report him.'

I thanked them and went into the jail where I was met by my least favourite guard.

'How are you feeling?' he asked, with all the sincerity he could muster.

'Just fuck off, you prick, and leave me alone.'

He turned his nose up at me, turned on his heel and walked away.

I went to see Harry and we got together all of our cigarettes and went around the inmates handing out gifts to those who couldn't afford tobacco. Modern day Santa Clauses we weren't, but it felt good to be giving stuff to those who had nothing. Normally we smoked where the cameras couldn't see us, but now we didn't give a shit. We brazenly puffed away in front of the cameras. We had been hit with extra charges and I had almost died on Christmas Day, how was a bollocking for smoking going to make things any worse?

I lay down to sleep that night feeling grateful to be alive. But I was worried that the Dubai authorities had now shown they had gone to war with us. Dragging me out of jail for illegal questioning to intimidate me had not had the desired effect and they had upped our charges on the day when they knew it would hurt us the most. It had worked, but I was more determined than ever to fight for justice, no matter what the cost.

20

A LUCKY NEAR MISS

I woke up on Boxing Day to hear the sound of a cockney voice as a new inmate walked down the strip.

'Fucking hell, mate, that's another East End boy,' Harry said. We looked at each other and ran out the door to find him. A stocky guy in his forties with weathered features was looking dazed and confused. And seriously hungover.

'Hey, brother, you okay?' I said. 'You look a bit rough.'

'Mate, I've had a proper nightmare.'

He introduced himself as Mike, and told us he'd got into a drunken fight with his best friend and a neighbour had called the police. He and his friend had both been arrested, but his mate had been let out after a couple of hours.

'Fuck, man, you're those guys off the telly. I've seen you on the news. Are you all right?'

'Yeah, mate, that's us. Yeah, we're okay. Well, you know.'

Mike was a gold trader who imported and exported the precious metal around the world. Wherever he went on the outside he was flanked by armed minders. The news of Mike's profession immediately sparked Jebillally's interest.

'So maybe we can do some business?' the affable African said a couple of days later as we sat in his cell. As well as being a bank robber, Jebillally had smuggled $200,000 of gold bullion into Dubai.

'I'm sure we can do that, mate,' Mike said.

The cockney was only expected to be inside for a few days as he was on a minor assault charge, so Jebillally worked out how to get Mike a sample of the gold when he was on the outside so he could start exporting it to his people in London. Criminal enterprise thrived behind the walls of Port Rashid.

The next day I was in my cell when I heard a high-pitched scream that reverberated down the strip. 'Yoooooooooooor!' two new Arab inmates screamed as they walked in. Baariq was at their side immediately, telling them to calm down.

Aboot and Abait were soon to be known as the two crazies, because they were seriously insane. Aboot was short and stocky with a small well-kept Afro and braces on his teeth. He had massive lips that dominated his face. Abait was a bit taller but chubby. He moved like he was a sloth on drugs with his head in the air. He had effeminate mannerisms but had the worst teeth I had ever seen. Some were missing while others were jet black. At the same time a small, mild-mannered, balding Senegalese guy had come in. He seemed bemused by the loud men beside him.

The lively new additions walked down the strip, screaming Arabic that I didn't understand at the tops of their voices. The jail was quieter than it had been for some time as more of the immigration cases had gone, but all of those remaining had come out of their cells to see what the drama was. Ayoop walked up to the pair and whispered in their ears. Within seconds they were laughing and joking. I didn't know what Ayoop had said to the pair, but I was impressed by how quickly he had calmed them down. I went up to Baariq to find out what was going on.

'You have to be careful of these boys,' he said. 'You heard them shouting? They were saying they were here to make trouble, and they would put anyone to the test if they think they are up to it.'

I realized that Ayoop must have been an even bigger gangster than I'd imagined as he had pacified them in seconds with a few words.

These guys looked insane so I decided to be wary of them. Aboot came into our cell later and shook Baariq's hand and then asked me for some tobacco. I introduced myself and we started talking about why they were inside. Aboot and Abait had been caught in typically stupid fashion for a typically ridiculous crime. They were having a street race and crashed their car into some parked vehicles. When they crashed they narrowly missed mowing down a group of men who had to dive out of the way. When the group justifiably complained they got out swords – the weapon of choice for young wannabe gangsters in Dubai – and attacked the victims.

'So just before the cops came we realized we had drugs in our system,' Aboot said. 'We would've been tested for sure as we'd crashed our car. So Abait told me to slash him good to make it look like the others had attacked him. They arrested both of us anyway.'

'But that doesn't make any sense,' I said. 'If they knew you had crashed, then the police would have tested you whether you'd been attacked or not.'

'Oh yeah, I guess you're right. Fuck it, we were high.'

When Aboot had left Baariq turned on me, an angry look on his face.

'People have got to stop coming to this cell for tobacco and *dokha*,' he said. 'We have phones and a lot of *dokha* in the cell. You guys have got to be careful.'

'All right, man,' I said. Inmates came in on a daily basis for smokes and it was doing Baariq's head in. To be fair, he had a point.

'No, it's not all right. You just care about yourself.'

'Calm down, Baariq, we'll stop.'

Things were getting tenser by the day with Baariq and I wasn't helping matters because I didn't give a shit. I walked out of the cell with Harry.

'Mate, I didn't tell you but I've met this guy who's a sick martial arts coach,' he said. 'His name's Adriano but he likes to be known as Coach.'

'All right, man, let's go and see him.'

We went out to the hoosh where the small Senegalese guy was training, doing an insane number of press-ups and then shadow boxing like his life depended on it. Harry introduced me.

'Ah, yes, you're Harry's case partner.'

'Yeah, man, I hear you're a coach in martial arts. I've done a bit of wing chun and a little bit of boxing. My dad was Roy Gumbs, who was British and Commonwealth middleweight boxing champion.'

'Okay, it would be really interesting to train you.'

Harry and I knew we were going to Central at some point so any help we could get that would aid us in defending ourselves was welcome. Coach had just come back from Central as he had served a sentence for fraud. But the moment he walked out of the jail he was arrested again for another case and immediately transferred to Port Rashid.

'Central is a crazy place, you don't want to go there,' he said. 'As soon as you get there they will take you to Building 1. Everyone is off their head and you never know, at any minute it can all kick off. Say you want to go to Building 2 otherwise you're in trouble.'

Harry and I looked at each other. This guy could clearly look after himself and he was telling us to avoid Central at all costs. The thought of going there sent a shiver down my spine and made me think of Tariq.

Coach agreed to teach me kenshi-kai, a martial art that was like something out of the computer game *Tekken*. He also agreed to teach Harry traditional Thai boxing. We were coached three times a week and we would pay him 100D a session. I was to discover that Coach was a very spiritual guy and just being in his presence calmed me down. I was uptight and angry with the world and this was exactly what I needed. I finally had something to focus on that helped me escape from the anger in my head.

After a couple of weeks of training, Coach posed a question that I couldn't really answer. 'Why do you do this corrupt stuff and get into arguments all the time? You are not this person.'

I was taken aback.

'Because I don't like taking shit from people.'

'But you are getting into stupid arguments that could get you killed. You are making a lot of enemies in here because of your attitude towards things. You and Harry are two British boys and you're basically running the jail. Some people don't like that. You don't need to be fighting every battle, sometimes you just need to let things go.'

I understood what he meant but there was a very real chance I would be rotting in a Dubai jail for a long, long time. I figured I might as well have a good time while I was here.

The training with Coach couldn't have come at a better time for Harry as well. He had received the news from home every single inmate dreads. He walked into the cell, looking ashen-faced.

'What's up, bruv?' I said.

'It's me and Sarah. We've split up.'

I'm not really sure why but I was overwhelmed with grief and I burst into tears.

'Why the fuck are you crying?' Harry said, laughing at my reaction.

'I'm just so sorry, bruv.'

'It's all right, mate. We're going to get through this and everything's gonna be okay.'

He was putting a very brave face on it but for the next few days didn't really get out of bed. It was only the training with Coach that kept him sane.

In the meantime things had been getting more and more tense with Baariq. I'd asked him again about the money he owed me for failing to get me out and he had scuttled off, his tail between his legs. I was starting to think he was one of the enemies Coach had been telling me about.

One day when I was bored I took a few pictures of the jail on my Blackberry and posted them on Twitter. I was watching TV shortly afterwards when I heard Captain Aziz shouting, 'Where's Black British?'

I walked back into my cell.

'Where's the Blackberry?' he demanded as I walked in. How did he know I had a Blackberry? It didn't make sense. Baariq was sat on his bed looking cool.

'What are you talking about, Captain Aziz? I don't have a Blackberry.'

'Shut up! I know you have the phone. Baariq, come.'

The angry captain and Baariq went a bit further down the strip. Ten minutes later Baariq came back in.

'Look he's really pissed. You're fucking stupid, you've been posting things on Facebook.'

I hadn't, but I played along to see what he said next. Baariq knew I had taken some pictures, but he had just assumed I had put them on Facebook. If Captain Aziz had discovered the pictures himself, he would have seen they were on Twitter. Somebody had snitched on me.

'Okay, man, no problem. We'll pay for it.'

'Fucking hell, mate, why did you post pictures like that?' Harry said. 'You're such a prick.'

Minutes later Jebillally came to see me. The big African spoke several languages and one of them was Arabic.

'Hey, Karl, you know you shouldn't be trusting Baariq, right? I overheard the conversation he had with Aziz. Don't you think it's weird out of everyone in the jail they have come to you for a Blackberry? Baariq has snaked on you.'

'What do you mean?'

'The guy is a snake. Did you even put photos on Facebook?'

'Nah, I put them on Twitter.'

'There you go. He's lying and he snitched on you.'

'I know he's a rat, mate, but I don't even care. It's just not worth it.'

One thing I did care about was Harry's opinion of me. I found him having a smoke. 'Look, bruv, I didn't even post anything on Facebook, it was on Twitter. Baariq snitched on me.'

'Never, mate! How do you know?'

'Jebillally overheard Baariq and Aziz. He tipped him off.'

It was annoying to have to give up the phone but the reality was that if it wasn't for Baariq and his connections with the guards we wouldn't be getting away with half the stuff that was going on. We just knew never to trust the guy.

*

Mike the cockney had been released from Port Rashid a couple of days before with the promise to Jebillally that he would sort out the gold bullion deal. Within a couple of weeks they had carried out three gold smuggling missions to London. Jebillally was paid when the gold reached its destination. This went off without a hitch three times. The fourth mission was not so successful. Having built up the trust of the big African, Mike sorted a $200,000 shipment. He was never seen again and the gold disappeared.

'Ah, mate, what are you going to do?' I asked Jebillally after he told me.

'Don't worry, one day our paths will meet,' he said, remaining totally calm. 'No problem. But when I do see him he is a dead man.'

In February we were called to the hatch to go to court for the second time. We had no idea what was going on and hadn't heard a thing from our lawyers. We knew that the embassy should tell us when our trial date was but we didn't have a lot of faith in them, so were concerned we might be facing our fate that day.

We went through the same procedure as before. Harry and I saw Tariq again and he was looking tanned and ripped. We were shown into the same court as before. The prosecution and the judge spoke but we had no idea what was going on. Again our lawyers didn't say a word. The court appearance lasted a few minutes but there was enough time for Tariq to hand us a box of cigarettes he had smuggled in his pants.

'Cheers, bruv,' Harry said. 'I'll balls these. We owe you, brother.'

When we arrived back at the jail we were met by Captain Aziz. He pulled me into a side room where I was searched thoroughly.

I was worried Baariq had snitched on us again and I knew imme-diately that there was no chance Harry was going to get the cigarettes in.

'Bruv, they're doing proper searches,' I whispered to him as I came out. 'You ain't getting those in.'

Harry walked into the room and pulled the cigarettes from his pants.

'This is what I've got, do your worst.'

'You will get a new case for this!' Aziz shouted.

'Mate, I'm on a drugs trafficking charge, you think I give a shit about a shitty charge for smuggling cigarettes?'

What was more worrying was the turn of events – first the phone and now this. I hoped it was just a blip and the tide hadn't turned forever. Apart from anything else, Coach was a constant drain on our cash. He clearly needed the money for something but it was getting a bit much. As well as paying for training we were loaning the guy thousands of dirhams. Baariq had seen how much time Harry and I were spending with him and didn't like what he saw. He came up to me and said, 'So I pulled Coach's case papers and it turns out he's a dangerous guy.'

'Oh yeah?'

'Yeah, he beat this guy so badly that when he ordered him to sign over his company he couldn't do it quick enough.'

I didn't know if Baariq was just meddling, but he had been right in the past. I vowed to be more careful with Coach, but I didn't think any less of him. When you're in jail with serious criminals it doesn't pay to be judgemental.

The following morning we were woken up by a commotion and shouting outside. Harry went to see what was going on and came back with all of the colour having been drained from his face. He looked like he had seen a ghost.

'Mate, they're calling people for Central and our names are down.'

'Fuck that, mate, I ain't going anywhere.'

Aziz walked in. 'Boys, get your stuff, you're going to Central.'

My heart sank and I started to sweat. Harry looked like he was about to pass out. This was our worst nightmare and there was no escape.

I called the British embassy and they helpfully told us there was nothing they could do. Knowing we had no choice galvanized us into action. Dozens of inmates owed us money for *dokha* and we went round trying to collect the cash. There were still bills of several thousand dirhams outstanding by the time we finished but we'd run out of time. We gave the money we collected to Baariq to put it in the business kitty.

'So what do you want to do about the cash and stuff?' I said.

'We can only do one thing which is split the money that we have at the moment three ways,' he answered.

'What?' I said, annoyed by his suggestion. 'But then you're going to collect the rest of the money we're owed and you get the *dokha*.'

'Okay, well, we split the *dokha* as well.'

Baariq was trying to stitch us up when we were at our most vulnerable. We were owed thousands of dirhams that couldn't be collected at that moment. It meant he would get the lion's share of the cash. He also knew we would struggle to sell our *dokha* at a reasonable price.

'Fucking hell, man, I can't believe Baariq has been such a cunt.' Harry said as we stormed out.

'I told you, mate.'

We went to see Jebillally as he had the most money in the jail and he agreed to buy our stash of *dokha* for a fair price. We also gave Coach a tracksuit and some of the Arabic tobacco as a thank you for all of the training he had given us.

'Look, boys, be careful,' Coach said to us. 'Central is a dangerous place. Keep your heads down and try to educate yourselves. Don't get into fights as everyone's got knives. They aren't scared to use them, so just take it easy.'

We shook his hand and made our way to the front of the jail. The Africans, the local gangsters, Baariq and the Pakistani murderers all came to say goodbye.

I was terrified. We had become comfortable in Port Rashid where we were big fish in a small pond. Now we were heading to one of the world's most notorious jails with the big boys. My throat was dry and I was struggling to hold it together.

'Hey, you two,' Baariq said. 'I'll call Tariq and let him know you're coming.'

We thanked him. Maybe he felt guilty about the money.

Aboot and Abait were shown into the van with us along with a few of the Indians. We were all silent as we made our way through Dubai. The tension in the air was tangible and the sombre mood lay heavy on us as we all imagined the horrors that were to come. I glanced at my fellow inmates and the looks on all of their faces mirrored my own feelings. They all portrayed a picture of absolute terror.

We were driven through the huge gates of Central Prison and into a garage. From there we were led into a massive cell where five uniformed police officers were waiting. A short Arab with a moustache was looking through the paperwork.

'Some of you can't come in here. You three,' he said, pointing to me, Harry and Aboot. 'You have to be over the age of twenty-five years old to be in here as it's too dangerous. A lot of guys have come from Port Rashid and been raped and stabbed, so now we're not taking younger people. Too dangerous.'

'But our friend Tariq's in here and he's not over twenty-five,' Harry said.

'Yes, but that was before, this is now. Too dangerous, *Yallah!* Go!'

I suddenly felt intense, pure joy and relief, like a guardian angel had plucked me from the gates of hell. I was high on life.

'Fucking hell, man, that was a close call,' Harry said, laughing.

'Yeah, I know. Look when we get back we need to get all of the money we're owed. When we go to Central we need to have enough cash to last us.'

He agreed. It was only a matter of time before we were both transferred. I was twenty-six in two months and Harry's twenty-sixth birthday was three months after that. The clock was ticking.

We walked back into Port Rashid and I felt like I was coming home, except nobody was pleased to see us. All of the inmates stared at us open mouthed. It was like we were back from the dead. Harry and I went from cell to cell like we were bailiffs on pay day. His first port of call was to go and see Qasim as he didn't like the guy.

'You owe me money,' he shouted. 'Give me my fucking money.'

The expression on Qasim's face was priceless. He looked like he was going to cry. He ran out of his cell and into Baariq's room. The foreman stormed out, a look of thunder on his face.

'What is this?' he shouted. He wasn't very happy to see us either. 'Why are you back here causing trouble straight away?!'

'Look, I'm not having any of it,' I said, rearing up. 'When we left you should've given us the money and got your share from the people who owed us. You're a prick and I'm sick of it.'

Baariq shook his head and walked off. Harry and I continued on our cash gathering mission. We went around and got our clothes back and collected every dirham that we could gather. It's fair to say we didn't make many friends. I was pretty sure the rest of the inmates wished we had been left to rot in Central.

After we'd done that I went out to the hoosh to get some fresh air. It was dark and stars twinkled in the night sky. Coach was by himself, doing a few laps, and called me over.

'You have been brought back to this jail and have been given a second chance,' he said. 'You could have been in hell. You didn't want to go to Central and now you are back here. You have a chance to make a difference.

'How you act in life now will shape your future. Forget all of your bad habits, the fighting and being involved in the corruption with the guards. This can be a fresh start for you. This is the only good thing about going to prison, you have a chance to change yourself, be a good person and make a difference.'

I was stunned into silence. What Coach said resonated so strongly with me that I immediately knew what I had to do. I had been aggressive, angry and generally an unpleasant person to be around. Admittedly I was in a hellish situation, but that didn't mean I needed to act like a prick. Coach's words were like an epiphany. I resolved to change my ways.

I went to find Harry and said, 'If you do business with a dickhead what does that make you?'

'A dickhead.'

'So why are we involved with this guy who should have given us the money when we left and instead tried to stitch us up? The guy's a snake. Look at what happened with the phone and our attempt to buy ourselves out. I don't want to be in business with this prick anymore. I'm gonna go into his cell and demand my share of the money and then I'm done.'

'Ceaze, come on, man, we don't need to do it like this.'

'Fuck it, bruv, I've had it with this guy. I'm finishing this now.'

Despite Coach's words a few moments before. I had worked myself into a state and there was no stopping me. I stormed into Baariq's cell. 'Look, Baariq, I don't want to be involved in the business any more. Can we split the money?'

If Baariq had been a reasonable person he would have seen that this was only fair, but he started ranting, 'No, you can't! I'm the one in control here.'

'I don't give a shit if you're in control, I just want my money and my *dokha*. I'm starting to get a bit pissed off now as you're telling me I can't have what's mine. I want my money and I want my *dokha* now.'

The look on Baariq's face was one of pure fury. 'You fucking little shit. Who do you think you are to come in here demanding my money?!'

'Furthermore, I want my money that you got from me with Matt,' I continued as I ignored him. 'You think it's okay to bump me? Well, it's not. I want all my fucking money now!'

Harry realized that this was getting ugly fast and tried to calm things down. 'Come on, Ceaze, why can't we all just get along?' he moaned.

'This guy's a snake,' I said, pointing in Baariq's face, 'and I can't deal with this shit. When we left the jail you should have given us the money. That showed me what kind of man you are.'

'I want you out of this cell this instant before I beat the shit out of you,' Baariq raged.

'What? Fuck off, you prick. Me and Harry would kill you.'

'Get out of this cell or you and I will have fight right now.'

'Fuck it, let's do this then. But I want my money and I want my *dokha*.'

'Ceaze, just go, man,' Harry said.

I stormed out of the cell, where a large crowd had gathered to see the action, and went to see Jebillally.

'What's up, man? I heard all the screaming.'

I told him what had happened.

'So why the fight? Why didn't he just hand over the stuff? I told you he was a rat. I told you he's a snake.'

Harry came and found me. 'Look, he's gonna give you your share of the money and the *dokha* but you have to move out of his cell.'

That was fine by me. A massive weight had been lifted off my shoulders. Although I was incarcerated I felt free for the first time in months. I hadn't realized how unhealthy it was for me to be involved in Baariq's business and the strain it had put on me. It had sent me slightly mad. I vowed to myself that I would no longer be *hiwan*, I was going to be the real Karl Williams.

21

THE REAL KARL WILLIAMS

The days after I moved out of Baariq's cell were some of the best I spent in Port Rashid. The pressure of being in business with him had slowly sent me crazy. Escaping being in his presence was like a pressure valve being released in my head. It was a time of quiet contemplation when I reassessed everything that was important in my life. I wanted to be a better person and get on with others rather than constantly looking for a fight. I'd never been one to look for a fight on the outside, although I'd always stood up for myself, and I didn't want to carry on my aggressive behaviour any more.

I spent a lot of time training with Coach and hanging out with Jebillally, who started teaching me German and French. We also spent a lot of time playing cards or Monopoly. Harry was being distant with me, though. In truth, the way I had behaved before moving out of the cell had constantly annoyed my friend, so it wasn't that great a surprise. I didn't try to build bridges with him because, although I had known Harry all of my life, when I needed him to back me up he shied away from it and stayed in the cell with Baariq. Even though I was upset, I also understood why Harry was doing what he was doing. Baariq was the fulcrum that made things happen in Port Rashid. Without him there was no smuggling business and without him there was no money. Baariq would tell Harry in front of my face that I was a prick and that I didn't care about him. I ignored the big Sudanese foreman and told Harry not to listen to Baariq but he would walk off. It was clear to me Baariq was trying to poison Harry against me.

I had moved into Aboot's cell, because he had a phone and was happy for me to share his room. We were joined by a cool guy called Hassla, a footballer with a colourful past, and a fat Arab called Adil, who was in jail for possession of drugs. Hassla was caught drink-driving but then compounded matters by beating up the cop who arrested him.

'So, man, I hear you've had troubles with Baariq?' he said.

'Yeah, man.'

'I've known him for a long time and he is not to be trusted.'

'I know, mate, he's a snake.'

Hassla loved to tell us stories about his excessive playboy footballer lifestyle. Apparently he often hired a harem of women for him and his mates to enjoy. His family were all gangsters and he had been in jail himself for drugs. Although I had heard sick stories of how some people had managed to get out of prison in Dubai, Hassla's story was the most extreme of all.

'I was arrested for possession of cannabis,' he said. 'I went to court one time and I was met by this very well-dressed guy from a top team. He said to me, "If you sign for us, all of this drugs stuff goes away."'

'Fuck off, mate.'

'No, seriously. I signed the contract and the next thing I knew I was being taken to a chauffeur-driven Bentley and driven to my new apartment.'

Unfortunately for Hassla his stock had fallen since that time and now he found himself back inside Port Rashid on another charge.

'The thing is, I haven't even told my agent where I am. He thinks I've just gone AWOL. He's going to go crazy when he finds out.'

Hassla showed me a picture of his wife, who looked like a supermodel. In the next breath he said, 'You know, Karl, if you have a boyfriend in jail it makes time go so much faster.'

I burst out laughing. 'Mate, what are you talking about?'

'Yeah, if you have somebody to stroke your hair for you, maybe suck you off, it is nice.'

'Nah, mate. If you were in an English jail asking people to do that you'd be in trouble.'

'You have never been with a man?'

'No, mate.'

'Why not? You might like it.'

Adil, who had picked up sex offence charges for shagging men in jail and had been sitting quietly on the bed, suddenly piped up.

'Yes, I fucked loads of boys in Central. Why do you think I caught so many cases? Some boys let me, some boys didn't, but I still fucked them good.'

I was repulsed that he had just admitted being a rapist, and that I had to share a cell with him. It made me feel sick.

'Mate, that's disgusting.'

'No, this is normal here. My wife knows I fuck men and she's okay with it.'

'Man, you've probably got AIDS.'

'Hopefully not.'

A couple of days later we were joined by two quiet Moroccan boys called Omar and Khalil. They had got drunk, beaten up a cab driver and stolen his taxi.

The two North African lads were very musically minded, always banging away on any item they could get their hands on to make a noise. I was playing poker one night with Harry, the Moroccan lads, Adil and the Africans, when we suddenly heard loud music pumping from the TV room.

Omar stood up. 'Where is this music?' he asked, before walking out of the room. We all quickly followed. 'Na, na na na gasoline!' was pumping out of the TV. What we saw will live with me forever.

Uno was on a table doing a crazy dance. He was quickly joined by Nayeeda, the huge Pakistani murderer, grinding up against him. It was one of the funniest things I have ever seen. We all wet ourselves laughing before joining in the dancing. The guards watching it on the cameras must have thought we had all gone mad. When the song finished we went back to our poker tournament.

'That was so funny, man,' I said.

'We need more music in this jail,' Omar said.

'Yeah, man, I know. Another night let's all listen to some music again.'

It was a couple of days later when I heard inmates running excitedly towards the hoosh. The Moroccans, Africans, Babar and Qasim and the local gangsters were sat around in a circle, banging on makeshift drums. Omar and Khalil had grabbed some empty water drums to use them as instruments. Nayeeda was stood up singing the most beautiful, haunting Hindi love song. I sat down, amazed at what I was seeing. Nayeeda had slit somebody's throat and chucked them off a building, but he had the voice of an angel.

The hoosh had twenty-five-foot-high walls and a cage over the top, making the music reverberate and echo around. We took it in turns to sing while the Moroccans provided the chorus of 'Why dididi dah dey dah dey, why dididi dah dey dah dey.' When it came to my turn I sang my own song called 'Yesterday', while several Indians danced in the middle of the circle.

At that moment I was the happiest I had been in Port Rashid. It was like we weren't in jail. All of us making music together created a beautiful unity. We had been forced together for multiple horrific reasons, but at that moment we could forget the evils of the past and enjoy the idyllic present before reality returned.

Because there were fewer people in the jail after the amnesty, there was a brotherliness that had been absent for the previous months. We all ate the same food, slept under the same roof and shared the same worries. It was like a big family and Port Rashid was home.

Although I felt more settled than ever life was not always easy. Baariq would put random, smelly new inmates into my room, just to annoy me. We would just kick them out and tell Baariq to fuck off. The constant risk of violence was still there, meaning you could never let down your guard.

A Ukrainian bloke called Anton was brought into the jail on a drink-drive case and was suspected of stealing from an older inmate. It's ironic that in jail nobody likes a thief. Baariq decided to set a trap. Aboot walked into his cell, dropped a 1,000D note and walked out again. Anton picked up the cash and quickly put it in his wallet. Moments later Aboot walked back into the cell and said he thought he had dropped a note.

'What are you talking about? Anton said, 'I've not taken your money.'

He was ordered to open his wallet. He slowly opened up a 1,000D note and there, drawn in the centre, was a middle finger in an 'up yours' gesture.

'Now we fuck you,' Aboot said. Anton's face dropped. Baariq,

Adil, Ayoop and a gang of locals dragged him kicking and screaming towards the hoosh.

'No, no, don't let them take me!' he screamed.

There was nothing anybody could do. Jail justice was being carried out. Baariq slapped Anton around the face and he fell to the floor sobbing, curled into the foetal position. Around fifteen people laid into Anton's body. His screams of agony could be heard in every corner of the jail. Some of his attackers had managed to get hold of broomsticks and they thrashed him until the sticks broke. A bin was smashed over his head while others stamped on his body. It was like Anton was an ant being obliterated. The group began to pull at his trousers, making a move to start raping him.

'No! Enough!' Baariq shouted. Things had gone too far. To Baariq's credit he stopped Anton from being raped but the Ukrainian was left with a broken hand and smashed ribs. The officers did nothing.

Anton wasn't the only inmate to suffer prison justice. At this time visits from the ninjas became more frequent and they always headed straight to mine and Baariq's cells. Despite constantly fighting with Harry I sometimes hid stuff for him. The ninjas were getting intelligence from somewhere, and that had to be from a snitch. Then a toothbrush with a razor blade melted into the top, sim cards and chargers were planted in Harry's bed and discovered by the ninjas. Somebody was stitching Harry up. He was taken out the front to see Aziz and came back in spitting blood.

'They're trying to give me another case for this shit. I've been fucked.'

Baariq went to see Feroz to find out what was going on and the cop told him that a young Egyptian lad called Mahmood was the snitch. We knew the small guy's mum had died while he was inside Port Rashid and he was always on the phone, crying as he spoke to his brothers at home.

Harry came to see me. Our relationship was tense but we were at least speaking.

'Baariq told me that Mahmood was so desperate to get deported back to Egypt for his mum's funeral that he sold everyone out,' Harry said.

'Shit, man.'

'I know, he's fucked.'

I heard shouting coming from down the strip. The cries of Mahmood could have been heard from a mile away as he was dragged outside to suffer the same fate as Anton. He was lucky to survive.

Meanwhile rumours had started to go around the jail that Port Rashid could be closing. It was a health hazard and the conditions we were expected to live in were inhumane. This was good and bad news. Nobody should have had to put up with the filth that we had to. But if Port Rashid was to close that could only speed up our move to Central.

'Come, come!' Captain Aziz said as he came into the jail one day. He was with five guards and they were carrying pots of paint and brushes.

'You!' he said, pointing to a group of Indians. 'You paint the jail.'

For the next two days the inmates were expected to paint Port Rashid. It turned out that the captain was expecting a visit from human rights officials at the UN. A lick of paint on the filth pit we called home was a bit like polishing a turd.

Harry was feeling the pressure of working for Baariq and it reflected in his moods. I was asleep when I heard Harry shouting and ran out to find him squaring up to a group of twenty Indians.

'Where's my fucking lighter?! Qasim's stolen my fucking lighter again.'

I rushed to help my friend while Baariq and Jebillally came to join the melee.

'If any of these Indians touch me I'm going to stab the lot of them,' Jebillally said forcefully, making sure the whole group of Indians could hear him.

Harry grabbed hold of Qasim and started to shake him, causing the two groups to clash, pushing and shoving each other. Baariq stepped into the middle to break up the fight.

'It's okay, I will get the lighter back,' Baariq said. The stand-off dispersed and Baariq did his best to keep the peace by trying to calm Harry down. But even when Harry was given his lighter back he went to find Qasim and tried to attack him again. Life was never dull.

I went back to my cell to find Adil, Omar and Khalil with a small Egyptian lad. I hadn't seen the boy before but he looked like a child.

'What's going on here?' I said. Everyone was smoking and passing the boy *dokha*. 'So who's he?' I added.

'He's my new lover,' Adil said, with a sinister smile on his face.

'What do you mean?'

'He's gonna be staying with us.'

'But, mate, there's no space.'

'It's all right, he's gonna be sharing my bed.'

I looked across at the wide-eyed boy and saw he had look of sheer terror on his face. My heart sank.

'Listen, he is not staying in this room,' I said.

Adil stood up. 'Come, come,' he said to me.

We walked onto the strip.

'Look, I just want to fuck him,' he said, suggesting it was perfectly normal behaviour and I was being unreasonable.

'No, mate, you're not fucking that kid in my cell.'

'How is it your cell?'

'I've been here longer than you and this shit isn't happening in the same room as me. You do that and I will cut you.' I never possessed a knife in jail but could easily have got one from outside.

'You don't want to be threatening me, boy,' Adil said, his voice rising.

'Come on then, let's have it,' I said, squaring up to him. I may have been a lot calmer than I had been, but I wasn't standing by as an innocent kid got raped.

Baariq and Harry had heard the fracas and came to see what was happening.

'What the fuck, Ceaze?' Harry said, looking disappointed at me. I couldn't believe Harry's reaction. He didn't wait to hear why I was squaring up to Adil, and had instantly thought it was my fault.

'You see?' Baariq said. 'This is what I said about you. You are always causing trouble.'

'Fuck off, Baariq, Adil wanted to rape the little Egyptian kid.'

That seemed to take the wind out of his sails and he turned to Adil and started to berate him in Arabic before sending the Egyptian boy to another cell. When I returned to my cell later, Adil and the Moroccans were there.

'Hey, Karl, you know we were only kidding, right?' Adil said.

'Where I come from this is wrong, you don't do this to boys,' I said.

'But in our culture this is okay,' Adil insisted. 'A little boy like that wants to get it.'

I was disgusted but didn't want to get into another row.

Harry thought I was causing trouble for no reason and wouldn't listen to my protestations that I was trying to change.

We were barely talking and we didn't even acknowledge each other, but I could still see he was the genuinely nice guy I called a friend. When new inmates came into the jail he would always try to look after them, to protect them.

One inmate he took under his wing was a small, frail Iranian guy called Harish. When he came in the old man, who must've been in his late sixties, was so thin that he looked like he could be snapped in two. He came across as vulnerable and Harry tried to look after him by providing him with *dokha* and cigarettes. Harish told us he was a multi-millionaire businessman who had been screwed by Dubai's corrupt system. He told Harry that he was owed £65 million by an Emirati family, but they told him they would only pay half. If he did not accept, they said they would find 'other ways' of dealing with him.

'Of course I said no,' he said with a slight Arabic accent. 'But when I refused the police raided my home. I had nothing to hide. But when they tested my urine they found morphine in it. This was crazy as I have never touched the drug. The Emirati who owed the money to me got a message to me. It said, "I told you I had ways."'

Harish had been for a blood test days before as he had been ill. There was no sign of any drug in his system.

'It was all a lie, they are just doing this as I was going through the court to get my money and I refused to drop it.'

Harry and Harish became close, with him allowing Harry's mum to stay in his million-pound apartment in Dubai when she came to see him.

With hindsight, there were pointers to suggest Harish wasn't just a simple rich old man. For instance, he walked into the jail with a phone and he had a sleeping bag.

'Woah, how did you do that?' I asked him.

'You know, I have my ways.'

Harish owned a container shipping company. He had businesses in Russia and Qatar and the only reason he couldn't buy his way out was because the family he was suing were pureblood Emiratis.

I was lying in my cell when I heard Baariq's name being called out to be transferred to Central and I ran out to say goodbye. I walked up to him and shook his hand and said, 'I want to apologize for being such an arsehole. I love you as a brother and I want to thank you for everything you have done for us. If it wasn't for you we wouldn't have had phones, the late night meals or been able to make money in here. It has all meant so much to me and I'm sorry for how I've acted over the last few months. The money I paid you for getting out you can forget about, take it as a thank you.' I still held a grudge against Baariq, but I was trying to do the right thing. I appreciated everything he had done for me but I still didn't like the guy.

A tear trickled down Baariq's cheek. 'You really have changed as a person,' he said. 'I'm sorry for being such a prick to you as well. I wish it had worked out perfectly. We were like brothers in here and I'd like to think if I came to England we could meet up.'

'Of course, man, without a doubt.'

He hugged Harry and me before saying, 'I have something to admit to you. I snitched on you over the Blackberry. The captain came to me and said they knew there was a mobile in here and they were going to tear the place apart. I gave you up as we weren't getting on and I'm sorry.'

'Mate, I always knew it. It didn't really make much difference to me. Forget about it.'

When Baariq left the first thing we did was have a cigarette in his cell. He had banned us from smoking in there for so long. I moved my stuff back in. Things were still tricky between us but I'd never hold a grudge against Harry. We had been through too much together.

'It's just me and you now, mate,' Harry said.

'I know, what are we gonna do?'

I decided to consider the situation over another cigarette when a familiar face walked through the door.

'You little cunt, I knew you would smoke in this cell as soon as I left,' Baariq said with a huge smile on his face.

'Mate, you knew exactly what would happen,' I said laughing.

There had been a mix-up with Baariq's paperwork and he was back with us for the foreseeable future. He was clearly delighted that he had managed to avoid Central. He invited me to stay in the cell but I couldn't face sharing a room with him again.

'Thank you, brother, but you know I like to be able to smoke where I sleep,' I said as an excuse.

I walked off and moved back into the cell with Adil. Despite his sexual preferences he never tried it on with me and in all honesty I had nowhere else to go.

Harry stayed with Baariq but was spending a lot of time with Harish. The older man valued my friend's opinion and sought out his advice. Harish had signed over various properties and businesses to associates as he was worried that he would lose his case and have to hand over his assets. Harry was constantly telling him to be careful and his advice was well founded, with some of the supposedly trusted friends disappearing without a trace.

'Thank you so much for your help and advice, I really appreciate it,' he said to Harry. 'Don't worry, when we get to Central it's in my hands and you will be looked after.'

Harry told me what he said. 'What the fuck does that mean?' I asked.

'No clue, bruv. Doesn't make any sense to me.'

'Maybe he knows people in there. I suppose it can't hurt.'

We walked out into the hoosh to have a cigarette. It was a muggy evening and the sweat dripped off of us. Suddenly the heavens opened and a deluge of water fell from the sky. It was the only time I had ever seen it rain in Dubai. The other inmates scuttled inside while Harry and I savoured the glorious feeling of rain on our skins. The torrent of drops fell onto the dirty mesh over the hoosh and the filthy water fell onto our faces. We didn't care, it felt like we were back in England.

I looked at Harry. 'This is a sign, we're going home soon,' I said.

It was more hope than belief. Harry and I had been getting more and more concerned that our gamble with the media had gone seriously wrong. There had been no movement for months now and Marc had no news for us. We started to believe what people had told us, 'Make noise and they will fuck you.'

We were in Harish's cell with Baariq soon after this and we were all discussing our cases. It wasn't looking good for any of us. In the current situation we had nothing to lose.

'We need to break out of here,' Daariq said. Babar and Qasim immediately said they were up for it. Harry and I nodded our heads in agreement.

'I can get the Iranians to hold onto Mo when he's on,' Harish said. 'They will pull him inside until he has given us the keys. Then Qasim and Babar can tackle the other guard and tie him up. When that is done we can escape out of the back exit and you will be on the motorway.'

It sounded so simple that it might actually work.

'I can get a gun from an old police friend and get it put on the outside,' Baariq said.

The plan was to escape through the desert to Oman. Once there, Harish would have one of his people waiting in a boat to get us to Pakistan. We would then head to the British embassy and request a permit to travel so we could fly home. The plan was set. In a week's time, on a weekend where Mo would have been one of the two guards on duty, we would make our break.

'Bruv, are you sure about this?' Harry said. 'If we get caught that's loads of extra charges.'

'Mate, I can't stay in this place.'

I was scared as well but I didn't see any other choice.

The following morning we were woken by Captain Aziz screaming our names.

'Kerrol Errol Williams, Harrison Michelle Jenkins, *Yallah! Yallah!*'

Our plans to escape had been shattered in one foul swoop. We weren't breaking out; we were on our way to Central.

22

ENTERING HELL

I lay still for a moment, willing it all to be a horrible dream. But within seconds the guards had come in and were harassing us to get our stuff together. They had clearly dispensed with the under twenty-six rule, as it was a few days before my birthday later in April. Harish had also been called along with a tiny Bangladeshi kid called Rajou who Harry had employed to clean his cell. It was a frail pensioner, a tiny guy who looked like a rape candidate and us who were off to Central.

We got our stuff together and shaved our heads with a pair of clippers. We had been told we would have our hair sheared off with a dirty, lice-ridden shaver when we arrived so we thought it would be better to do it ourselves.

'Don't worry, we'll be looked after,' Harish said. 'Don't forget your friend Tariq's there and there will be lots of people who have been in Port Rashid. It will be like one big reunion.'

He seemed remarkably calm for an old man who was about to enter one of the world's most dangerous jails. Rajou wasn't faring so well.

'When I get to Central I will be raped,' he whimpered. 'Look how small I am.'

Harry was trying to console him as we were led to the windowless prison van. An eerie silence descended on us. It was déjà vu, except this time there was no going back.

Baariq had previously told us that Central is the second-most secure jail in the world. Towering walls, electric fences, watch towers and guards with guns and dogs made up its impenetrable ring of steel. We were driven through the gates and into the processing centre we had seen before, but this time there were also inmates there coming back from court. Menacing prisoners who looked like Osama bin Laden on steroids scoped us out. Most had their faces and bodies covered in tattoos while others' skin was criss-crossed with unsightly scars. Bizarrely, a couple wore designer sunglasses.

We were all told to undress and put on white prison clothes that resembled thick, loose-fitting pyjamas, before we took it in turns to have our mugshot taken. We were handed ID cards that were to act as our way of paying for food. There was no cash in Central and you had to hand all of your money over. This was then put onto the card to purchase goods. Those without any money had to survive on prison food. Then we were led down a dimly lit corridor that must have been half a mile long. We walked downhill for what seemed like an age before we hit a gradient heading up to the surface. We were to learn that the reason Central was so secure was that this claustrophobic twenty-five-foot-wide corridor that burrowed deep underground was the only way in and out of the jail.

At the end we walked through a series of metal detectors and then onto a spiral staircase that took us to the surface. We found ourselves in a booking area that resembled an airport security zone where bags are scanned. We walked through more metal detectors and then we were made to line up against a window. I looked through the glass hoping for a glimpse of the outside world but could only see the uninspiring sight of a car park where officers left their vehicles. One by one we were led into a small bathroom.

'Take your top off,' the guard said.

I was then told to take off my trousers and pull my boxer shorts forward. He ran a metal detector up and down my body and close to my dick.

'Why so close, man?' I asked.

'Sometimes people cut themselves open before they come to prison and put razor blades or drugs inside their testicles.'

I'd heard some crazy things but this was sick. 'You're kidding me?'

'I no joke. Pull your pants down, squat and cough.' This was swiftly followed by the metal detector being run over my balls again.

After that I went back into line to wait for the others to go through the same process. Finally we were told to put our belongings on a conveyor belt to be scanned before we were led outside. We found ourselves on a well-kept path with neatly cut grass on either side. Towering fences with rolled barbed wire on top lined the walkway. Beyond the fences were the two biggest prisons I had ever seen. The two-storey modern blocks had dark windows and spread as far as I could see. Each had several exercise areas while I could see a football pitch and cricket pitch in the distance.

I looked to my left and in the distance saw a little Indian I recognized immediately.

'Tariq!' I shouted, and Harry joined in.

'Bruv, you're finally here!' he shouted. 'Make sure you come to Building 1. It's my gaff! It's my gaff!'

Harry and I burst out laughing. 'Shut up, you little dickhead!'

'Tell them you wanna go to A6. I'm just gonna have my visit

but then I'll be there. People know you're coming so you'll be looked after.'

The guards didn't seem to mind our brief chat, and when we had finished we were walked down the pathway to the end. A couple of the inmates were taken to the right where Building 2, which housed those on fraud cases and less serious assault offences, was situated. We were taken to the left to Building 1, home to rapists, murderers and Mafia lords. Despite Tariq's assurances I was terrified.

The front of the building was all glass, except we couldn't see through to the inside. As we approached we could hear a hum of noise that increased as we got closer. When we got to the door the wall of noise was deafening. People were banging on the windows. This was our welcoming committee.

'Here we go, bruv,' I said to Harry. I felt sick with fear. 'Time to cover our arseholes.'

Harry laughed but it wasn't really funny. It looked like the other inmates were preparing for our arrival. We were fresh meat.

The guards opened the main entrance to the jail and our senses were immediately attacked by the intense noise and the smell of smoke which hit me like a hammer. Around a dozen Arabs were screaming and shouting while an alarm was going off. *Wayo! Wayo! Wayo!* it blared. *This is an alarm condition, please remain calm and await for further notice.* It repeated incessantly. There was a riot going on somewhere in the prison. The haze of filthy smoke was so deep it was like a fog. The guards walked us in before swiftly making their exit.

I looked up and saw the glass on the inside was cracked and there was blood on the walls. A minute after we walked in we saw a large Arab man with a sharp blade shearing the skin off his arm. Blood sprayed out like a fountain. I felt my stomach rise to my mouth as I tried to supress the need to vomit. The police, in a glass bubble above the main reception area, could see what was happening but carried on without a care.

Police officers rarely entered the jail, preferring to monitor the inmates from the bubble. Other Arabs walked past him and berated him, but left him in a pool of blood.

Harry, Harish, Rajou and I pushed our backs to the wall, unable to comprehend the horror in front of us. Rajou was in tears and I could understand why. Two guards came in the main entrance and dragged the bleeding Arab away.

More muscle-bound Arabs, many of them looking psychotic, started staring intently at us. Some came up close and sniffed us and tried to touch Rajou. 'Indian, you come to our wing,' they kept saying. Rajou responded with more tears.

I was getting prepared to defend ourselves against the crazed-looking Arabs when the sea of men looking at us as potential targets parted and around half a dozen huge, shaven-headed Russian gangsters stormed towards us. I'd watched enough gangster documentaries to know what their tattoos meant. Star tattoos adorned their shoulders, a sign that they were senior members of the Mafia, while tears were inked on their faces, showing their murder tallies. I thought I was going to explode with fear. Then I heard the cockney voice of an angel.

'Hey, you Somalian pirate, what you doing?'

Tariq swaggered in and I have never been so happy to see him. He handed us chocolate milk and Galaxy bars.

'What the fuck?' Harry said, as we both wolfed down our gifts. We had only had chocolate at court. None was available in Port Rashid.

'And here you go, boys.' Tariq got out two packets of cigarettes and handed them to us.

'Ah, man, thank you,' Harry said as we immediately got a smoke out.

'Cheers, Tariq, do you have something to light this with?'

He got out a weird contraption. It had a white plastic casing and a wire at the top. He pressed a button and the wire went red as it heated up. The home-made lighter was made out of batteries and wires. Smoking was allowed in Central but lighters weren't. That didn't stop inmates making their own.

The scary-looking Russians were all taking it in turns to kiss Harish on the head.

'Who's the old guy?' Tariq said.

'That's Harish, he's with us,' Harry said. 'He's a really good guy.'

We introduced him to Tariq.

'So you're Karl and Harry's case partner? Great to meet you.'

A light-skinned Arab in his mid-twenties with a receding hairline had joined the Russians talking to Harish before he came over and started addressing Tariq.

'Tariq, you silly little Indian, I told you to bring your friends straight to our amber when they arrived.' They called the wings ambers in Central.

'I know, I was bringing them but they were too busy saying hello to everyone.'

'You need to listen more, Tariq, you don't listen.'

Harry and I were laughing. Tariq looked like a schoolkid getting told off.

'Don't you recognize that geezer?' Tariq said, pointing to the Arab who had told him off.

'No, I don't think so,' I said.

'Don't you remember Sofian? He was the guy who was high as a kite in the holding cell at police headquarters after we were arrested.'

'Fuck me, of course,' I said, suddenly remembering him.

One of the big bald Russians turned to Harish and beckoned him forward. 'Harish, time to go.'

I couldn't believe what I was seeing. The little, frail pensioner Harry had taken under his wing was a serious player with the Russian Mafia. All of the tough gangsters were here to protect him. Harish came over to me and Harry to say goodbye.

'Guys, I guess I'm going to see you around,' Harish said. 'I have to go with the Russians.'

'No, it's okay,' Sofian said. 'These Russian boys are on my wing and we're all going to the same place. All of you boys are coming onto my wing.'

Harry and I looked at each other with massive smiles on our faces. Harish chuckled.

'Thank you so much, Sofian,' I said.

'No problem, any friend of Tariq's is a friend of mine. Plus you boys are famous! You've been on the news.'

'I told you! I told you I was a boss in here,' Tariq said excitedly. 'This is my gaff.'

'Shut up, Tariq, I bet you're getting bummed by everyone,' Harry said.

'Fuck off, mate,' Tariq responded.

'Yes, this little Indian, we all fuck him,' Sofian said, laughing. 'No, seriously, we all like Tariq as he's such a nice person and he's always making jokes.'

During all of this time a terrified-looking Rajou had been quietly edging closer to Harry in the hope he would protect him. Now he glanced up at Harry with a pleading look in his eyes.

'Mr Harry, can I come with you?' Rajou said.

'It's not up to me, mate.'

'But I will do the cleaning for everybody.'

'Sofian, is that okay? Can Rajou come?'

'No, we have too many Indians on the wing already.'

'Come on, man, please. He was my cleaner, he makes my tea and everything for me.'

'Yeah, come on, Sofian,' I said. 'Please.'

'Okay, but if he does anything I will kick him straight off.'

Even though there were some seriously tough-looking Russian gangsters on the wing, Sofian was foreman, having won a vote for the position. There may have been no democracy in the Arab state, but there was honour amongst thieves, murderers and rapists.

We were led out of the reception area into a long corridor, where a smoky haze still hung heavy in the air.

'So what happened to that guy who got raped?'

'Fucking hell, that was bad,' Tariq said. 'He was passed around the wings as a sex slave before he told the police. The cops opened up a case against Salim but they also opened one against the guy he raped. Salim said the sex was consensual so they charged the poor bastard as well for having gay sex.'

I was speechless. The thought of what he had been through was one of my worst nightmares.

'That ain't gonna happen again on our wing. Sofian might be foreman but the Russians control it, and as soon as what Salim had done came to light they kicked him off. Not much has been done to Salim, though, as his family are proper gangsters.'

We were heading to wing A6 which would be our new home. Central prison Building 1 is separated into a sentenced and un-sentenced side. Inmates can go wherever they like during the day. On each 'side' of the jail there are twelve wings, six on the ground floor and six upstairs. The wings were next to each other in a circle around a main central area. The jail held 2,000 people in Building 1. There was a large hoosh area for each wing which was covered. I only ever saw police officers come into the jail to speak to the jail boss, collect prisoners or body bags. The jail was run entirely by the inmates.

'So we saw this guy cutting his arm up and the guards in the bubble didn't do anything,' I said.

'Mate, that's normal,' Tariq said. 'When their medication gets stopped or denied they start slicing themselves open to prove they're mad. Everyone's got knives in here and at night-time you can hear them sharpening their blades.'

'How do they get knives in here?'

'They snap metal trays and then sharpen them to make a blade. The cops don't care. There have been quite a few murders. You boys are lucky you have come now as a few months ago people were being carried out in body bags on a daily basis.'

'Fuck, bruv, have you had any grief?'

'Nah, nothing major. I've had a few arguments but nothing serious. No one's gonna mess with me, I run the wing.'

'Yeah, all right, bruv.'

'Being serious, the Russian Mafia is looking after me. Our wing is the cleanest, most peaceful and safest place in the jail. We'll be all right here.'

'So what are the sunglasses all about?' Harry said.

'Only the bosses are allowed to wear Prada, mate. It's part of the uniform for them.'

We were led onto our wing through a small TV area with a flat screen on the wall. A white guy with brown hair and a beard stood up as we walked in.

'Tariq, are these the boys, yeah?'

'Yeah, this is Harry and this Karl. This is Ben.'

'I've heard so much about you boys. Tariq said you're good friends of his. How are you doing?'

'We've heard loads about you too when we spoke to Tariq on

the phone, man, good to meet you,' I said. 'I heard you're into music?'

'Yeah, mate, it would be good to have a chat. Sorry to hear about the torture stuff.'

'Ah, man, it's no problem,'

'Tariq's told me about it all and I've seen you on the news. It's gone to Tariq's head. He thinks he's the guy.'

'No it hasn't, you prick,' Tariq laughed. 'I've always been the guy.'

There are some people in life that you have an instant connection with. Ben was one of those people. He was a well-spoken, privately educated lad from Hampstead and I was an East End boy, but I instantly knew we would be friends.

Two of the towering Russians came up to us. 'Come, come, you must come and drink tea with us,' one said.

We followed Harish and the Russians into a cell with six bunk beds. The cell was slightly bigger than those in Port Rashid and had the luxury of a shower and toilet en suite. Pictures from glossy magazines of Rolex watches, Ferraris and men kick-boxing covered the walls. The room was so clean you could have eaten off the floor. A blanket was on the floor along with a table made out of cardboard boxes. The first bald Russian invited us to sit and as soon as we took our slippers off he put them in a neat line. Everything was regimentally organized. It was like we were in a boot camp.

A six-foot-four, broad and muscly Russian in his thirties introduced himself. 'I am Mice, this is Ravi,' he said, pointing to a stocky, square-headed guy with big eyes. 'Would you like tea and biscuits?'

This was surreal and I had to pinch myself. I didn't expect to be having tea and biscuits with the Russian Mafia. Ravi brought out a chest with Nice biscuits, custard creams, Pepsi, 7 Up and chocolate. More Russians came into the room and were chatting away to Harish.

Harish pointed at us and said to the Russians, 'These are my guys. Treat them as you would treat me.'

This was music to my ears. We were going to be protected by the Russian Mafia. I looked across and could see Tariq playing the joker.

'Hey, Mice, you silly meathead, you say you kill me? No, I kill you!'

Mice was laughing. 'No, you crazy little Indian, I kill *you*!'

It was a hilarious sight. Mice could have snapped Tariq in two yet Tariq was comfortable enough to be able to have banter with him like this. It was good to see.

When he had finished chatting to Mice I turned to Tariq and said, 'So how does it work in here?'

'Sofian is the foreman of the wing and then there is the foreman of the jail called Akrim. He's a Russian Mafia lord and runs the prison with the other Russians on our wing. He's been in here for sixteen years and is a mythical figure. You would never want to cross this guy.'

Sofian came across. 'Okay, boys, it's time to get you all beds. One of you can go to Tariq's room and the other can come in my cell.'

We decided Harry would go with Tariq.

'Okay, Karl, but just so you know the other guy in my cell is a complete nutter and hates Tariq, so just stay away from him. He's facing a fifteen-year sentence so he's under a lot of pressure. Also, don't go upstairs to the wing up there, it's like a jungle.'

'Okay, man, no problem.'

We went first into Tariq's cell and were introduced to Alfonso, a short, fat Filipino with jet-black hair. In a bizarre twist Alfonso was the father of Danny's girlfriend who had snitched on him.

The small guy had been found with a woman's body in his car boot. She had been stabbed repeatedly.

His other cellmate was a Geordie called Geoff, a bald-headed and stocky man in his forties who was wanted for an attempted murder in the UK and had been caught while on the run from Interpol.

Then Sofian took me next door to his cell where I was introduced to Abu Moosfoot, the nutter he had mentioned before. He was a short, bald Arab, but the hair he did have at the sides of his head had grown long and stuck up in the air, and he had a long beard and moustache. He grunted at me. It was obvious he was off his head on the prescription drugs given out by the jail.

'You are the Indian's case partner?'

'Yeah.'

'I no like this Indian. He makes too much noise. Always giddy giddy,' he said, making a talking movement with his hand.

'Ah, Tariq's lovely.'

'No, he too noisy.'

After dropping my books and toiletries off I went to see Harry and Tariq.

'Bruv, there are two guys called Abra and Shekai upstairs who told me they wanna see you.'

'The Crazy brothers?' I said. 'But Sofian said upstairs is like the jungle.'

'Yeah, that's them. Mate, it's nuts up there. You have all of the Africans and all the local gangsters.'

'Should we not go up there?'

'Nah, mate, I go up there all the time. Sofian's just shook,' meaning he was scared. Tariq led Harry and me up the metal staircase. The upstairs part was exactly the same as our wing. We walked straight into their cell. Crazy Hair was scrubbing the bathroom while Crazy Beard was sat down playing on an iPad, powered by dozens of batteries linked together by wires.

'Ah, my brothers, good to see you,' Crazy Beard said. 'Don't worry about my brother. He's taken some pills and always cleans when he's high.'

Crazy Hair's head popped over the top of the swing doors to the bathroom. 'Hey, how you doing, British? I can't stop, I have to clean!'

'I see your case on the news,' Crazy Beard said. 'Keep going, boys. You have to fuck these Arabs. Fuck them.'

After spending a few minutes with them we went back to our wing and met up with Ben.

'Hey, man, wanna take a wander?' he said, so I went outside with him to explore my new home. The sun shone down and the heat was intense but there was a hive of activity outside. Inmates were playing football in one area while another load were engaged in a game of basketball. Others were sat on the sandy-coloured concrete playing cards and others were simply lying in the sun.

As I looked across I could see a large rectangular glass fronted building shimmering in the sunlight a couple of hundred yards away. It was an exact replica of the building I was currently living in and contained another sixteen wings. Tinted windows covered the front of each building but the frames were metallic blue.

'So what do you think of Central?' Ben said.

'It's like a dream compared to Port Rashid. We never got any sunlight and we couldn't even smoke.'

'Yeah, mate, you'll be all right here.'

I had been dreading the moment we were going to enter Central Prison but a simple act of kindness in giving Rivas a phone had meant Tariq had been protected by the Russians. Now they were protecting us. In addition, Harry taking Harish under his wing when he thought he was just a humble old man had ensured total loyalty from the same gangsters. Because of what had happened before we had dodged the demons that had seen so many others perish in one of the world's most dangerous jails. We were some of the fortunate few; we were being protected by our own guardian angels.

23

SLEEPOVERS AND TATTOOS

There are many things that I never expected to happen in my life and having a slumber party with Russian Mafia henchmen is definitely one of them.

On our first evening we sat in Tariq's cell eating a delicious dinner of chicken, hummus and salad. While we could get free prison food from the canteen, a special menu was also available for a price. Compared to the slops in the canteen it was like eating in a Michelin-starred restaurant. Food orders came on a daily basis and had to be ordered from a menu a week in advance. It seemed ironic that the convicted gangsters and murderers ate so well, while the inmates in Port Rashid, who hadn't even been charged, were fed food that wasn't fit for a dog.

'Come on, boys, *Lord of the Rings* is on tonight,' Mice said as he put his head around the door. He stared at Tariq and said, 'I kill you!' before walking off.

'Boys, at night-time when there's a good film on we put our mattresses in front of the TV and pass around chocolates and drinks,' Tariq said.

'What, like a massive sleepover?' Harry said.

'Yeah, kind of, but it's with the Russian Mafia.'

We all dragged our mattresses to the TV room and cocooned ourselves in our blankets. Chocolate, Mirinda, which was a fizzy orange drink, and banana milk, were passed round. I felt like I was a teenager having friends over to stay, except these were all cold-blooded killers.

Mice was the reason he and his friends were all in jail, as he had got into a row with a large gang of men. There was a hundred man fight in a square which ended when Mice's friend Zachariah stabbed a man to death. Zachariah, a mountain of a man and leader of the Russians on our wing, said, 'I didn't have any choice. Either I killed him or they killed us.'

Russian mobsters weren't the only dangerous characters on the wing.

'Boys, you have to meet this guy called Raga,' Tariq said the next morning. 'He's one of the most dangerous people you will ever meet. He doesn't look it, but he's proper scary. He's a serial killer who says he murdered fifty-two people. He's number two in the Indian Mafia and a complete nutter.'

'Woah, fucking hell,' Harry said.

'Yeah, mate, come and meet him.'

Tariq took us into his cell and introduced us. Raga was a slight, skinny man with a weasel-like face, big, boggle eyes and an unkempt goatee beard. His buck-toothed appearance didn't suggest he was a dangerous killer. I wouldn't have even looked twice at him on the outside.

'Hello, how are you?' he said in a posh English accent.

I was wary about talking to a man who was capable of murdering so many people so decided to keep my head down, but Harry was fascinated. Raga's case sheet was multiple murders, money laundering, racketeering, prostitution, drug trafficking. He was the epitome of organized crime.

'So what's your case?' Raga asked us and Harry retold our story.

Raga was happy to talk about his crimes. If anything, he was a little too happy. He talked about killing like it was buying a loaf of bread.

'There was one person who stole heroin from me in Afghanistan,' he said to Harry. 'I hung him up and cut his throat to let him bleed. I could not let him get away with what he did. I always used to have a technique when I was younger where I would put the knife in and twist and pull up sideways so it would rip up his insides. It was quite effective.'

He looked excited as he told each story. He explained how he cut off another man's fingers and made him eat them before ending his torment. When I looked in his eyes there was nothing there, no feeling or empathy. He was a cold-blooded sociopath and a calculating killer who would not have thought twice about making one of us victim fifty-three.

He went on, 'I have judges and politicians in my pocket in India. You think they are going to keep me? You are crazy. I will pay rupees and they will let me go. Within two months of going back to India I will be back on the street.'

I had heard enough, and made my excuses when I heard a British accent from down the wing. After that I made sure I kept my distance from Raga. There are some people you should always avoid and he was top of my list.

Harry and I went outside where we saw the owner of the squeaky north London accent, a bald Indian guy.

'This must be the little mugs then,' he said. Ash, who was in his late thirties, had a well-kept grey beard and a belly hanging over his waistband. 'So you're the little mugs who ended up on TV for having some fake cannabis.'

'Yeah,' I said, smiling.

'How'd you get on telly?'

'A human rights charity approached us after they heard about our case.'

'Wicked. I was caught with a load of coke. I was sentenced to death but dodged that bullet. My lawyers got it down to fifteen years.'

Ash, who was from Camden, had accepted his fate. 'Fuck all I can do about it now,' he said. 'Just gotta get on with it.'

Ash had been in Central for six years and was a respected member of the jail community, running the paid-for canteen food. He would come by to deliver menus and take orders. He was standing with a big Bangladeshi guy who had a nineties' curtains haircut and glasses. He was holding a clipboard.

'This is my accountant Mandeep. As you guys came in in the middle of the week you haven't got any food coming, but if you come and see Mandeep at about six o'clock when the food arrives he'll give you something. Just give him a sleeve of cigarettes.'

Mice, Zachariah, his brother Vlad and Ravi came out onto the landing in shorts with black plastic bin liners over their bodies to make them sweat more, with holes cut for their head and arms.

'Get out the way or I kill you,' Mice said jokingly as they walked out.

'What are they doing?' Harry said.

'They train every day, running around until they almost pass out,' Tariq said.

'But it's like 50 degrees out there,' I said.

'I know, they're machines.'

I looked out of the reinforced glass to see them sprinting around. They had filled water bottles with sand and tied them together to make dumbbells. They were really going at it. I was pleased they were on our side.

Tariq had a miniature radio he had bought from the canteen so we went to listen to some music in his cell.

'All right, lads?' Fred – Tariq's cellmate – said as we walked in. His face dropped as we put on the music.

'Keep it down, lads, will ya? You lot laugh like a bunch of hyenas.'

'All right, mate.'

When I met Fred my immediate impression was that he would be a perfect member of the British National Party but he was always okay with us, apart from moaning about the noise we'd make. Even so, I always thought he was holding his tongue.

'So, Fred, are there many black and Asian people where you come from?' I asked one day.

'No, mate. If I was in England, I wouldn't be hanging around with people like you.'

'What do you mean?' I said.

'Well, coloured people.'

We laughed awkwardly but I knew my initial assessment was right.

The first few days in Central had passed quickly and we soon adapted to the routine. Although the jail was full of menacing characters I felt fairly safe because of our association with the Russians. It was calm, but I was still constantly wary that it could kick off.

I had been unable to call Amy for several days as our cards hadn't been activated and we didn't have a mobile phone any more. It was coming up to Faith's first birthday on 18 April and I was missing her even more. My birthday was the day after and I was dreading spending it inside. The chances were that it would be the first of many.

'I've been so worried about you,' Amy said when I called her on a payphone.

'I'm sorry but we were moved jails and I had no way of calling.'

'You know it's Faith's birthday tomorrow?'

'Of course.'

'I'm going to have a little party for her and her friends and then I'm going to take her to your mum's at the weekend for another one. I really wish you were here.'

'I know, me too.'

I was devastated not to be there but there was nothing I could do. I had to stay strong. We had been told by the embassy that our trial would be soon. Our date with destiny was drawing near.

I went for a wander to clear my head and bumped into somebody I recognized straight away. Bobby was walking down the corridor and when we spotted each other we both stopped. My immediate thought was that he would try and get me done over and I'm sure he was worried I'd tell people he was a snitch.

'Hey, man, how you doing?' I said, feeling awkward.

'I'm all right, man, how's your case? I've seen you boys on the news so keep going.'

We made small talk for a couple of minutes before making our excuses and leaving. It was clear we were both wary of each other after everything that had happened before.

On my birthday I woke up and called home again, speaking to my mum as well. I could tell she was upset that I was in jail and not with her but was trying to stay strong for me. Then the Russians came down to say happy birthday.

'Tonight we have a party,' Mice said.

'Ah, thank you, brother, that's real nice of you.'

Later that evening we all met in Harry and Tariq's cell. Zachariah came in with a cake they had made for me despite having no access to an oven. They create this jail delicacy by crushing biscuits to make a base. Then several broken-up Swiss rolls are put on top and melted Nutella on top of that.

'That's really good of you but I can't eat it as it's got nuts in it,' I said.

'What?' Mice said. 'You no like cake?'

'No, I'm allergic to nuts.'

'Why you allergic to nuts?'

'I don't know!' I said. We all burst out laughing.

'We have another treat for you,' Zachariah said as he brought out a couple of plastic water bottles. 'We have brew,' meaning it was home-made hooch. It was the first time I had seen alcohol in months and it tasted like tropical fruit juice.

That night we cranked up the music and partied the night away. I was far away from home and all of the people I cared about most, but getting drunk with the Russian Mafia as we all danced in Tariq and Harry's cell was the perfect antidote to my melancholy state of mind. I spent a lot of time talking to Ben. We were on the same wavelength and he was keen to get into the music industry. He confided in me that he used to be a heroin addict and was hooked on the prescription drugs he was able to get inside.

'Mate, you have to get off that shit,' I said.

'I know, but it's not that easy.'

'Look, I will be your sponsor. If you ever have urges, come and find me. You can do this.'

We became good friends and would go for a walk every morning and hang out all day. He told me that the only reason he was inside at all was because his dad was trying to teach him a lesson.

'I know my old man is going to get me out,' he said, 'he's just trying to punish me as I've been in and out of rehab for years. He sent me to rehab in Dubai to fix my drug problem but I ended up meeting somebody there who knew how to get hold of heroin. That guy snitched on me and I was arrested. My dad was pretty pissed at me, but when he's calmed down he'll get me out.'

If he was right, it was just another example of *wasta* being more important than the law.

Mice came in a couple of days later and proudly proffered his arm. 'Look! Tattoo!' he said. The awful artwork of a badly drawn fist surrounded in barbed wire looked infected.

'Okay, mate, nice one,' Harry said.

'Come to the HIV wing later and we get you a nice tattoo!' He could probably see from our faces we didn't think that was a great idea. 'It's okay, you no catch HIV,' he added.

The tattooists used a beard trimmer to print the skin, and had one for those with HIV and another for those who weren't infected. As they had no ink they used rubber from the edge of the football pitch, which melted in the sun.

'I think I'll pass on that to be honest, mate,' Harry said.

Mice looked like he was going to argue but the moment was broken when three Russians I hadn't seen before walked onto the wing.

'Fuck me, bruv, that's Akrim,' Tariq said.

Akrim was a tall, muscle-bound, shaven-headed Russian in his late thirties with olive skin. He was wearing sunglasses and walked with the air of confidence of a man who was in control. Akrim, who was flanked by two massive henchmen covered in tattoos, went into Mice's cell. Moments later Harish came out to see us. I hadn't seen much of him since we had arrived at Central.

'I'm going to be moving into the other Russians' wing and I will be staying in Akrim's room,' he announced.

Although it was clear how revered Harish was by the Russians, it was only now that we realized what a huge player he must be.

Nobody shared Akrim's cell with him. He was king of Central. But our little friend was so important that he was being invited to share his cell.

'That's great, mate,' Harry said.

'Those boys have lots of connections so if you need anything come and see me. Actually, let me settle in and all of you come over and have dinner at some point.'

We had been invited to eat at the top table and we gratefully accepted.

While outwardly we were coping, inside I was struggling to hold it together as our trial was looming. I was grateful of my morning walks with Ben as I found it difficult to speak to Harry and Tariq about it as we were all in a pretty dark place.

'I'm not sure I can do this, bruv,' I said to Ben. 'If I'm convicted of trafficking and sentenced to twenty-five years, there's no way I'm going to be here. I'll have to end it.'

'Come on, mate, be positive,' Ben said. 'You're helping me achieve something I never thought I could do in getting off the drugs. Whatever happens you can do this.'

'I'd honestly rather kill myself than be here for the rest of my life.'

'I know you're stronger than that. You've helped me, Karl, I'm going to help you through this.'

I was grateful of his support but I had my doubts. It would be easier to take the coward's way out. A lifetime in Central was no life.

We hadn't heard from Marc in a while so I called him from the payphone.

'Hey, Karl, how are you getting on?'

'We're in Central now and we've been told we're going to court soon. Hopefully we can get sentenced before Ramadan.'

I realized there was little chance of us getting off the possession charge, as the drugs had been found in our hire car and that was enough – it seemed the prosecution didn't need to prove it was ours. But if we were cleared of the more serious charges against us then there was a chance we would be sentenced to the minimum term of four years. That would mean, according to the Dubai legal system, we would get a pardon at Ramadan and be sent home.

'The lawyers are saying that your case is looking good as there is literally no evidence against you. When you go to court you won't understand what's going on and you won't get to give evidence. They will just use your statement about your torture while the police will use the ones you gave after you were arrested.'

'Okay. Is there much happening with the media?'

'Yes, we are going to have a media push before your trial and we are going to try to get the BBC to cover the court case.'

I thanked him and hung up.

It was terrifying enough knowing that our court appearance would decide whether we were going to spend twenty-five years in jail or face a firing squad. Knowing that the media would be there covering every word was an added pressure. There had been some articles in the Dubai press calling us liars and branding us drug dealers and I was concerned about what would be written about us.

I went for a walk with Tariq and Harry in an attempt to clear our heads. We spotted a familiar face in the distance through the fence in Building 2 walking along a pathway.

'Shit, is that Mohammed?' I said.

'Fucking hell, it is!' Harry said excitedly.

'Mohammed! Mohammed!' We all shouted.

Our old friend's face lit up. 'Oh, my British drug dealer friends!' he shouted as he ran towards the fence. 'How are you?'

'We're good, mate.'

'So you like Central?'

'It's pretty good, man,' Harry said. 'We can eat what we want, smoke when we want and we don't have to swap Mayfair for it.'

'You must always bargain, though, my friends. Hey, you should all come over here to Building 2. Over here I'm big drug dealer, I run the place.'

We were all laughing at our crazy Arab friend. The lightening of the mood was exactly what we needed.

'Thanks, Mohammed, but we're happy where we are,' I said. 'It's all right here.'

'Okay, but if you guys ever wanna spend time with a real drug dealer you know where to come.'

It was typical Mohammed. We were with some of the most serious criminals in Dubai yet he was still insistent he was the biggest drug dealer in the place. We said our goodbyes, grateful that Mohammed had distracted us from our dark thoughts for a few minutes.

The next day we heard our names called over the loud speaker system. Harry, Tariq and I walked to the bubble and a guard opened the glass and said, 'Your embassy is here to see you. Wait here and guards will come and get you.'

Two officers came into the reception, handcuffed us and led us to a visitation area near Building 2. We were led into a visitation building to wait. It was like a different world. Paintings of flowers were on the wall and there were comfortable armchairs for us to sit in. It was clear the authorities wanted visitors to believe people were well looked after in Central.

I glanced out of the window and saw Bill, the club promoter

and my old mate from Dubai, being led across the courtyard. He looked wide-eyed and kept trying to walk off in random directions even though he was handcuffed to the guard. It looked like a comedy sketch but I could tell something was wrong. He was brought into the room with us.

'Bill, what's happened to you, man? Are you okay?'

'Yeah, I'm okay. I just keep having these bad dreams.'

'What do you mean?'

'It's all in the dreams, they keep talking to me in my dreams.'

He started pulling his pants down and the guard was going crazy at him.

'Keep it together, Bill, man, you're gonna be out soon,' I said.

'Yeah, I know. I'm going home soon.'

He was meant to see representatives from the embassy but the guard had had enough and pulled him away, with Bill trying to pull down his pants as he went.

'What the fuck has happened to him?' I asked.

'I forgot to tell you,' Tariq said. 'He was doing loads of drugs, running up loads of debts with people. He was running around naked, asking people to fuck him and crawling around like a dog. He lost it completely, man.'

Bill was a victim in the starkest form of the Dubai system. He had completely lost his mind and the cops didn't get him treatment, but put him in solitary instead.

We were called into the office where Mandy was waiting.

'Hi, guys, I've got some progress on your case.'

'Oh yeah? Progress, yeah?' Tariq said, laughing.

'We've had a letter from the Dubai authorities.'

She handed it over. It said, 'After reviewing the pictures of your injuries and after further investigations we have decided not to look into your claims of torture as we believe them to be untrue.'

'You call this progress?' I said. 'All they've done is illegally question me. This bit about pictures is a lie as they didn't take any. If they took photos, there wouldn't have been the need for an investigation as they would've seen the evidence themselves.'

'Call this fucking progress?' Tariq said. 'It's more like a kick in the teeth. I've had it with you embassy lot coming down and talking rubbish the whole time. Guards! Get us out of here.'

'I can send another letter if you like?' she said.

That was it. We demanded to leave. We were fuming. The Dubai authorities were trying to sweep everything under the carpet after another pack of lies.

'I can't fucking believe this,' Harry said. 'The lying cunts.'

'Let's call Marc as soon as we get back and see what he's got to say.'

'This is perfect, boys!' Marc said when I got him on the phone. 'This is what we wanted. This proves they were liars. There were never any pictures taken and there was no proper investigation. It shows they're scared of conducting an investigation as they know we'll catch them out.

I was amazed but delighted by Marc's reaction. What had seemed like a kick in the teeth could actually go in our favour.

'Look, it's good that you've called as we've just heard that your trial is going to be in a week's time. Stay strong, I am confident that it's going to be okay.'

I was terrified. It was the news we had been waiting for but the news we were also dreading. We had been in limbo for months but now we had to face a horrific reality.

I went and told Harry and Tariq.

'Fuck, man, here we go,' Harry said, a look of fear crossing his face.

'Nah, man, this is cool!' Tariq said. 'You never know, we might be allowed to go home.'

'Fuck off!' Harry said. 'That's never gonna happen.'

I thought Harry was right and we had to wait a long week until our trial.

We all dealt with the pressure differently. I would get up early and would go walking with Ben while Tariq and Harry spent a lot of time in their cell.

'How are you feeling, man?' Ben asked the day before.

'I'm scared, man. I know I'm innocent but that doesn't count for shit.'

'It's all right, man, you'll be okay.'

I know he was just trying to make me feel better but nobody could know what was going to happen. The night before I lay awake thinking about the life I would have if I got out, and about the horrific prospect of spending the rest of my life in a Dubai prison. The latter didn't bear thinking about.

The following day we were called to the bubble, along with Mice and his pals. We were on our way to trial. Wearing our prison uniform, we were taken through the tunnel and out into a large police van with several other prisoners. The Russians going to court that day were led into their own police van and accompanied by an armed escort of two police cars. The cops weren't taking any chances when transferring the Russian Mafia. When we arrived at court the Russians were given their own cell while we were with the other random suspects.

Tariq, Harry and I sat reflecting on what was about to happen to us. Our future would soon be decided and I felt like I was going to puke.

A couple of the Arabs had cigarettes but nothing to spark them with so one had the idea to try and dismantle a light fixing and use the live wire. We all laughed at their desperate attempt. It was one humorous moment in two hours of waiting.

When we were called we were led up a flight of stairs and into the courtroom which was rammed full. Rows of journalists were sat staring at us, writing notes in their pads. Zain and Ross were sat in court to support us. Tariq's sister and Harry's mum and brother were also there. I looked across and nodded at them before the judge walked in. We were put in the dock with two guards wearing black uniforms standing behind us. The room was cool but I felt like I was burning up, sweat running down my back. We were asked to confirm our names and asked how we were pleading. We all said not guilty.

For fifteen minutes our legal teams and the prosecution spoke to the judge in Arabic. We had no idea what was going on. Eventually we were led back into the holding cell before heading back to Central. Once there I called Ross to see if he had managed to speak to the legal team.

He said, 'They were just talking about the charges but in a couple of days the officers will be giving evidence.'

'Okay, thanks bruv.'

Those two days were among the hardest I experienced in jail. We were all quiet and nobody wanted to say anything. Even the normally jovial Russians were stony-faced. Tension hung in the air.

We repeated the process two days later and found ourselves in the dock again. The witnesses were called and Ferrari cop walked into the box.

'That's the one!' Tariq screamed. 'That's the one who beat me. That's the one who tortured me.'

'Quiet! Quiet!' Tariq's lawyer said, trying to calm my friend down as a guard came over and grabbed hold of him.

'Calm down!' the guard shouted, but Tariq was going crazy.

'Mate, calm the fuck down,' I said. 'You're making things worse.'

He seemed to finally take notice and kept quiet.

Ferrari cop was standing in the witness box the whole time looking worried. He spoke for a few minutes before leaving the courtroom.

After that we were taken back into the holding cell. 'What was going on, man?' said an Egyptian guy who had been in our van from Central. 'I could hear shouting.'

'We saw one of the cops who tortured us and Tariq went crazy.' We all laughed. It wasn't particularly funny but in our state of extreme stress it appeared to us a moment of dark humour.

When we got back we found our faces plastered across the BBC. 'Today the British prisoners were on trial for allegedly trafficking synthetic cannabis, called spice, into Dubai,' the report said.

We were desperate to talk to our legal teams and find out what had happened. I went to use the phone to call my lawyer, who I still hadn't spoken to, but when I picked up the handset it was dead.

I went up to Sofian to ask him what was going on.

'Mate, I don't know, but these phones have never gone down.'

'Fuck, we need to speak to our lawyers as we'll find out our verdicts tomorrow.'

'Man, this must be because of your case. They don't want you using the phones. Your case is a big deal here. This has never happened in Dubai before. Nobody's ever stood up to them the way you boys have. You have to be careful as some very powerful people want you to be quiet.'

Even in the most serious of times we still managed to have a laugh. We knew there would be a big press pack in court the next day so Tariq and I devised a plan for a bit of fun.

'I'm gonna faint in court and see if the press report it,' I said.

'Yeah go on, that would be sick, bruv. Let me see what you can do.'

I dragged my mattress into the hall and fell onto it several times. Tariq was giving me marks out of ten while Harry sat on his bed, unimpressed by our antics.

'Will you two please grow up and stop being such immature pricks?'

'Come on, bruv, it's just a laugh,' I said.

I had to do something to keep me sane.

It was the middle of the night before the phones came back on. I called Amy and she was being so supportive. She was my rock.

'Don't worry, you're going to be home soon in my arms. And I've got some news. Faith's taken her first steps.'

A big smile spread across my face. 'That's amazing! I miss you both so much.'

'Look, you have to stay strong. You will be home soon.'

I went to bed and lay there thinking about tomorrow. It was one of the most important days of my life and I had no control over what would happen to me. My friends' destiny and mine was in the hand of a judge and I could only hope that he would give us the justice we deserved. I fell asleep praying for freedom and for our nightmare to finally be over.

24

EXPECTING THE WORST, HOPING FOR THE BEST

The night before we were sentenced I had a dream of freedom. Harry and I were riding on huge bumblebees and we were trying to catch an Emirates airline plane. We managed to cling onto the wing, and as we flew over Wanstead I turned to Harry and said, 'It's time now, mate.' We parachuted off as we flew over my mum's house, landing on the conservatory roof.

'Boys, I think we're gonna be all right,' I said to my friends the next morning.

'What are you talking about?' Harry said quizzically.

'I had this mad dream that we were flying on bumblebees to freedom.'

'Mate, we need more than silly dreams for us to get out of this place.'

'Yeah, shut up, mate,' Tariq said.

My friends' reaction was fair enough. We were all stressed about the day ahead and in a sombre mood.

Realistically our best-case scenario was to get cleared of the more serious charges of trafficking and intent to supply and be sentenced to the minimum sentence of four years with deportation.

But knowing how annoyed the authorities were about the amount of noise we had made, I feared the worst.

As we walked off the wing our faces appeared on BBC News.

'Three English men will today appear in court to hear their verdicts on drug trafficking charges in Dubai,' the newsreader said. We stood stunned, watching the TV, as people on our wing started to cheer.

We were taken through the same process to get out of Central and driven across Dubai to court. I tried to hold it together as I thought about my little girl.

We were called into court and made our way into the dock. I looked across and saw Ross and Zain who nodded at me. The press gallery was rammed with reporters and there wasn't a seat free in the court. We confirmed our names before the judge spoke for two minutes in Arabic. The court was air-conditioned but I was drenched in sweat. I couldn't stand still and started twitching.

I whispered to Tariq, 'I'm gonna faint.'

'Yeah, bruv, do it.'

'Will you two shut up?' Harry hissed.

'Go on, do it, Ceaze, faint.'

'You are not going to faint!' Harry said through gritted teeth.

I was stood in the middle with an angel on one side telling me to behave and a devil on the other. By the time they had stopped bickering the judge had finished speaking and we had no idea what had just happened. I looked across at Ross and he had a big smile on his face. I didn't understand what there was to smile about. We were seriously expecting the worst and hoping for the best.

One of the guards behind us said, 'Come, you go now.'

'Wait, what did they say?'

'You go home Ramadan.'

'What?'

'Yes, four years, deport, go.'

Relief flooded through my body. I have never felt so elated in my whole life. We had taken on the system and won. We had been cleared of all of the most serious charges against us because of a lack of evidence and we were going home! All three of us hugged and squeezed each other tight.

'Yes! We're getting out of here, boys!' I said.

'Yaaaaaaar!' Tariq screamed.

'Yes, we're fucking going home, mate,' Harry shouted.

'You're gonna get to see your baby girl, bruv,' Tariq said.

'I know, bruv, I can't believe it.'

We walked down to the holding cells screaming in delight, but stopped when we remembered there were murderers waiting to get into court who would be handed the death penalty.

I had been preparing myself for a sentence of at least ten years in jail, so although being found guilty of possession was an injustice, all we cared about was getting out of jail and going home. We had already lost nine months of our lives for something we didn't do.

When we returned to Central we were greeted like conquering heroes. We had stood up to the authorities and had won.

'You're going home!' Zachariah said as he shook our hand. 'You're all over the news.'

We could hear the BBC journalist on the TV reporting that we had been sentenced to four years.

'You fucked the system,' Sofian said. 'Fuck them!'

I called Ross and then Amy who was elated.

'I've heard the news!' she squealed down the phone. 'I'm so happy. Do you know when you'll be coming home?'

'No, not yet. We should be going home during Ramadan in a couple of months as that's when the sheikh issues pardons for people sentenced to four years.'

'That's great news I can't wait to have you home and for Faith to see her daddy again.'

'I can't wait either.'

I called Reprieve and spoke to Kate. 'I want to thank you so much for everything you've done for us,' I said.

'No, don't thank me yet, you're not home.'

'Yes, but we were facing the death penalty and got a sentence of four years after all of the exposure you got us. I definitely think I need to thank you. If it wasn't for you and Marc, we could have been stuck here forever as our case would never have been highlighted and they could so easily have screwed us.'

'This is the first step. We need to make sure those people who did this to you are held to account. We're thinking about doing another media push, getting your brother Alex and Tariq and Harry's family to go on the sofa on *Daybreak* to try and put a bit more pressure on them to get you home as soon as possible.'

'Okay, that's great, and thank you again, Kate.'

When I finished the calls it was time to celebrate. We were playing music in our cell and dancing to songs on the radio. Favourites were 'Come & Get It' by Selena Gomez and Macklemore's 'Can't Hold Us'. The sentiment behind the last song couldn't be more fitting.

Fred was irritated by our high spirits and I don't think he was very happy that we had been given the chance of going home.

'You lot need to get out of here when you're smoking,' he moaned.

'Nah, mate, I was in this cell before you so don't sit here and tell me I can't smoke in my own cell,' Tariq said.

'Fucking pricks,' he said as he stormed off.

Nothing was going to dampen our spirits. The Russians, Ben and Sofian all joined us for a party. Our worst nightmares hadn't materialized. We would be free men soon.

The next day Alex appeared on the breakfast programme *Day-break* with Tariq's sister Davina. They spoke about how we had been tortured and demanded an investigation into the treatment we had suffered. David Cameron was due to meet His Highness Sheikh Khalifa bin Zayed Al Nahyan, the Dubai leader, at 10 Downing Street a few days after their appearance, so Davina used the programme to urge the prime minister to speak to him about our case and try to get clemency for us.

What was even better for us, and a stroke of genius by Kate in terms of timing, was that David Cameron was due on *Daybreak* the following morning. This allowed the presenters to ask him about our case and what he was doing about it. The question came as a surprise to the prime minister as it wasn't on the list of things he had been told he would be asked.

Mr Cameron said, 'What we've said, and the point I will make today, is that we think there needs to be a proper, independent investigation into these allegations of what happened.'

The noise was rising and we were hopeful we would be released soon. I called Kate, who said, 'This is really good for your case as now Cameron *has* to say something to the sheikh. Hopefully it will mean the sheikh feels he has to do something about you and let you go.'

Kate wanted to do more media pushes but when I spoke about it to Harry and Tariq, we realized we were concerned speaking out more could affect our chances of freedom. Although those who get four years are normally given a pardon by the sheikh, we didn't want to annoy the authorities so much that they refused to let us out. Much as we wanted the police officers who tortured us to be prosecuted, we'd prefer it to happen when we were in the safety of our own homes. I called Kate again to tell her this.

'Okay, I understand,' she said, 'don't worry about it. We won't do any more media until we know if you're on the pardon list.'

We also heard the news that Port Rashid, the place where we had spent the vast majority of our incarceration in Dubai, had finally been closed. Obviously the inmates' paint job hadn't been enough to disguise the squalid state of the place and the authorities had closed it down before the human rights inspectors could get in there.

Even though we had been in the system for several months, once we had been sentenced we had to go into quarantine to make sure we didn't have any contagious diseases before being moved to the sentenced side of Central. We had been told that quarantine was one of the worst experiences of jail in Dubai, as it was where inmates with infections were kept. We packed extra T-shirts and trousers, as it was bitterly cold in the segregated building. They apparently kept the temperature so low so that germs don't get spread.

'Fuck, man, there are people in there with TB and that's properly contagious,' Harry said.

We were all worried. We had already given up nine months of our lives to this hellhole, we didn't want to get a serious illness as well. Two guards from the quarantine police came to get us and led us across the courtyard and into a small building with ten cells. As we walked in we saw three people wearing surgical masks.

'Fuck, they must be the ones with TB,' Tariq said.

'I'm gonna call home and find out if our BCG vaccinations will stop us from catching it,' Harry said.

We were all in our new prison outfits, which had a yellow stripe across the middle that signified we were sentenced to four years. To me the yellow stripe was a symbol that we would be going home. It also showed we had fucked the system. Those with a green stripe were sentenced to two years or less, blue was up to ten years and red was those unlucky enough to be in Central for more than ten years.

We walked into the dining area to see a large window at the end. Through the glass I could see several very effeminate-looking men. The ladyboys were kept in a separate section as they would have been raped in two minutes in the main Central jail.

We spent three miserable, tedious days in quarantine, staying in our cell almost the whole time. There was no television and no interaction with the other inmates. When we were released back into the main jail, some of Tariq's mates from the sentenced side came to see us. Mareed, a stocky Indian guy, who was Bill's case partner for dealing spice, Nada, a bald-headed Indian with a big pot belly and a long beard, and Andy, a South African in for twenty-five years for smuggling cocaine in his stomach came across.

'Well done, man, we're so happy for you,' Andy said, in a South African accent.

I felt quite humble. 'How is it that you can be so happy for us when you have a red stripe and we have a yellow?' I said.

'It's because we can see you going home is a step closer to us going home. We can feel your energy and the way you have all fucked the system. It has given us all hope.'

This was pretty deep and made me realize what we had done in taking on the authorities had made a difference to a lot of people. Over the next few days prisoners I didn't even know would come up to me and say, 'Thank you for helping us.'

'How did I help you?' I would ask.

'Because of you we are going to get a fair trial now.'

It made me feel like the year inside hadn't been for nothing. We had at least given others hope.

'Look, boys,' Sofian said, 'you're going to have to find yourselves a bed on the sentenced side. The guards are pressurizing me to move you.'

We knew this was the system in Central so we went to see Ash. 'You boys can come onto my wing if you like. It'll be a pleasure to have some more Brits about,' he said.

We went up to where he was living. It was immaculately clean and quiet as a church. All of the prisoners were in for over fifteen years so just wanted to have a quiet life.

'Wait, Ash, we can't stay here, mate,' Harry said.

'Nah, it's good, it's nice,' he said.

'Mate, we're just gonna make too much noise for you lot.'

'Why, what you all doing? Fucking?'

'Nah, we just laugh loud and piss about all the time,' Harry said.

'And you don't want us with a bunch of lifers. We're going home Ramadan so it'll be like rubbing your faces in it,' I added.

'Fair dos, boys, so what you gonna do then?'

'We could try and stay on our old wing, I suppose,' Tariq said.

'I tell you what,' Ash said. 'I'll come down and have a word with the Russians for you.'

We all walked back to our old wing and went to see Zachariah and Mice, who were happy for us to stay and came with us to see Sofian and plead our case.

'Look, I don't mind you staying and can speak to the guards about it, but promise me there will be no trouble. Tariq, you promise me?'

'God's honest, bruv, no trouble.'

We were delighted. We were comfortable and didn't want to move. The only downside was some of Harry and Tariq's stuff had gone missing when they were in quarantine so they asked me to keep their things in my room.

It was while we were at Central that we learned of another bizarre foible of the Dubai justice system. If you could learn and recite ten sections of the Qur'an off by heart you would be freed. This was ridiculously hard to do as you had to get it word perfect and very few tried and passed. It was just another crazy aspect of Dubai's messed-up system.

The first signs that the Dubai authorities weren't willing to roll over and let us go home came a few days later in May. I was called to the bubble where a police officer was waiting for me.

'You British, come, let's go, let's go.'

'Where am I going?'

'Come, there are some men who want to speak to you.'

I didn't like the sound of this and turned on my heel and ran back to my wing. 'Tariq! Harry! The police are trying to take me out for another illegal questioning. Call Marc and Kate.'

The next moment the police officer came walking onto the wing. 'You stupid?' the officer shouted. 'Why you running?'

'I had to come back and make a phone call.'

'Okay, I understand,' he said. 'So you're the British from the news, yeah? What happened to you was a disgrace. Stay true to your cause.'

It reinforced my opinion that not all of Dubai's police officers are bad.

I was led across the prison to an office where I was told to sit down. Two generals in cream suits with stars and eagles on their lapels walked in. One sat down and the other leant on the desk.

The officer who was standing up said, 'So, all this beating and all this stuff that happened to you? Why don't you just forget about it and you go home? Ramadan is soon and *inshallah* you go home.'

'Can I have a phone call?' I asked.

'No, no need for phone call.'

'You know this is illegal? You are questioning me without a lawyer or my embassy. Can I go now, please?'

'You sure you want to go? Are you sure you want to make things hard?'

'No, I don't want things to be difficult for me, but I have to do this properly as the last time I was with the prosecutor he said a whole heap of lies. This time I want to make sure things are done properly.'

'Okay, no problem, enjoy your stay in Central.'

I walked back to my wing and told Tariq and Harry what had happened.

'Fucking hell, mate, why do they keep taking you?' Harry said.

'I don't know, mate.'

'So what did you say? Did you say we'd drop the case?' Tariq said.

'No, I said what they were doing was illegal.'

'Mate, we don't want to be pissing them off,' Harry said. 'I want to go home at Ramadan. You should've just said you'd drop the allegations.'

'Mate, there's no way I'm even thinking about that.'

'Come on, think about Faith,' Harry said. 'Don't you want to see your little girl?'

'Yeah, I do but at the same time what they did was wrong.'

The whole episode was a massive concern. It just showed that they weren't finished with us and were going to make our lives as difficult as possible. But no matter what they said to me I wasn't willing to give up after everything we had been through. It was a matter of principle even more important than my freedom.

Alfonso the Filipino guy was always moaning at me when I ate my food in Tariq and Harry's cell. For the most part I ignored his whining as I felt quite sorry for him. He was a lonely old man whose one form of communication with the outside world was to write letters to the prosecutor. He would never let anyone see what he was writing.

On one occasion I was outside the cell looking in and saw the top few lines of the letter. It said, 'I didn't kill the woman found in my boot. She was a whore. She was having sex with me all of the time and was trying to bribe me and get money out of me but I refused to pay and when I refused to pay her she jumped off the building and stabbed herself.'

This man was clearly messed up. When I told Tariq and Harry they burst out laughing. Tariq said that the true story was that he stabbed his victim, threw her off a building and put her in the boot of his car. The car alarm went off so security came and found her.

A couple of days after the generals' visit I was eating dinner in Tariq's cell and put my plate in the sink. I had been pretty lazy with the washing-up and had swerved the chores by saying I was a guest. When I left my dish again it wasn't a great surprise when Alfonso started moaning at me.

'You fuck! Why don't you ever clean your dishes?'

'Look, I'm waiting for everyone to finish and then it's my turn to wash everyone's plates.'

'You aren't a guest anymore so get your arse in there and wash up. Clean those fucking dishes.'

'Alfonso, man, I'm a guest,' I said jokingly.

'Fuck you, man,'

'Alfonso, I'm only joking. I'm just waiting for everyone to finish.'

'No, you fucking do it now!' he screamed at the top of his lungs. 'You fucking black shit!'

The whole room went silent. Harry looked at me and said, 'No,' as he knew I was about to lose it.

I felt a sudden burst of rage. My immediate thoughts were to attack him, but I realized I couldn't as he was an old man. I looked at him, gritting my teeth, and said, 'Something has to happen.'

I got up and kicked a table Alfonso was making out of bread and water papier mâché. It flew against the bars and made a highpitched ringing sound. It tumbled to the floor with a huge dent in it. Alfonso ran out of the room and came back with Sofian who was swiftly followed by the Russians.

'This boy, Karl, he kicked and broke my table I made for the mosque,' Alfonso shouted.

'What did you do this for?' Zachariah said.

'He was racist so I could have either kicked him or kicked the table,' I said. 'He's an old man so I kicked his table.'

'What is this racist?' Zachariah asked with a perplexed look on his face.

'Let's say I called you Russian scumbag, said that Russian women are only good for prostitution, this is not good, right?'

'Yes, yes, this not good.'

'This man said the same sort of thing to me.'

'This old man is crazy. He said the woman stabbed herself while jumping off the building. You pay attention to this, man?'

Sofian had heard enough. 'Tariq, come here!' He dragged him out of the cell. 'I told you, any trouble and you have to leave.'

'Come on, Sofian, man, this was Alfonso's fault.'

He turned to me again. 'Why you do this? I told you boys no trouble and you go and do this.'

'I'm sorry,' I said. 'But where I come from we don't tolerate racism.'

'You all must leave.'

'No, Sofian, it's not my friends' fault. Let them stay and I will go.'

'Okay, you're a good man. You cannot live on this wing anymore but you can come back here whenever you want, you can come and eat here no problem. I have to show some kind of authority.'

I went to see the Russians and apologized. They didn't want me to leave but I insisted, as I knew I couldn't go against Sofian's authority. I collected my stuff together and took it with me to Tariq's room.

'Look, let's go over to the other side and see if you can stay with Nada and those boys,' Tariq said.

We walked over to B3 and Tariq explained to Nada what had happened.

'Of course you can stay with us, dude,' he said. 'You're all right. Just look out for Dawood,' he said, pointing at a tall Petan Pakistani. 'He's a bit fruity.'

Dawood, who was sitting on the top bunk, laughed. 'Fuck off, no I'm not.'

'I'm only joking, dude. Karl, you're gonna have fun here. We play a lot of poker and we'll teach you some of the Indian games.'

This sounded like my kind of place. I was gutted to have been kicked off the wing with Tariq and Harry, but I was lucky enough to be helped out by a genuinely good bunch of people. If things went our way, we would be going home soon and the incident with Alfonso would pale into insignificance. Despite the cops' final efforts to fuck us, I felt like I was on the edge of a new dawn in my life. Nothing was going to ruin my new-found optimism and the belief that I would soon have my little girl in my arms.

25

GOING HOME

Moving wing was like a breath of fresh air. I loved Harry and Tariq like brothers but spending too much time with anybody can become unhealthy. They never really liked getting out and about from their wing and I found it quite restrictive. Central Prison was huge and I didn't see the point in staying in one place.

I was extremely grateful to Nada for letting me stay in his cell, especially as it was already full to capacity when I arrived. Mareed, Dawood and Nada were living in the cell with Bruffin, a small Bangladeshi guy who made clothes out of bed sheets, Bowman, an Iranian in his forties who was jailed after he fell asleep on a bench while smoking marijuana, and Ali, a bald Pakistani guy who had long fangs and looked a bit like Dracula. As well as those six, a tall, light-skinned Pakistani who spoke perfect Queen's English called Dabir would always come by and stay in our cell.

Nada offered me his bed and said he would sleep on a mattress on the floor and I gratefully accepted.

The wing was made up of people like ourselves on shorter sentences and the older bosses. There were only about ten bosses in the entire jail, and we had three on our wing. Señor Gonzales was the main man. He was an Arab but looked more like a Mexican. He always wore aviator sunglasses and had thick black greased-back hair. He was on a twenty-five-year sentence for drug trafficking, was a gangland boss and was one of the friendliest people you could meet.

I was playing poker in my cell with Dabir one day when Señor Gonzales walked in.

'You play poker? We play game?'

'Yeah, man, no problem.'

'I get the Iranians and we play.'

It may not seem like a great idea to be playing poker with gangland bosses and drug traffickers, but I never felt uncomfortable with them. Prison is a great leveller and I got on with them all.

'I fuck lots of women if I come to England?' Señor Gonzales said one session.

'Yeah, mate, the English birds will be falling over themselves to get to you,' I lied.

'Good, good, me want to fuck.'

As well as poker there was always music blaring out down the wing. While a riot had been going on Salim, the rapist, had ripped out a speaker from the public address system. It had been wired into a Qur'an reader – a device that you could play the Qur'an on – and Salim had now put it inside a water drum to make it even louder. The music came from an iPod that belonged to the Russian Mafia on Akrim's wing. I would often go over and borrow it from them and parties would rage all night.

Other times I would go onto Akrim's wing to see our old friend Harish and play backgammon. Akrim was always polite to me, nodding to me as I came in the room, but I knew he could have snuffed out my life in seconds. A Mafia boss on the outside, he had been convicted of murder after he rescued fifty Russian call girls from an Arab gang of sex traffickers. He freed them all and gave them their passports back but had killed a man in the process.

I made sure I still kept in touch with Harry and Tariq, going to see them every couple of days, but whenever I was there they would just sit on their beds and read. I constantly invited them over for a game of poker and, despite saying they would come, they never did. After a while I gave up going across as there is only so much effort you can put in when you're getting nothing back. I understood it was my fault I had been kicked off the wing, but I had thought they would at least come and see me. We were in a dangerous jail and I was effectively by myself. I felt like they had abandoned me to a certain extent.

I was in the cell with Nada and Mareed one day, playing poker, when the subject of Bill came up. It turned out Bill had snitched on Mareed after the former DJ had been caught selling spice. Mareed was given ten years for Bill's betrayal.

'Yeah, man, Bill's a snitch but he didn't deserve what he got,' Mareed said.

'What did he get?'

'He went properly mad.'

'Yeah, I know, I saw him.'

'Well, he was going round nicking people's slippers when they were praying and would start to strip off. He'd walk around on all fours, barking like a dog. One time he stripped off and came into the cell and started trying to lap dance with everyone. He was asking people to fuck him and wouldn't stop.'

Nada was good friends with Bill, and they used to buy the prescription drugs that sent Bill mad from an Iranian enforcer called Hassan on Akrim's wing. As there was no money in Central you would have to pay for things like drugs by giving items bought from the canteen. Bill had built up a huge debt before he had been whisked away to solitary, and the Iranian enforcer was determined someone was going to stump up his cash.

I was in my cell with Nada, sitting opposite him on our beds, chatting about raves in Bali, when Hassan came into the room. He was six foot five, stocky and rippling with muscle. His head was bald and he had a long black beard.

'I want my money!' he said.

'Hey, dude, I told you I haven't got it. You know Bill was the one who owed the money.'

'You and Bill are friends. You used to buy the drugs together. Bill's not here so you have to pay the debt. I know you did half the drugs.'

'Look, dude, you need to give me more time. I haven't got it.'

'No, no more time.'

'Fuck, dude.'

'You say fuck!' Hassan spat. He looked furious. The next second he dragged Nada off the bed and my friend curled into a ball on the floor. Hassan started to beat the life out of him, punching him repeatedly in the face and chest.

I stood up ready to help before realizing this was not a fight I should get involved with. I felt guilty, but Hassan was a player and was on Akrim's wing. If I was to get involved and beat this guy up, he could come back with some even more serious characters and there would be nothing I could do to stop both of us being killed.

After Nada had received his beating he lay groaning on the floor.

'Mate, I'm sorry, man,' I said, 'I was gonna help you out . . .'

'No dude, I'm glad you didn't. If we'd beaten that guy up, we would've had serious trouble.'

Two days later I was in the TV room with Nada and Mareed when we heard a commotion coming from Akrim's wing. We looked across and saw Hassan having a heated argument with an Arab. Hassan went to punch him but the Arab ducked as he produced a home-made knife from his sleeve and stabbed Hassan in the armpit.

'Fuck!' I shouted. 'Look at that!'

The others turned around and we watched the carnage unfold as the jail alarm sounded. Hassan fell to his knees and what happened next was like a pack of wolves ripping apart their prey. He was set upon by a group of Arab men stabbing him repeatedly as he lay on the floor. Others stamped on his head. It was an assassination; there was no way he could survive. Within three minutes there were fifty inmates, all armed with spears and knives, beating and stabbing each other. One had part of a metal girder sharpened down. It was solid rusty metal crafted into a deadly blade. Others were using broom handles and some were trying to break the glass to get out an extinguisher.

The fight made its way up the stairs and our view was blocked. We quickly ran up to our wing to get a better vantage point. Moments later, a group of fifteen Russians, including Mice and Ravi from Harry's wing, ran into the battle zone. They had small knives protruding through their knuckles with a piece of cloth attached and wrapped around their wrists. They ran into the wing and swept the opposition aside. It was like an unstoppable force, a tidal wave cutting its way through the enemy. The second their blades cut someone it was like a small explosion of spurted blood. I saw men get stabbed in the neck and others get sliced down their faces. One guy was being throttled by one attacker as another elbowed the victim in the face. Blood splattered every surface as prisoner after prisoner was sliced.

The carnage eventually abated with a death toll of three and dozens of casualties. The only response from the police during the entire riot was to put on the alarm. Officers only entered the jail when the paramedics arrived to carry away the bodies.

'Fucking hell, can you believe that?' I said.

'I know, dude,' Nada said. 'Two days ago he was in my cell beating me up and today he's being carried off in a body bag.'

'The world works in mysterious ways, my friend.'

The jail went into lockdown for three days and we were only allowed out of our wing to get food.

The day after the riot I saw the main captain of the jail, who I recognized as one of the men who had questioned me weeks before, speaking to Akrim as they walked across the courtyard. It was the Russian Mafia boss's job to maintain control and he was being read the riot act. It turned out Hassan had attacked another guy on the same day he attacked Nada. A group set out to get revenge and, because Hassan was on Akrim's wing, the Russians had to get involved.

When everything had died down and we were allowed out as normal, Dabir came to see us. He was nervous as he was due to be sentenced the following day.

'I was with a friend of mine called Rajeeb at his place smoking some hash,' he explained. 'Somebody called asking if he could buy a spliff's worth and Rajeeb asked me to go and drop it to him. I didn't even think about it. It was an undercover cop sting and I was arrested for dealing.'

'Fuck, man.'

'Yeah, and the thing is I admitted handing it over so I'm really worried.'

Dabir went to court the next day and came to see us afterwards. He was ashen-faced and looked sick, chain-smoking one cigarette after another.

He had been sentenced to twenty-five years in jail for handing over a gram of hash. The sickening thing was that his case partner Rajeeb, who was effectively dealing, had been given a four-year sentence for possession. Rajeeb would be going home at Ramadan while Dabir would spend most of his life in Central.

'Don't worry, man, your case will go to the court of appeal and they will cut the sentence right down,' Nada said. 'You'll be okay, dude.'

We were all deeply affected by Dabir's plight. It showed the ridiculous inconsistencies in the Dubai justice system. A young man's life had been destroyed for handing over a tiny amount of hash while the actual dealer had escaped with the minimum sentence. It made me sick.

Seeing Dabir jailed for twenty-five years also made me think of my own situation, and I wondered if we would ever get out. I called Kate to see if there was any update.

'There's some good news,' she said. 'We had a report commissioned by a torture expert and his findings are that you were telling the truth about what happened to you. He took the notes made by the British embassy and he said your injuries were consistent with being electrocuted.'

'Yeah, I know. I don't need a bit of paper to tell me that.'

'Yes, but it's the proof that we needed that the police lied. That means we can go after them when you get out.'

I was more concerned with the getting out part at this point. It had been several weeks since we had been sentenced and there was no sign of us being released. Our prayers were answered when I called the embassy a few days later on 10 July, the second day of Ramadan, to hear the glorious news that we were on the pardon list.

'Fucking hell, yes!' I said to Nada. 'I'm going home!' I called Amy immediately and told her the news.

Even though I was delighted I still feared they might try to screw us. Were they really going to let us go? I walked over to Harry and Tariq's wing to tell them the good news.

'Fucking hell, bruv!' Harry said as he gave me a big hug. 'We're fucking going home.'

'Yeeeeeeeeees!' Tariq screamed. 'We're going home, boys!'

'Where's Ben?' I asked. I wanted to share the news with my friend.

'He's gone, mate.'

'Where's he gone?'

'Fuck knows, mate. He went to quarantine a few days ago.'

'Fucking hell, I bet he's been released! He always said his dad would get him out of here.'

This was doubly good news. I hoped my friend was far away from Central, enjoying a drug-free life.

It only took a couple of days for our dream to be shattered. My friends and I were called to the bubble. I immediately feared something was up.

'Fuck, man, what's going on here?' Tariq said.

'Fuck knows, mate, they're probably just trying to fuck us up again,' Harry replied.

An officer in the bubble slid across the glass and said, 'You three, wait there. You go and see the general prosecutor.'

This was bizarre. We had already been sentenced yet we were going to see the top prosecutor in Dubai.

'I think you're right, bruv,' I said. 'I think we're gonna get fucked.'

We were met by two police officers who took us through the whole process of getting out of the jail and put us into two different BMWs. Tariq and Harry were together and I was by myself along with two officers. We were driven across Dubai and pulled up outside a building I recognized only too well. It was the prosecution building we had been taken to when we were first arrested.

We were led through a different entrance and upstairs through the plush building with its walls of light grey marble and darker stone pillars. We were led up a marble staircase, which was lined with mahogany panels on the walls, to sit outside a large office.

I was nervously preparing myself for the worst when I tuned in for a second to Tariq's conversation with the police officers. 'I'd love to bend your missus over,' he said. They just smiled at him and nodded as they didn't have a clue what he was saying. Tariq enjoyed abusing police officers with language they didn't understand.

'Come, come,' the guards said to me and I was led into a big office with plush cream carpet and marble walls. A man sat in the corner typing away and an old man I hadn't seen before with glasses dressed in full Arabic dress sat at a large desk in front of me.

'What am I doing here?' I said aggressively, standing before him.

'You made a claim of torture so we are investigating.'

I laughed in his face. 'You told us weeks ago that you had already investigated and found our claims were untrue. How does that work? I can't say anything without my lawyer present.'

'Well, if we don't drop your allegations today then you won't be going home for Ramadan.'

I was angry and upset. They had waited until we were on the verge of release to play their trump card, making it very clear that our freedom was in their hands and unless we played ball we weren't going home. There was no way I was going to let them get away with what they did to us, no matter what the cost. We had fought for this long and I wasn't giving up what I believed in.

'That's blackmail,' I said.

'What is this blackmail? You black man.'

'You blackmailed me.'

'What is this?'

'You're threatening me.'

'Yes, I don't care.'

'Will you say the same thing in front of my lawyer and the British embassy then?'

'Yes, I will.'

'Why do we need to be in the country for you to carry out your investigation?'

'We need you to be here to identify people.'

'But you can send us pictures for us to identify people.'

'No, you must be here so we can't deport you.'

'Okay, well, will you repeat what you have told me to my lawyer and the British embassy then?' I repeated.

'Yes, when do you want a meeting?'

'I'd like it for tomorrow.'

He agreed and I was sent out of the room. I told Tariq and Harry what had happened.

'Fucking hell, Ceaze, I told you,' Harry said. 'We should just drop this shit. I wanna go home, mate.'

'Mate, I'm not dropping it.'

'Well, I'm just gonna tell them I don't want to do this any more. I just wanna drop it.'

'Fuck that shit, man,' Tariq said. 'Let's fuck these cunts.'

'Thank you, Tariq,' I said. 'How can you do this, Harry, after a year of what we've been through? What about all of the people who believe in us? What about the difference to people's lives we are making as we are standing up to them?'

'Look, I don't care, I wanna go home. You two are a pair of muppets.'

Tariq was next and he was as good as his word as he refused to back down.

'Fuck those cunts, man,' he said as he came out of the office twenty minutes later.

'Fucking idiots,' Harry said as he was taken in.

I was disappointed in Harry, but he was the one who got beaten the least. In his head the torture wasn't a big deal as he was barely touched in comparison to Tariq and me. There was no way I would ever have rolled over and I was annoyed that my friend had caved in. We continued to have a go at Harry on the journey back but he didn't care. He wanted to go home and didn't want to do anything to jeopardize that so he was sticking to his guns and wasn't willing to fight this last battle. With hindsight, I understand, but at the time I was angry and emotional.

As soon as we were back in the jail I called Kate.

'What?' she said, clearly shocked by the new development. 'No way have they done that? Are they stupid?'

'I know, it's insane.'

We called the embassy and Hibba promised us they would be at the prosecutor's office the next day with our lawyers.

Ash came later that evening to drop our food off. 'Mate, I heard what they did to you. This is some crazy shit. In all the six years I've been in here I've never heard of this happening. You gotta stay strong. Keep it up and don't give up. They're running scared.'

He was right and I knew I had to stick to my guns. I called Amy and told her what had happened.

'Don't give up,' she said. 'You have to keep on going. I want you home but you have been through too much to stop now. I have faith in you.'

*

The next day we were picked up again and taken to the prosecutor. Harry was moaning as he didn't see why he should have to go when he wasn't continuing his complaint. I met my lawyer and he introduced himself. Even though he had defended me in court he had never come to see me in jail or spoken to me on the phone. I told him what had happened the day before.

'Oh my God, I can't believe that,' he said. 'This is illegal.'

I was called in along with my lawyer and Hibba.

'So you came back?' the prosecutor said.

'Of course I did. Will you repeat what you said yesterday?'

'Yes, of course. If you don't drop this case you will not go home for Ramadan.'

My lawyer just shook his head in disbelief.

'You still want to continue?'

'Yes, I do.'

'Okay, tell me what happened.'

It took three hours for me to recount our tale of arrest and torture. I was doing what I could to help by answering the incessant questions, but the prosecutor was trying his utmost to make me look like a liar. There was no way I was going to back down. When I was finished Tariq did the same. Harry was kept sitting outside for six hours and wasn't happy. When Tariq was called in I waited for a bit before asking if I could go back to Central. The officers eventually agreed. I didn't feel the need to hang around for another few hours, especially for Harry who was just caving in.

The following day we heard Danny had been released. He was on a ten-year sentence yet had got out before us. I was worried we had made a terrible mistake.

A few days later Nada ran into the cell with an excited look on his face. 'They're reading out the pardon list!' he said. Names started to be read over the loud speaker system. This was our moment of destiny. I was so excited but terrified at the same time. I waited with baited breath, desperate for them to read mine and my friends' names. The list went on for what seemed like an age, but then I heard a beautiful sound.

'Harrison Michelle Jenkins,' the cop said. I smiled, knowing my friend would be released, and waited on tenterhooks for my name to be read out. Another name was read before I heard what I wanted to hear.

'Kerrol Errol Williams.'

I punched the air in delight. I was going home. The prosecutor's threats had been a big bluff, but Tariq and I had held firm and we'd won.

Tariq's name was next. Adrenaline rushed through my body as I ran as fast as I could to find my friends. I met Harry halfway across the courtyard coming to see me.

'Did you hear our names, mate?'

'Yeah, mate!' he said with a smile on his face.

'Where's Tariq?'

'Mate, Tariq's been given another case,' he said, his smile disappearing.

'What the fuck?!'

'Yeah, he's been taken to another jail for the rental car,' he said. 'The police have kept hold of the rental car all of this time and the company had been charging Tariq for it. He didn't know about it and obviously hasn't paid. Now they've charged him. Tariq's in bits. He was stuttering and in tears when they led him away.'

I was devastated. I had just heard the news I had been dreaming of for a year and never thought would happen, but my friend had been shafted at the last minute. I went back to my cell with the most extreme mixed emotions I have ever felt. I called the embassy and Kate to try and find out what was going on and they confirmed that he was arrested for not paying for the hire car. Kate said they were trying to get him out but warned it could take a few days.

Harry and I were called into the dining area with the other people who were being pardoned. We were asked if we had our passports in the country and if we could get them to the jail. My brother had mine and Danny's parents had Harry's. When we had our passports we would be sent for an eye scan. When you enter Dubai they scan your eyes and our biometric data would now be put on a list of people banned from coming into the UAE.

The next day our passports were brought to the jail and Harry's name was read over the tannoy, calling him for his scan. I waited to hear mine called but it never came. My heart dropped. Was this the final piece of cruelty? Was I being kept here because I was pursuing the case against the police? I was panicking, my heart beating out of my chest. I called the embassy in a desperate state.

'I think they're trying to fuck me,' I said. 'I think they've taken my name off the list.'

'It's okay,' Hibba said. 'They have just made a mistake. Your eye test is booked in for tomorrow.'

I breathed a huge sigh of relief, but in the back of my mind I still thought they were going to screw me at the last minute.

The next day was Harry's birthday and it was the day before he was being released. It was a proper double celebration. After my eye test I walked across to his wing with the boys from my cell bringing a few doughnuts as a present. Ash and Harish had come to say goodbye while the Mafia boys were joining in the fun, drinking hooch, listening to music and generally having a laugh.

The following morning I heard Harry's name over the public address system and ran down to see him. He had a huge smile on his face and gave me a hug.

'It's finally over, you're going home,' I said.

'Mate, I won't believe it until I'm on that plane.'

'Shut up, you prick, you're going home.'

We were joined by all the Russians, Nada and Mareed. Everyone shook Harry's hand and followed him down to the bubble where two police officers came to collect him.

'I'll see you back at the Ends, man,' he said, using an East End phrase for our area.

'Look, make sure you have everything ready for me when I touch down – I want to go hard.'

'Don't worry, mate, I will.'

We hugged and he walked to the door. As he exited for the last time he turned around and smiled. I choked up as I waved him goodbye. I was so happy he was going home, now I had to hope tomorrow would really be my turn.

Later that evening I was with Ash when Nada came running in looking worried and said, 'Dude, the Russians are looking for you.'

'Fuck, what do they want?'

'I dunno, but you'd better go and find out.'

I went back to my old wing to see Mice and Ravi. 'What's up?'

'I want to kill you,' Mice said, staring intently at me.

'What?'

'No, only joking. We want to call Harry to make sure he got home okay.'

We went back to my wing and I phoned our mate Craig as I knew he would be with Harry.

'Bruva!' Harry shouted, when Craig gave him the phone. 'I made it!'

'Yeah, mate, what you doing?'

'I'm with Al and Craig and we're going for a few in the Golden Fleece.'

'Don't you worry, bruv, I'll be there tomorrow.'

'Give me the phone,' Mice said. He grabbed it off me. 'Harry, I will kill you,' the big Russian said. We all burst out laughing.

My old life felt so close as I heard my friends in London talking in the background. 'We'll see you tomorrow, bruv,' they shouted as I hung up. I was desperate to see Faith, Amy and my mum, before meeting up with my friends to have the mother of all parties.

The following morning, on 18 July 2013, I heard the sound I honestly never thought I would hear. 'Kerrol Errol Williams *affraj*!' I froze and terrible thoughts flooded my brain. If the police wanted to get revenge on me for all of the noise I had made, they could arrest me as soon as I walked out the door. What if Amy had found somebody else? What if Faith wouldn't like me? I hadn't seen her for a year and she wouldn't know who I was.

I tried to put the dark thoughts out of my mind to say my goodbyes. My mates from my wing followed me to the bubble. The Russians were there and we all hugged. It was one of the happiest moments of my life but also the saddest. There were people here who would probably never get out of jail. Throughout my prison experience I had tried to help people, and by fighting the police we had given others hope. But when we were gone they would still be here, languishing in hell. Some of these guys were like my brothers and I was leaving them to their fate.

As I walked out the door I looked back and waved at all of the crazed psychopaths and Mafia lords who had become my friends.

I struggled to contain my emotions as I walked away never to see them again.

Two policemen took me through the tunnel to the outside. I was given my clothes and belongings back and swiftly changed into a blue tracksuit I had had in Port Rashid. I was then driven to a deportation centre at the airport. I was about to go through to the departure lounge when I heard Ross shouting at the door. 'Wait! Wait! Wait!' He was with Zain and they came running through. Ross gave me my suitcase and I changed into a pair of jeans and a brown Gabicci top.

'Bruv! I can't believe they let you out,' Zain said. 'They should never have let you out!'

'Shut up, you prick,' I said with a huge smile on my face.

'*Yallah! Yallah!* Go!' the guard said. I quickly hugged Zain and Ross and said goodbye.

In the departure lounge I bought cigarettes and a bottle of Grey Goose vodka from the duty free. I had just sat down at O'Grady's pub to eat my first meal as a free man, a BLT with a pint of Stella, when I looked up to see my face on the news.

'The second British man accused of drug trafficking in Dubai has been released from jail.'

The guy next to me looked at me and said, 'Is that you?'

'Yeah, mate.'

'Fucking hell. I heard about that back in England. Hats off to you for enduring that.'

My English phone I had handed into the guards at Central was going mad. Amy called, weeping with joy, and my friends were hollering down the phone. On the plane I tucked into the booze to celebrate. It took me two hours to fly to Qatar where I changed before the eight-hour flight home.

When the flight touched down it was late. Alex picked me up

and took me to my mum's. I walked up to the front door of the house where I had lived all of my life. It was so surreal. I was scared and excited to see Amy and Faith again. There were times when I never thought I would see my home again. My mum opened the door and she threw her arms around me and told me how relieved she was to have me home. Then I hugged Amy tight and she was crying her heart out.

'I missed you so much,' she said. 'I'm not letting you out of my sight again!'

I was desperate to see my little girl. I made my way upstairs and Faith was asleep in her cot in my room. She opened her beautiful brown eyes and immediately put her hands up towards me. As I picked her up and held her tight I was the happiest I had ever been. I hung out with Amy, Faith and my friends, enjoying being able to see them all, catching up on everything I had missed.

The following day I stayed with Amy, my mum and Faith to try and catch up on some of the months I had missed. Harry, Craig and Mytus came round to see me and it was a moment of pure elation as I hugged my pals. When I saw Harry I gave him a huge embrace. We had been through so much together and neither of us could believe we were home.

They said my good friend Plan B was performing at the Lovebox festival the following evening, 20 July, and he wanted to see me. The next night a large group of us headed to Victoria Park in east London to celebrate mine and Harry's homecoming. The moon was in the sky and I was in a drunken haze when I was at the side of the stage watching his performance. I truly felt I was home.

I stood there trying to make sense of what had just happened to me. I had been to hell but had come out the other side. I knew at that point I had been blessed and given a second chance at life.

I was determined that the experience was not going to break me; it was going to make me a better person. I was going to make sure I made a difference to those I had left behind and ensure those who weren't as fortunate as me are never forgotten.

EPILOGUE

When I woke up in my bed that first morning I immediately thought I was in Dubai, before the beautiful realization dawned that I was home. Faith was in a cot by my bed and Amy was lying next to me.

I heard the next day that Tariq had been moved to an Out Jail deportation centre for the rental car case. His family paid the cash owed to the company and he was released two days after I was. Harry and I went with all of our friends to the Hoxton Pony nightclub to welcome him home. We all got drunk and didn't really discuss the case. We'd been through hell for the past year and the last thing we wanted to do was talk about it. We wanted to savour our freedom and to try and forget what we had been through.

I felt that I'd started to drift apart from Harry and Tariq when I was in Central and this continued when we were released. I've only seen Tariq a few times since we got out and my relationship with Harry has been altered fundamentally, our outlook on life now very different. The trauma we had been through changed us all but I still hope we will always be friends.

We had agreed that we wanted to do something to raise awareness of the other inmates' plight in Dubai so we all did an interview with the *Sunday Mirror*, were all on the sofa of *Daybreak* and I did the Victoria Derbyshire show on 5 Live. After that, we needed to return to normality, but adjusting to being back in the UK was tough. I was paranoid and always looking over my shoulder. Being out in London was surreal, almost overwhelming. It was as if my senses were heightened and I could smell and taste everything. I was having horrific nightmares about being tortured, being attacked by the Russians in Central or my family dying. I didn't want to get out of bed and face the world. Sometimes I wanted to cry for no real reason and couldn't comprehend why. I felt depressed and empty.

Kate from Reprieve suggested I go and see a counsellor at the Helen Bamber Foundation, which is a charity that supports people who've been subject to human rights violations, including torture. Part of me was reluctant, not ready to admit I needed help, but in the end I went. When the counsellor asked me how I felt and what I'd been through I tried to resist by telling her I didn't have any nightmares and that the ordeal hadn't affected me, which was obviously untrue. By the third session I realized I wasn't helping anybody by spinning her a load of lies and opened my heart. She asked me about the torture in depth and I told her everything. It was very cathartic but completely span me out. There was a huge weight off my shoulders and I felt light-headed and in a daze. I couldn't believe I had offloaded everything in my mind to a complete stranger and wandered around Camden for two hours not knowing what I was doing.

I had weekly sessions for six months and in the end they said I was suffering from post-traumatic stress disorder, the same condition that many who have spent time in war zones suffer from. It made me realize there was something actually wrong with me, and that in turn made me very defensive and argumentative with Amy, my family and Harry. I felt like I was being judged by them, and I refused to go on the treatment course as I couldn't face it. I even lied to my mum and Amy, saying that I was still going to therapy as I didn't want to admit I was suffering from PTSD. I would have random outbursts and eventually admitted to Amy what happened during one row. I told her I didn't need the treatment as I was feeling better.

I realized I needed to do things that made me happy so I started recording music again. I went to Bulgaria with a grime MC, Dee Double E, to shoot a video for one of his songs. I've released the single 'Tell Them It's Over' and have toured with Maverick Sabre. I also have an album coming out soon.

I've also been chosen as the face of clothing brand Gabicci and have been collaborating with them on future projects. We are in talks about releasing my own signature range called Gabicci London.

I feel like I have come out the other side of the mental illness that affected me after our release. I no longer feel paranoid or depressed and I don't lash out like I used to. It has taken a long time but I feel I am in a good place with exciting projects on the go.

Reprieve continued to badger the Foreign Office to get reports on our torture claim but nothing was ever done. When we were out of sight the Dubai authorities swept it all under the carpet. I felt cheated that we had been through this ordeal and yet nobody was willing to do anything about it. It made me worried for the world that this sort of thing can happen and nobody is held accountable. However, I have given assistance to the Foreign Consulate Service, advising them on how they could better their service for Britons in jail abroad. I told a panel about our case and what they should have done to help us. They should have taken statements when they saw us, taken photographs of our injuries and made sure we received the correct medical care. If they had done more than just sending letters asking for an investigation we would have stood more of a chance of getting some form of justice.

As far as I know Baariq is still inside a jail in Dubai. He never made it to Central with us. Zain is still in Dubai and I have seen him a couple of times when he has come back to the UK. He is as crazy as ever.

Despite being jailed for ten years Mohammed was released from prison in 2015. He always said he'd be out years before his sentence ended. He called me that summer and said, 'My British brother! How are you? I told you I would get out. Being big drug dealer like me is very helpful.'

'Ah man, I'm so pleased to hear your voice.'

He said he was concentrating on his legal businesses and wasn't dealing drugs any more.

As for me, I am making it my mission to highlight the plight of those still incarcerated in Dubai through my music and this book, grateful that I was one of the lucky few who managed to escape while so many are left to rot with no justice and no one to hear their voices.

ACKNOWLEDGEMENTS

Karl Williams

I would like to say a big thank you to Reprieve for working around the clock on our case and ultimately helping us to get freedom. If it wasn't for Marc, Kate and their team I think we would've been stuck in that sandpit forever. I would also like to thank my missus Amy for being my rock while I was in jail. Thank you for looking after our daughter and raising her to be such a pleasure to be around. I would also like to thank my brother Alex for supporting me 100 per cent of the way.

A massive thank you to Tariq's sister Davina and Harry's parents for all of your hard work and persistent campaigns for our release.

A big part of our release is down to the team at ITV1's *Daybreak*. You guys didn't have to raise our case with David Camcron. I owe you a massive thank you as you could have got into trouble for not clearing the questions with him first!

I would also like to thank all of my friends who showed so much love when I came out. It hasn't gone unnoticed, but there are just too many to mention you all.

When I came out I hooked up with the Jungle Brown Boys and you guys helped me to record my first few songs after my release. You then took me on an adventure performing around France, so thank you.

A big thank you to D Double for taking me to Bulgaria as this helped me regain my confidence.

I was able to assist Maverick Sabre on tour and had a fantastic time. I can't thank you enough brother. It has opened my eyes and made me see my worth in the industry. A big thank you to Paul Wilkinson and MAK Studios for all your hard work, helping put together my album.

I also want to thank Gabicci for their support.

A big thank you to my agent Robert Smith and to Ingrid at Pan Macmillan for making this book possible.

I would also like to say a big thank you to Richard Evans from Rich London PR for all your help over the years and sparking my love for Gabicci clothes. If it wasn't for you, Rich, I wouldn't have met Justin and been able to write this book.

Writing this book has probably been one of the most tedious tasks for Justin and I bet it has been one of the strangest. I want to say thank you for putting up with my crazy behaviour and me turning up late and very hung over for sessions. I have had a great time and I believe what started out as just a business relationship has developed into a friendship.

And finally, a special mention for the people we left behind in Port Rashid and Central. Thank you for your support and belief throughout our ordeal. You have not been forgotten.

Justin Penrose

When I met Karl Williams in August 2013 I was the crime correspondent on the *Sunday Mirror* and I had agreed to interview him about his arrest, torture and imprisonment in Dubai. At that time Karl and his friends had not spoken to any media outlets about their ordeal and I assumed they were guilty of the allegations against them. But when I heard their horrific story I realized that here were three lads who had been on holiday, targeted and subjected to brutal torture, all for a crime they didn't commit.

We met at a studio in Brixton where, surrounded by clothes for various photo shoots, they told me of their shocking story. When the article appeared Karl called me to say how much he liked it and asked me whether I wanted to write this book. It was the start of a two-and-a-half-year ride where, through the hundreds of hours of interviews, I felt like I had entered Port Rashid and Central Prisons and met the colourful characters that inhabited Karl's life for the year of his incarceration.

Of course I have to thank Karl for asking me to write the book in the first place, the mammoth backgammon sessions when we should have been writing, testing my patience to breaking point and for generally being a great guy. I feel honoured to be able to call you a friend.

I would like to thank my agent Robert and my editor Ingrid at Pan Macmillan for making this all possible.

Thanks also to my friends Ants, Steve O, Jay, Sheps and Sam for the poker and the nights out. To my mum for the constant love and my sister Elaine for always being there to help me out of a hole. Thank you to my children Evie, Lydia and Barney for keeping me on my toes and making me laugh.

No acknowledgements would be complete without thanking Jess, for providing the love and support that has helped me get through the toughest of times.